From Generation to Generation

*A story of intermarriage
and Jewish continuity*

Jane Larkin

FROM GENERATION TO GENERATION:
A STORY OF INTERMARRIAGE AND JEWISH CONTINUITY.

Library of Congress Catalog

ISBN-10: 1495301524
ISBN-13: 9781495301520
Library of Congress Control Number: 2014901694
CreateSpace Independent Publishing Platform
North Charleston, South Carolina

For Cameron
Words seem an inadequate way to express my love
for you. Thank you for your endless support of and
involvement in this journey.

For Sammy
You are my guiding light and Jewish star. I love you.

ACKNOWLEDGMENTS

While I am the author of this book, I received much guidance and input along the way. Thank you to my readers, Sara Kaplan, Laura O'Neill, Renee Karp, Mimi Zimmerman, Rabbi Oren Hayon, Rabbi Debra Robbins, and Nancy Shanks for your time, patience, encouragement, and thoughtful suggestions and comments. Your input made this a better book and me a better writer.

This story might not have been told if it had not been for Ruth Abrams, my first editor at InterfaithFamily, who encouraged me to share my story, and for the ongoing support of my work that I have received from Ed Case and Lindsey Silken. It is a pleasure to work with people who care deeply about expanding Judaism's tent.

To the CreateSpace team who helped to make this book a reality.

To Stuart Matlins for taking the time during a Vermont blizzard to share publishing wisdom.

To Nicole Kalish, a long overdue thanks for your generosity of spirit and friendship.

To Robert Kern, my friend and youth group adviser, thank you for nurturing my Jewish identity.

I am lucky to have parents who have always believed in me and who saved all of the articles from my days as a freshman reporter for *The Daily Orange*. I love you.

Thank you to my in-laws for welcoming me warmly into the family and sharing in this journey.

To my grandparents and great-grandparents for leading by example.

Finally, thank you to Cameron and Sammy for your unconditional love and support during this project. You make all of this possible. I love you with all of my heart.

CONTENTS

PREFACE

"We'll start the meeting by going around the room and introducing ourselves. Please say your name and whether you are the Jewish or not Jewish partner."

"My name is Jane Larkin, and I am the Jewish spouse."

So goes the opening at every meeting of the Interfaith Moms group at my temple in Dallas. The twelve-steps-style introductions seem appropriate since all of us in attendance are in a way admitting that we have a problem. We have chosen a spouse or partner from outside our faith, and now there are issues with parents, in-laws, siblings, children, temples, churches, Jews, and non-Jews, just to name a few. Add the label "biggest threat to Judaism's future" given by some family, friends, strangers, academics, and religious leaders alike and a heavy dose of guilt, Jewish or otherwise, and you can understand why we always serve wine at our get-togethers.

Of course, it is easy to see why people tell those of us in interfaith marriages that our challenges are self-inflicted. With 5.3 million Jews[1] in the United States, the advent of JDate, Jewish organizations on college campuses, and young-adult programs in major cities, falling in love with another Jew should not be that difficult. Yet, according to the 2013 Pew Research survey on Jewish Americans, 44 percent of married Jews are intermarried, and the intermarriage rate for those marrying between 2000 and 2013 was 58 percent. This is concerning when compared to the intermarriage rate in the 1970s, which was about 30 percent.[2]

But while the rate of intermarriage among recently married Jews has grown, the overall rate has remained relatively static since the mid-1980s.[3] Still, the alarm within the Jewish community is understandable. Leading Jewish sociologists suggest that rather than aggressively reaching out to intermarrieds in order to encourage them to engage in Jewish life, the Jewish community should focus its outreach efforts on deepening the Jewish identities of *inmarrieds* (two Jewish partners) because that is the group from which three-quarters of future Jews will come.[4] The recommendation to shore up the religious bonds of Jews today in order to prevent intermarriage tomorrow sounds reasonable. As it has often been said: "The best offense is a good defense."

At the same time, other groups—such as the Jewish Outreach Institute, InterfaithFamily, and the Reform movement—have, in recent years moved to recognize the value in communal efforts to strengthen Jewish identity and choices among intermarrieds in order to drive affiliation and engagement, among other things. The Central Conference of American Rabbis (CCAR), the leading organization of Reform rabbis, issued the following statement on intermarriage during the group's March 2010 convention:

> While in the past the Reform rabbis focused discussion on how to prevent intermarriage, the CCAR today affirmed that intermarriage is a given and should be approached with the goal of engaging intermarried families in Jewish life and living. Rabbis can and should work to improve the effectiveness of their efforts to encourage intermarried people to embrace Judaism for themselves and their children.[5]

The Interfaith Moms group at my Reform synagogue would not have been possible if not for clergy and lay leaders who recognized the importance of drawing interfaith families into the Jewish tent several years before CCAR's statement. Driven by a commitment to two stories fundamental to Judaism—the story of Abraham welcoming guests and embracing the stranger in Genesis and Ruth, the Gentile who aligns herself with the Jewish people and faith—Interfaith Moms has been allowed to grow, flourish, and expand to include initiatives targeting interfaith fathers and families.

It also helps that my temple has adopted interfaith-friendly policies, such as allowing the not Jewish partners of intermarried couples to serve on committees and cochair events such as our temple-wide Sukkot celebration and mitzvah day. This has been one of the reasons my family has fully embraced Judaism, and we are not alone. The welcoming and supportive environment at our synagogue has helped many interfaith couples and families find a religious and spiritual home and a Jewish identity. It is not just that the congregation provides support, but we have also learned the importance of supporting one another. Like other kinds of support groups, we help each other as we navigate the path or minefield known as intermarriage.

As a participant in the inaugural Interfaith Moms meeting and later as cochairwoman of the group, I have seen the effectiveness of outreach efforts firsthand. My own family is a testament to how engagement can encourage interfaith families to embrace a religious identity and bring additional meaning to their lives. As the former chair of the outreach committee at one of the largest Reform congregations in the United States and the largest in the Southwest, I have had the opportunity to guide our efforts to connect families like my own to Jewish life and encourage Jewish choices.

What I have learned through my own experience and outreach work is that inmarried Jews often consider all intermarrieds to be the same—all some shade of interfaith. But while we may face common issues, we do not always have common solutions; and we are not all in the same place emotionally or spiritually in how we navigate the joys and challenges of being an interfaith family. Each of our stories is different.

The unique nature of our stories has been reinforced through my involvement with InterfaithFamily (IFF), the premier resource for interfaith families exploring Jewish life and advocate for more welcoming Jewish communities. Four years ago, I began writing articles for IFF about my family's experiences creating a Jewish home with one not Jewish parent. These personal essays described our rituals, choices, challenges, successes, and failures. Recently, I became a writer for the site's parenting blog. I have always been deeply grateful for the positive reaction most of my work has received and have been equally thankful for the discussion some of it has generated.

Encouraged by the feedback from the IFF staff, clergy, friends, temple colleagues, and strangers who have commented about these pieces online, I have considered sharing many times over the past few years my family's story. I wanted to offer more detail so that rather than providing a snapshot of how we handle a few situations in one moment, I could paint a bigger picture of how our ideas, positions, and actions evolve. There are many books about interfaith relationships, including ones that offer advice, history, an academic perspective, examples of different arrangements, and stories culled from interviews with couples but written by someone else. Often these anecdotes depict how a family deals with one particular situation such as telling grandparents what religion grandchildren will be raised or how a couple deals with the December holidays. Other books are a compendium of personal essays written by various writers and mixed with advice from professionals in the field, or they give the male partner's point of view. I feel that there is room in this mix for the female voice—a mother's voice—as well as a more in-depth look at how one family handles a variety of situations over time.

Life is fluid, and so is the spirituality of an interfaith family. We have unexpected joys, surprising challenges, victories, and defeats. Those issues we thought we handled come up again. Our religious life, celebrations, and concerns go beyond the classic "December Dilemma" discussion. It may surprise you to learn that inmarrieds and intermarrieds can be more similar than different when dealing with parenting or other family situations, and that there are actually non-Jews who *actively* engage in raising Jewish children.

I hope that my family's story will encourage you to think differently about interfaith families. For those in an interfaith relationship, I want you to see that there is room for you, if you choose, in Judaism. You may need to scratch a little harder in your community to find welcoming spaces, but they do exist. No Jewish family is perfect, nor is any family. We all make trade-offs and compromises in our relationships, religiously or otherwise, and the ones that my husband and I have made may not be ones that work for you. The choices we have made have helped us to build a foundation from which to impart a shared set of beliefs and values to our son and to create a rich identity and community for all of us. My wish is that this book sparks ideas of your own.

For those who have children or grandchildren who are intermarried or heading down that road, I hope that my family's experience makes you think about how you can engage the interfaith couple in a positive way. Maybe the rituals we have started in our home are things you will choose to invite your family to participate in at yours, or you will get an idea of how to handle or not to handle a particular situation.

And for those who work within Jewish organizations either as professionals or lay leaders, I hope that this book demonstrates that outreach does matter. Do not let the vision of the perfect Jewish family, Jewish parents, and offspring be the enemy of a good Jewish family—an interfaith couple with Jewish children. Rather than lament about the number of Jews choosing to marry outside the faith, do something to bring them into Judaism's tent.

My family's story highlights an interfaith marriage between a Jew and a Christian, creating a Jewish home, but many of the issues we confront are consistent with those faced by others in mixed relationships, whether they are between different races, cultures, or religions. You may find some part of your own story in these pages. I hope that this book encourages you to connect with others in a similar situation and, through the sharing of your narrative, to find your voice.

Now, I invite you to follow my family's search for religious identity and meaning. Share in our Jewish journey. Perhaps, when you are finished, you will be inspired to welcome an interfaith couple into your community, create a more robust outreach program for interfaith families at your synagogue, or embrace your child's not Jewish girlfriend or boyfriend. Maybe you will reach out to your intermarried children in a more meaningful way, investigate ways to connect your family to Judaism, seek out Jewish choices, explore your own beliefs or family history, challenge yourself to learn more about your or your partner's faith, or even start an interfaith families' group of your own.

INTRODUCTION

Most people who intermarry, including me, do not set out to marry outside their faith. In an open society, it happens. And, it has been happening for a long time.

Jon Entine, founding director of the Genetic Literacy Project and author of *Abraham's Children: Race, Identity and the DNA of the Chosen People*, shared the results of studies on ancestry among Ashkenazi Jews (Eastern European) in a Spring 2008 interview with *Reform Judaism* magazine. He said, "DNA evidence shows that 80 percent or more of Jewish males have direct Semitic ancestry, two major studies of Jewish female lineage suggest that only about 50 percent of females trace their ancestry...to the Middle East. The other 50 percent or so of Ashkenazic women today...appear to be descended from gentiles."[1]

Entine says that studies point to the small Jewish communities established in Europe by traveling Jewish traders as the reason for the significant number of Ashkenazic women with non-Semitic lineage. He states that the Jewish men frequently took local, Gentile women as wives. The women raised Jewish children, but most never underwent a formal conversion.

Before Jews migrated to Europe, intermarriage happened in Babylonia around the time of the destruction of the First Temple in 586 BCE. Jews' high rate of marriage to non-Jews distressed the priests so much that they codified the concept of matrilineal descent (religious identity passed through the mother) and encouraged Jewish men to leave their non-Jewish families behind when they returned to Israel. In the Bible, there are many instances of Israelite men married to non-Hebrew women, raising Jewish children, often with no evidence that the women converted to Judaism. Examples include Bilhah and Zilpah, two of Jacob's wives and the mothers of Dan, Naphtali, Gad, and Asher; and Asenath, an Egyptian married to Joseph and mother of Ephraim and Manasseh. Even Moses, the great leader of the Jewish people, married outside the tribe. Zipporah, his wife, was the daughter of Jethro, the Midianite priest who advised Moses on leadership and management. Jethro was the person who suggested that Moses set up a system of judges to assist him with conflict resolution, which Moses did. And then there was Ruth, the Moabite, who, because of her love for her dead husband and mother-in-law, joined herself to the Jewish people to ensure that the family would live on after her husband's death. Ruth goes on to become the great-grandmother of King David. As the Messiah will be a descendant of David, the story of Ruth demonstrates that greatness can come from anywhere, even non-Jewish lineage.

There are examples of intermarried Jewish women in the Bible too: Bathsheba, the wife of Uriah the Hittite, later married King David; Esther, the wife of the not Jewish king Ahasuerus, used her position to save the Jewish people from genocide in Persia; and Jael, wife of the Kenite Heber, who killed the Canaanite general Sisera during the battle for Canaan.

Like these early interfaith families, the families who my family has become involved with through my synagogue's Interfaith Moms group have a strong desire to build a connection to Judaism. Sometimes this drive to be a MOT (member of the tribe) is driven by the Jewish spouse, and other times, the non-Jew is the driver. Regardless of which partner initiates the family's involvement, in this circle, there is an overall wish to belong, a commitment to raise Jewish children, a will to learn the traditions, and a yearning for spiritual engagement. Yet, our interfaith families are different. Both parents are not card-carrying members of the tribe called *Jew*. And unless the non-Jew converts, he or she cannot claim as the people in the American Express ads do to be a "member since..." Our best hope is that our not Jewish husbands and wives will be welcomed as honorary members for their dedication to a Jewish identity for the next generation and for the link to the Jewish people and religion that they feel in their hearts and exemplify through their actions.

My temple's commitment to making this hope a reality is essential to the success of its outreach initiatives. For those of us who are lucky enough to have had a welcoming environment as one of our first interactions with a synagogue, it is frustrating to hear the alarms still being sounded about intermarriage. It is common for us to have women come to an Interfaith Moms event and tell us how this is a last-ditch effort to join their families to Judaism. These women's stories are sad: unaccepting family, High Holiday sermons that talk of the travesty of intermarriage and how it will only bring doom and gloom to the Jewish people, and synagogue membership inquiries rebuffed. It always amazes me that these women have actually darkened the doors of another Jewish institution after having been repeatedly rejected. It has been said that the act of doing the same thing repeatedly and expecting a different outcome is the definition of insanity. Maybe you need to be a little insane to want to align yourself with a minority that has been persecuted off and on for over two thousand years. I often wonder: would I have persisted if my family encountered the same?

Because of what these moms have experienced, they need more than just an empathetic ear; they need to know that they and their families belong, and it takes more than one meeting with a warm welcome. These moms start to get involved slowly: first some meetings and then possibly a moms' dinner before working up to attending a family event. At this point, the welcome wagon needs to turn its attention to the husband or partner to reassure him or her that our congregation has space for interfaith families. This is not easy since, after the previous hurts, the spouse is skeptical that this Jewish experience will be different from past ones. Words of welcome are helpful, but interfaith programming is what draws these families into the community. Standing in a room with twenty other interfaith families while a rabbi leads the group in the singing of Hanukkah songs or Havdalah says more about the openness of our community than any website, conversation, or membership pitch. These events feel so warm and welcoming that they make you want to put your arms around your neighbor and break into song.

We have never actually done this, but it would be appropriate. The image of people swaying together in song is associated with human unity, closeness, compassion, and connection. Jewish engagement and identity, whether it is for inmarrieds or intermarrieds, starts with connection. And connection is built through stories.

Storytelling happens to be something that Jews do well. It is an integral part of the Jewish tradition. Judaism's master stories (think creation, the Exodus, Purim, and Hanukkah, to name a few) are how we communicate our fundamental beliefs and values, derive meaning and our ethical attitudes, and form our worldview. Continuously retelling these stories not only helps to ensure the continuity of our people but also gives us an opportunity to reflect on how they relate to us personally. They influence our perspectives, and hearing them time and again offers us the opportunity to find new meaning at different stages of our life.

Stories also bring us together by telling us that we are not alone in our struggles. Storytelling enables us to find common ground, and this connection to one another is the cornerstone of the success of Interfaith Moms. Whether our stories are told at a social event for moms or families or at an educational program that includes a heavy dose of interaction and sharing, our tales of challenges and joys help to bond us together. We laugh with each other, cringe with each other, cheer for each other, and empathize with each other. While we may sometimes receive advice, more often we find wisdom and inspiration from within the stories themselves.

As we learn through the reading of Judaism's tales and through the sharing of experiences with others in our everyday life, Jewish stories come in many packages. There are no straight paths. That is what is so interesting about each of our stories. Yet, interfaith families are often judged collectively. It is assumed that our relationships are more difficult because there is always religious tension, or that we all have the same challenges, such as whether or not to have a Christmas tree. This type of thinking is naive and one-dimensional. Just as all inmarried families are different, so, too, are interfaith ones.

When I met my husband, I had no idea the road we would travel regarding religion, nor could I have predicted the central role that Judaism would come to play in our lives. From determining the religious identity of our family, to figuring out what it means to us to live a Jewish life, to exploring our own beliefs and handling prejudice inside and outside our faiths, no situation has been without its share of surprises. While we have chosen to create a Jewish home, our choice is by no means the only choice or right choice. But through trial and error, peppered with some good advice and luck, we have managed, like our ancestors before us, to create a strong religious identity for our family, even with the last name Larkin.

Jews come in different guises, and now more than ever before, we come with traditionally non-Jewish last names. In many congregations, we see these families as the faces of interfaith—but why not as a reflection of the diversity that is Jewish life in America today, and that will be tomorrow? Let us face it, in the years ahead, there will be many more Larkins, McCartneys, Johnsons, and O'Briens listed in temple directories. Jews with these names will be passing on our master stories to the next generation, and quite possibly, some will even be Judaism's future leaders.

I think of my own son and how he will add his Jewish journey to our tradition. I hope that, like the stories of Ephraim and Manasseh and other children of interfaith families whose names we do not know, his story is absorbed into Judaism's larger book and becomes part of who we are as Jews. Just as we find wisdom and inspiration from the retelling of the great old Jewish stories, so too can we find it today in each other's narratives.

My story begins as my first marriage to a nice Jewish boy is falling apart, and I realize that I chose religion over love and pleasing my family rather than pleasing myself. What follows is not something I ever imagined: marriage to a non-Jew. Nor did I ever think that by marrying outside the faith, I would find my Jewish voice. But the path I have taken has turned out to be one filled with discovery at every turn, whether it is about Judaism or my own beliefs, and I find that more than ever before I have to *think intentionally* about what it means to be a Jew and to create a Jewish life.

I hope that in these pages you find some part of my story that resonates with you, as well as a new perspective on interfaith families and their place in the Jewish community. Beyond that, my hope is that this book inspires you to tell your story.

Note: most people do not desire to have parts of their lives shared publicly; therefore, I have changed all names in order to try to protect their identity. The only exceptions are my husband, Cameron, my son, Sammy, and relatives who are no longer living.

Parts of this book have previously appeared in essay or blog form on InterfaithFamily.com, and are used by permission.

ONE

FROM INMARRIAGE TO INTERFAITH DATING

It was the morning of Memorial Day 1998. I lay in bed on my side, facing outward, with eyes closed, starting to wake. After the sleepiness began to fade, the events of the night before began to come back to me. As they flashed across my memory, my only thought was: *Please, God, let this be a dream.*

It was a familiar feeling—one I remembered from college: that feeling you wake with after having had too much to drink the night before, and the memories of what you did come flooding back. My typical response would have been to groan, shrink under my covers, and when I did finally emerge, hunker down in my room for the day.

But that was not an option on this morning. I needed to face the day. I took a deep breath and opened my eyes. I was not in my small New York apartment but rather a New Jersey hotel room. I lay on my side, facing the windows, dreading the reality that I would find beside me in bed. I rolled over and there was Mike sleeping soundly. My heart sank, and a pit formed in my stomach—not because of Mike, but because I knew long before this moment that he was not for me. Last night was not a dream—it was my wedding.

While I had made many mistakes in my twenty-seven years, this was one of the bigger ones. I could not talk my way out of it or make an apology. Although, years later, as our marriage was falling apart, I would try both.

As I turned over on my back and stared at the ceiling, I wondered how I let this happen. Not wanting to face the disappointment and anger I felt at myself, I quickly dismissed the thought and focused on the facts: *Last night was my wedding, and I am now married.* It seemed pointless to think about how I got into this situation. For better or worse, I was in it. "Suck it up and make it work," I told myself. And that was what I did. Embracing my role as wife and sometimes mother, I turned off all emotion, woke my husband, and told him to get ready so that we could greet our guests at the brunch downstairs before leaving for our honeymoon.

This idea of "when the going gets tough, the tough get going" had served me well over the years (and frankly, it still does). I was practiced at pushing emotions away and forging ahead. Whether it was dealing with my physically abusive father, my parents' divorce, childhood hurts by friends, an admonishment from my mother, a breakup with a boyfriend, or a school or work challenge, this "I'll show them; I'll prove them wrong" attitude had gotten me through some difficult times. By shutting off my feelings, I could move on—endure.

I have always been proud of this ability and have seen it as a sign of resilience. But this brand of resilience has also come with consequences. Being adept at emotional shutdown has often left me cold, lonely, and lacking empathy. At times, it has caused me to be insensitive. I cringe when I remember the time I told my friend Natalie to "suck it up and deal with it" as she was pouring her heart out about a relationship we had discussed several times before. Later, Natalie would provide unconditional support for me when I was getting divorced. I am lucky to have had friends that were willing to do for me what I did not do for them.

I learned to turn off my emotions at a young age. I remember that sometime before age ten, I was crying about something in front of my mother. I cannot recall what the tears were for, but today I can still hear my mother's response: "Only babies cry!" Ever since, I have taken that to heart and have worked hard at being tough. I remember putting my mother's directive to work one summer at camp. I had tripped and fallen on pavement, scraping my knee. I can still see myself sitting on the ground, hugging my leg that was in pain, and biting my lip to try to stop the tears from coming out of my eyes. My counselor asked if I wanted to go to the nurse. My mother's words echoed in my head, and, playing the tough guy, I responded, "No, I'm fine." What I really wanted to do was cry and get a hug. But life went on, and after about a half hour of pretending to be fine, I believed I was.

Over the years, it became easy to assume an uncaring attitude when I was emotionally hurt. When, during my sophomore year of high school, the girls I hung around with decided that they did not want to be my friend any more, I just shut down. Although I was deeply hurt and confused as to why all of a sudden they did not like me, I did not discuss it with anyone or shed a tear. Instead, I reminded myself that strong people do not throw pity parties for themselves, and I chose to handle the situation by ignoring the pain and my former friends.

For a long time, I thought that my mother's admonition about crying was just a sign of her sometimes lack of empathy and compassion, but as I have reflected on it, I understand the context in which her words were delivered. My mother was dealing with my father, who was physically abusive to her, as well as my brother and me. In order to keep our life as normal as possible, she suppressed a lot of her own emotion—at least in front of us kids. She seemed to be sucking it up. A child's cries were insignificant to the emotional baggage she was carrying and wanting to unload. Instead, she created an aura of strength and toughness, one that I know was a very critical part of what got her and us through the eighteen years of their marriage.

Do not get me wrong: I am not giving her a free pass on her role in any issues I have discussed on the therapist's couch. Part of accepting our parents is to understand how life and circumstances affected their parenting. I never thought about this until I became a parent myself. Unfortunately, we are not able to be the parent we want to be or envision being every hour of every day, and our parental behavior is often influenced by what else is going on in our lives. All we can do is admit our mistakes, apologize, work to do better, and hope that our children recognize that even though we are imperfect, we love them very much.

So how did I let myself get married? The answer was sheer determination to prove my family wrong and actually marry someone who was Jewish. Considering that I had been living in New York City, had graduated from Syracuse University, and had mostly Jewish friends, this should have been easy. But a quick review of my dating history made it easy to understand why it was not.

When I was a teenager, the closest I came to having a serious Jewish boyfriend was on my Israel teen tour when I was sixteen—a six-week romance that ended when we returned to the United States. The distance between my home in New Jersey and his in Alabama made the long-distance relationship too difficult. My high school boyfriend was Catholic. Most guys I dated in college were of one Christian denomination or another, prompting my mother to ask, "How is it that I sent you to Syracuse, and you've managed to date every guy with a vowel at the end of his name?" At the time, Syracuse University's student body was 15 to 20 percent Jewish. As I prepared to graduate into the "real world," my mother reminded me that it was just as easy to date Jewish men as not Jewish men. My divorced mother followed this with "marriage is hard enough when you're the same religion." My father, with whom I had a strained relationship after my parents' divorce, had little to say about my choice of dates.

The summer following graduation, I met Jack, a nice Jewish guy from Boston. I was a counselor on a teen tour, and he was with another group from the same company. We dated for two years. While the relationship did not last, I proved to myself (and my mother) that I could date a Jewish man. In my mind, I had reached a milestone: a long-term relationship with a Jew.

The ironic thing was that I never envisioned myself marrying a non-Jew because my Jewish identity is—and has always been—important to me. I had a bat mitzvah, completed confirmation, marched on Washington on behalf of Soviet Jews, was president of my temple youth group, and traveled to Israel. I just assumed that I would have a Jewish home and children.

After Jack and I split up, I met Mike. We were introduced by a mutual acquaintance at a Syracuse vs. St. John's basketball game at Madison Square Garden. The following night we ran into each other at a GMAT prep class as we were both preparing to take the entrance exam for business school. Mike was tall, good-looking, and fun. He was often told that he resembled Harrison Ford or Richard Gere. He had graduated from Syracuse a year before me and was a frat boy in one of the socially acceptable fraternities that my sorority mixed with, so our social circles overlapped and mixed well. After our second date, I remember speculating with my friends about whether or not he was Jewish as it was not obvious from his last name. During a conversation on our next date, religion came up, and I mentioned that I was Jewish; he said he was too. I breathed a sigh of relief. I liked this guy, and so did my friends.

We dated for two years and then became engaged. Before the engagement, there were several signs that Mike was not the right one for me, but my family and friends seemed to like him, and he was Jewish. I put my blinders on and forged ahead, determined to silence the doubters in my family. I was so close to the finish line that there was no turning back.

Why I did not have confidence in my own feelings to walk away remains a mystery to me. I was confident in my decision-making abilities at work and in other areas of my life, and I always felt that my gut instincts were good. Was I afraid that I might not get another shot to grab the brass ring, or was I just hell-bent on proving my mother wrong? Maybe I was following my pattern of being a pleaser and knew that the decision would get me the pat on the back I craved. Maybe the answer was "D—All of the above."

A traditional Jewish wedding followed with flowers from a New York florist that counted Donna Karan as a client and custom-made tablecloths for which my mother had dragged me around New York's garment district to find fabric. While I grew up Reform, I wanted to incorporate many Jewish traditions into the ceremony, although my mother and rabbi talked me out of performing the Seven Circles.[1] Accompanied by a trio from the New Jersey Symphony Orchestra, my grandfather walked me down the aisle to the music of *Shalom Rav*, my favorite blessing. My father, who I had repaired my relationship with, was present as a guest. It was exactly the kind of wedding my mother envisioned. I, on the other hand, had pictured something in a more beautiful location, not a luxury hotel in New Jersey. Marrying someone because you think it is what your parents want is never a good idea.

Four months after my second anniversary, I told Natalie, over lunch at Sarabeth's on the Upper West Side, that I was leaving Mike. I shared how unhappy I was, how I felt trapped, and how I had met someone I was attracted to and wanted to date. While nothing had happened yet, it had made me realize that I needed to leave before the marriage became more complicated by kids. To my surprise, Natalie was not shocked.

"Jane, do you remember the conversation we had three years ago when we were sitting outside, having dinner at the restaurant on the Upper East Side?" she asked.

"I remember the meal; it was an Italian place," I replied.

"You told me that night that you weren't sure that Mike was the right one for you. I figured that you worked out whatever questions you had since you never mentioned it again and went through with the wedding," she said.

The conversation with Natalie came flooding back to me. I could see everything. We were sitting at an outside table on the side street, not the avenue side that the restaurant was on. Natalie sat on the west side of the table; I, on the east. I could hear the words as I replayed the meal in my mind.

Those concerns were not the only warning. The first summer that Mike and I were dating, we each had a timeshare in South Hampton. We often went out on the same weekend so that we could see each other since we were in separate houses. One weekend Mike did not come, and I was out with a group of my friends to celebrate one of their birthdays. My share house had a party, and I met a guy named Jon. He had sandy-blond hair, was nice, funny, and Jewish. We were outside alone on the deck talking when one of my friends pulled me back inside, whispering to me that Mike was a great guy and not to ruin the growing relationship.

My friends were well aware of my limited ability to stick with a guy for very long. Not only did I have commitment issues, but I had break-up issues too. Not wanting to hurt anyone's feelings, I often avoided telling boyfriends that I was not interested in them anymore, preferring not to return phone calls or avoid places where I knew they would be.

Over the next week, Jon called me several times to invite me to a Grateful Dead show and dinner. I said no, even though I wanted to say yes. I remembered what my friends said and reminded myself that my typical dating behavior was to cut and run when a relationship started to get serious. I figured that I could do worse than Mike, a nice Jewish guy who my friends liked and who my mother had predicted was the one I would marry after meeting him only once. I challenged myself to stay the course, and I did for another year and a half, at which point we moved in together and shortly thereafter became engaged.

Engagement had been my stipulation for moving in, but the order was switched, which left me feeling like I had egg on my face after making my public pronouncement to my friends about not moving in with Mike until I had a ring. Once he did propose, I felt that I had to accept in order to save face.

During the engagement, I would sit at my desk in the office, occasionally daydreaming of things I would do with my next husband or of the qualities that he would have. If my wanting to date someone else earlier in the relationship was a sign that I ignored, this time my subconscious tried the flashing-neon-Times-Square kind to get my attention. I knew my thoughts spoke the truth, and that I would not grow old with Mike, but I dismissed them and tried to stay focused on my work. Thankfully, the sports marketing job I had both pre- and postmarriage often required me to travel on the weekends, the only time we had together.

Similar signs flashed several more times after we were married, but I shut them out, refusing to acknowledge them until after I graduated business school and started a new job at GE Card Services, General Electric's consumer finance business in Stamford, Connecticut. One of the things that I loved about my new job—besides the challenge and its intensity—was the camaraderie. There was a group of us that commuted from New York each day on the train, and we bonded on our rides—about an hour each way. We dubbed ourselves the "Train Crew" and would often grab drinks and dinner during the week when we arrived back in the city. This new community filled a void left by the changing nature of my college friendships. As we approached thirty, our lives were evolving. We were no longer a big group of girls that got together to watch episodes of the original *90210* and *Friends*, have picnic dinners in Central Park during the free summer concerts, or go out in a pack on the weekends. Now, we had other commitments. We had jobs that were more demanding, husbands, and for some, babies. And the exodus out of the city to area suburbs was slowly beginning.

Not only did I enjoy the social part of my new job, it delayed the inevitable return home. The changes in my work situation made it increasingly clear to me how unhappy I was in my marriage. I started to avoid seeing Mike as much as possible. Several mornings a week, I would get up at 5:00 a.m. to go to the gym before catching the 7:15 a.m. train. On nights that I had no plans after work, I would work out when I got back to the city. Most weekdays it was 9:00 p.m. or later when I would get home and see Mike for the first time.

Not surprisingly, Mike became resentful of my new coworkers. If I did not tell him of my plans to go out, he would be furious when I got home, telling me that he was upset because he did not know where I was. When I suggested that we go out with GE friends and their spouses, he showed no interest. When he finally agreed to go, he was disinterested and uncharacteristically rude. I was embarrassed. He became increasingly resentful as I became more involved in my work life. At the same time, the freedom I felt from commuting out of the city and from starting a new chapter in my career made me realize how trapped I felt at home. I felt that Mike was holding me back.

One Sunday in August, we drove to my uncle's house in Connecticut to swim and see my family. As Mike drove, I stared out the passenger-side window, and tears came to my eyes. My chest felt heavy, and I started taking deep breaths to try to calm myself. I felt miserable. I desperately wanted out of this marriage.

Then I met Cameron, a nice non-Jew. Cameron also commuted from the city to the office in Stamford. He was a friend of my group leader, Maahir. I had not formally met him during the commute because we often were on different trains in the morning, but I recognized him from the evening ride. I remember thinking that he was attractive, but I was not attracted to him. I was dealing with what was going on at home and did not give him much thought beyond that initial observation. That changed one morning in the office.

I was going back to my desk after a meeting, and Cameron was walking toward me. I smiled and was about to turn into my office when Cameron said hello and introduced himself.

"Hi. I'm Cameron; I see you on the shuttle to the train station," he said.

My heart started racing, and I felt nervous.

"What are you working on?" he asked.

"I'm an MLP (Marketing Leadership Program), working for Tamara Stone on risk-based pricing, in Maahir Urdu's group. Jane—nice to meet you," I responded, hoping to end the conversation.

Cameron was not letting me off that easily. "Have you considered taking an assignment abroad—a STIR, a short-term international rotation?"

"Uh, no," I answered.

I had been in my job for less than two months. I had not thought about much more than getting up to speed, and going abroad seemed out of the question because of Mike and the hassle of finding him a job.

Cameron pushed back again. "Why not?"

I just wanted this conversation to end quickly. "I'm just not able to do it," I mumbled.

"Why not? It's a really great opportunity."

I thought, *Please just leave me alone.*

"I'm married," I said as quickly as possible, hoping it would be too fast for him to catch. "Gotta go. Nice meeting you."

My heart sank as I walked to my desk, and I wanted to cry. I did not want to be married; I wanted the freedom to take on interesting career opportunities— it was one of the reasons GE appealed to me, and at that moment, I did not want this cute guy to know that I was married! Clearly, I felt some attraction toward him. I recognized this, and I thought that this could not have happened at a worse time, when I already had mixed feelings about Mike. Looking back, maybe that is why it happened in the first place.

The conversation haunted me the rest of the day. By the time I got home, I was depressed. I had to deal with the situation with Mike, but I was scared. I started to realize why people stay in bad marriages: it is comfortable. Being with Mike was like putting on an old pair of jeans. We had a shared college history. Even though we did not know each other at the time, our social circles overlapped while at Syracuse, and we had many of the same experiences. This was comforting in the fact that there was this understanding—this "I get it-ness"—that you just do not have with someone you meet later in life. It was part of the reason getting involved with Mike was so easy in the first place. It was like going back to college and reliving the magic.

Our relationship was like a college one, only with more money and greater independence. Leaving would be like graduating again and finally having to grow up. It would also be admitting failure. Besides, the logistics of going out on my own seemed daunting, and losing Mike's half of our friends as well as saying good-bye to his family—all who I truly loved—made me sad. I was not sure that I had the strength to walk away. This college-like bubble was easy, safe, and familiar. Maybe this attraction to Cameron would pass.

My feelings did not fade; they intensified. After we had arrived back in the city one night, our group went for drinks at a bar in Grand Central Terminal. Following drinks, we walked to an Indian restaurant farther uptown. Cameron and I walked together, talking about books that we were reading. I remember thinking, "Books—he reads books!" I had never seen Mike read anything other than the sports section or *Fortune* magazine.

We read *Fortune* like a bible, putting its suggestions to work in our online trading account that we managed ourselves. It was the tail end of the Internet bubble, and it seemed like every week another website was going public, and twenty-somethings were becoming millionaires. E-commerce was a business buzzword, and many young professionals dreamed of being the next Jeff Bezos and their sites the next Amazon.com. We even knew a few people who had struck Internet gold. Mike was in sales, but he wanted a piece of the dot-com bonanza. He often said that we needed to come up with an idea for a website, to which I would respond in a snarky tone, "Oh, you mean a get-rich-quick scheme."

As Cameron and I talked more, I realized that he had an intellectual curiosity that was appealing and that engaged me in a way I had not experienced in a while. We arrived at an upscale Indian restaurant. It was dimly lit and not very busy, which allowed us to linger. We were seated at a long table, and Cameron and I sat next to each other. We had a lively and delicious meal, with everyone talking and in good spirits. It was one of those perfect moments—one that you wish you could bottle up and save.

Twice during the course of the meal, while we were each speaking to other people, Cameron's leg brushed against mine. My heart raced, and I got that warm, almost tingling sensation that you get when someone you are attracted to touches you. I continued talking, but I was no longer present in the conversation, my mind busy analyzing the movement. Had he done it on purpose? Was it a sign that he was interested in me too? Would it happen again?—the crazy thoughts of someone attracted to another. Later on, Cameron would reveal that he did not even remember our legs brushing together.

A week later, Maahir hosted a team get-together at his apartment in the city after work. The team was mostly women, and even those that did not live in the city took the train in for the party. On the platform in Stamford, Cameron mentioned that he was joining us. After arriving in the city, we walked from the subway toward Maahir's apartment together. He said that he was going home first and would come by the party later.

When Cameron arrived, we were already engaged in conversations and had started drinking Pimm's Cup, an English drink usually made with Pimm's No. I, which is a gin-based alcohol, chilled lemonade, club soda, mint, and slices of cucumber, lemon, and orange—a perfect drink for the late-August evening. Maahir was from Bangladesh by way of England and had shared this popular British drink with Cameron when they had worked in Prague together before they had moved to the GE business in Stamford, but it was new to the rest of us. It was refreshing and went down easy—maybe too easy.

Toward the end of the evening, I was talking to Cameron about our shared love of running; we were near the entry to the small kitchen.

"I've run four marathons. Right now, I'm training for New York in November," he said.

"I've done a half marathon, but I don't think I can do a full one. I can't imagine spending four hours running," I said. A few months later, Cameron talked me into registering for the Spring 2001 Vermont City Marathon in Burlington. On May 27, after four hours and fifteen minutes, Cameron and I crossed the finish line together.

At the moment, I was interested in his training regimen, and as someone that enjoys cooking and healthy eating, I wanted to know what type of diet he followed leading up to the race. "What do you eat during training and before a race—a lot of pasta?" I asked.

"Peanut butter sandwiches and Ensure," he said.

"What? That doesn't sound very healthy," I said with eyebrows raised. And then I lost all power over my rational self and added, "You can't train for a marathon and only eat that. I'm going to make dinner for you."

Cameron replied, "I'll have to take you up on that offer."

Immediately I thought, "Really Jane, how are you going to do that? Are you going to invite him over for a secret dinner one night when Mike is out, or is it going to be a meal with you and your husband from whom you want a divorce?" Thankfully, my manager Tamara, who lived a few blocks from me, came over and asked if I wanted to share a cab home—saved! I gladly accepted before I did anything else irrational.

By the time I got home, my head was spinning from alcohol and conversation with Cameron. It was late, and Mike was already in bed. I washed, undressed, and got into bed too. I lay awake the entire night, unable to calm my racing heart and mind. I tried deep breaths, meditation, and lying in shavasana, the relaxation pose typically used at the end of yoga practice. Nothing worked. I replayed the events of the evening and previous weeks. I resolved myself to tell Mike that I wanted out. Mentally exhausted but feeling a physical rush of adrenalin, I got out of bed at 5:00 a.m. and went to the gym.

After slogging through the day at work, I got home around 7:00 p.m., prepared to talk to Mike that evening. After dinner, I said that I had something I wanted to discuss. I told him that I wanted a divorce. Trying not to sound like a cold-hearted bitch, I resorted to the old break-up line, "It's not you; it's me." I explained that I was unhappy, and that I just did not want to be married anymore. I gave examples of behaviors that I did not like and how they made me feel—ones, that in retrospect, were attempts to validate leaving and avoid being completely honest, which, at the time, I felt would be too hurtful. Telling someone that you never really wanted to marry him and that you did it to prove something to your family seemed heartless and a poor excuse for turning someone else's world upside down. Mike was shocked. He thought I was crazy, and that we could work it out. The conversation resolved nothing, but at least how I felt was out on the table. We got in bed.

Mike easily fell asleep, which should have been an indication that he did not really understand how serious I was. I, on the other hand, lay awake, trying to quiet my thoughts of what would happen next—and of Cameron. It did not help that being in the same bed with Mike made me tense. Sharing such an intimate space with someone that you do not want to touch you, even in the slightest way, is not very conducive to a good night's rest. This began a pattern of sleepless nights that would continue until I finally moved out. Looking back, I wonder why I did not move to the couch, especially since I felt so physically and mentally exhausted—a clear sign of how sleep deprivation distorts ones thinking.

Besides lack of sleep, I began to lose weight. By the time I left, I had shed ten pounds and weighed ninety-three pounds. I had a small appetite and could not keep much food inside. I had never before used the bathroom so consistently.

A card-carrying member of the "Clean Plate Club," halfway through a meal I would uncharacteristically push my plate away. While the body-conscious you-can-never-be-too-skinny girl in me enjoyed how I looked in a bathing suit, I knew that the weight loss was neither healthy nor sustainable.

In the meantime, Mike and I continued to discuss separating, without making much progress toward agreement. I repeated my reasons and examples. He still believed that we could work it out. What he missed or did not want to accept was that I never had any interest in working it out. The train had left the station. I felt that I had finally worked up the courage to extricate myself, and I had no intention of being derailed. I just wanted out as quickly and painlessly as possible. I would have snuck out quietly via a back door without anyone noticing or telling anyone if I could have. This type of exit was in line with my break-up history. Unfortunately, this time I would have to face the person and the conflict head on.

The Saturday following our initial discussion was Labor Day weekend, and we had plans to spend the night at my mother and stepfather's in New Jersey. While just the thought of the trip was painful, I did not think I could cancel. My family had no idea about how I felt or what was going on, and I thought it was best to wait to tell them until we agreed to separate—no need to get everyone worked up until it was necessary.

We drove out to Jersey on Saturday morning and spent the afternoon by the pool in my mother's townhome complex. I read in a lounge chair and would occasionally lie down, trying to relax. Mike and I did not speak much to each other. I daydreamed of Cameron. Something inside me knew that he was the one I would one day marry. At that point, the fact that marrying Cameron would be an intermarriage—which was what I had hoped to avoid—did not cross my mind. When I closed my eyes, I even pictured sitting by the same pool with Cameron and our children, two blond-haired, blue-eyed boys. (This might give the impression that I was dreaming of Aryan poster children, but Cameron and I both have blue eyes, and I have blond hair.) For me, the marriage to Mike was over, and I was ready to move on. But the reality that I was still married was painfully clear that evening at dinner.

During the meal at a nice Italian restaurant, the conversation turned to my work hours and how often I was gone. My mother and stepfather sided with Mike in admonishing me for my new lifestyle. I defended myself by explaining the culture at GE. They continued to apply pressure. I felt that they were ganging up on me. At one point, I looked at Mike and thought that I saw a hint of a smile. He looked to be enjoying himself and the support he was getting. I stopped talking and just wore a stone-cold glare on my face.

When we returned to my mother's, she and I went for a walk. It was a hot, humid, and buggy night. As we started to walk, my mother wanted to know what was wrong with me after the episode at dinner. Feeling that there was no other way to get her to understand my behavior, I told her that I was leaving Mike. We sat down on a bench near some tennis courts, and I repeated the reasons and examples I had given him. I just wanted out. Telling her this seemed easier than having to explain why I had gotten married in the first place. I feared that the real explanation would make her angry or result in her telling me that I was stupid and careless. She had left my father after eighteen years in an abusive marriage. Leaving because I married for the wrong reason and had now met someone that I wanted to pursue a relationship with just did not seem acceptable. At twenty-nine, I was still scared of my mother and wanted her approval.

Much to my relief, my mother was immediately supportive. Having divorced my dad when I was sixteen, she had a good understanding of what I was going through and how I wanted out as quickly as possible. We talked until the swarm of gnats flying around us got to be too much. On the way back to the house she told me that she would help me, including putting me in touch with her lawyer and asking my grandfather to pay my legal fees.

One thing I can say about my mother, stepfather, and father (when I told him) is that they all were unequivocally supportive of my decision. None of them pressured me to stay in the marriage or to even try to work it out. Maybe they knew my personality and realized that once I made up my mind there was no changing it, or they just felt that parental desire to provide unconditional love during a difficult period in their child's life; regardless, my parents supported me.

After the weekend, Mike continued to push to stay together, suggesting that we see a marriage counselor to help us work out our issues. I continued to push for separation. As each of us grew more desperate to get the other to agree to our position, we threw out anything that we thought might turn the tide in our favor. Mike used guilt, saying that his best friend and his wife had moved to the town next to my mother in New Jersey because they thought that one day we would follow suit. I responded by saying that I thought that was a ridiculous reason to choose a place to live.

I threw a jab and revealed that I had met someone else. Mike replied that he did not believe me. I tried to persuade him otherwise. While I had not done anything, I felt that because of the intensity of my feelings for Cameron, that in my heart, I had cheated. Mike insisted that he did not believe that I was the type of person to cheat. Drained, I finally said that I did not love him, and that I just wanted out. I could see how deeply my comment stung—so much for not being a cold-hearted bitch. Mike agreed to separate if I would consent to marriage counseling. I relented, knowing at that moment—before an appointment was even scheduled—that I would go in order to say I tried it and check the box, but that I would not give in. I was done.

At the same time the discussions with Mike were taking place, I was in charge of planning the next Train Crew outing. I sent an e-mail to the group, asking for suggestions on what to do on September 22, which was two weeks away. I got several responses, including one from Cameron. I replied with the other suggestions I had received. He wrote back, giving me his vote for the activity and asked if I had plans on Friday night. My heart raced with nervous excitement, but I was not sure how to respond. Mike and I had agreed to separate earlier in the week, and I felt that I now had a "get-out-of-jail-free" card. On the other hand, I had consented to have dinner with Mike on Friday, and I knew that if I wanted the separation to go as smoothly as possible, I could not break the plans. I remembered that Mike planned to go to my friend Tate's fiancé's bachelor party the following night, and that he would be out late. I thought about what to do. Was it okay for me to go out with someone else? While technically still married, we did agree to separate. During the separation period leading to divorce, millions of people date, don't they? My brain, which was being more rational, told me to say I already had plans. My heart said, "Go out with this guy—this is your chance." At the moment, my heart was stronger than my head.

I e-mailed that I had plans, but that I was free on Saturday night. Ping! I clicked over to my e-mail, hoping it was Cameron's reply. I was giddy but afraid to open his response. I waited a few minutes before reading it. He responded that he would be up for a late dinner after he returned to the city from a golf outing in Connecticut. I agreed. Cameron said that he would make reservations and call my cell on Saturday with the place and time. It was a date.

That Thursday I grabbed drinks after work with some other women on the marketing team and listened with interest as they discussed trying to set up one of the single ones with Cameron. I did not share my situation or that Cameron and I were going out that weekend. Friday night I went through the motions at dinner with Mike at a new Spanish restaurant I had wanted to try on the Lower East Side. It might be on record as the quietest meal ever, with the exception of each of us asking to taste the other's food. We walked home in silence with a fair amount of distance between us so that I could avoid having Mike try to hold my hand.

The next day, I went to the gym early and then to meet Natalie at Sarabeth's. After making her my first friend to know that Mike and I were separating and sharing that I met someone else, I told her that I had a date with the person that night. If Natalie thought that what I was doing was wrong, she never showed it. She even offered to let me move in with her until I found a place to live.

As we left lunch and walked around the Upper West Side, I felt a jumbled mix of conflicting emotions: excitement, nervousness, and uncertainty. Excited for the date, nervous that it might not go well or that Mike might catch me and make the separation process difficult, and uncertain about whether or not going on the date was actually cheating. Unfortunately, separation did not come with a handbook that explained what was and was not acceptable behavior; and living in the same apartment only complicated things. The situation would get easier once I moved out, but that was still two weeks away.

In the meantime, I was going on a date with a nice Episcopal boy who was friends with my manager and who worked down the hall from me. I was too excited to see the red flags or the sign that said, "Danger! Do Not Enter!"

—•—

DIVINE INTERVENTION

As I stood on a Maui beach in the late afternoon sun, I thought about how much excitement I had managed to pack into the last two years—a new job, separation, divorce, engagement, and now marriage again. I never did heed those stop signs when it came to Cameron. In fact, I did not even yield. It is funny how the heart can overcome our more rational mind.

As my yoga teacher, Sandy, says, "We often don't trust ourselves to know where we're going or what we can do, but our heart knows, and it will lead us." After two years, my heart led me to Hawaii to be married by an aging hippy with long, wavy gray hair, wearing a tie-dye T-shirt. He spoke of the spirit wind blowing in our family and friends so that they could be, in some way, present at the ceremony. As I tried not to laugh at Spirit Wind Man, I thought about the last twenty-four months; they had been a journey and a long, strange trip.

The path to my marriage to Cameron started with that initial Saturday night date at Mesa Grill. It was a beautiful late-summer evening, one of those perfect New York nights when it is easy to love the city: sidewalks buzzing with people and conversation, warm temperatures, clear skies. Cameron and I arrived about the same time, and we grabbed a seat at the bar while we waited for our table. I sat down next to a woman I knew from religious school. We said a quick hello. I wondered if she knew that I had been married and noticed that I was not wearing my ring. Once I told Mike that I wanted a divorce, I stopped wearing both my engagement ring and wedding band. I assumed she realized that I was on a date. I knew she had recently broken off her own engagement. I looked at her with envy, wishing I had the courage to get out before saying, "I do."

Seeing her also made me self-conscious. Even though I had not been friends with this woman or seen her for years, with the exception of the occasional High Holiday service, her mother was my mother's real estate agent, and I was not sure how public my mother had gone with the news of my separation. Most people have at some point felt self-conscious, whether it is when they enter a room and know no one, start a new school or job, or during the teen years. But this feeling was different and new. I felt naked, as if my life were completely exposed and on display for the world to see and judge. Beyond feeling like everyone who looked at me knew I was heading toward divorce, I felt ashamed. I became hypersensitive to how others, even strangers, perceived me, most often assuming that they labeled me as a failure, a deserter, selfish, or a bitch. It is hard to believe that in the twenty-first century, with divorce a common marriage outcome that I could feel this way (at the time, almost one-quarter of all marriages in New York City ended in divorce or separation[1]), but as I learned, these are common emotions for someone in my situation. Still, I found no comfort in knowing that I was like other divorcees. I still felt like Hester Prynne, walking around with a badge of shame.

At the same time, I was excited about being with Cameron. As we were seated at our table, Cameron, who was not one to shy away from discussing difficult subjects, began the evening by saying that he thought I had said I was married when he had asked me about taking an assignment abroad.

I said, "I am, but my husband and I are separating. We've agreed to split, and I'll be moving out over the next two weeks."

With my marital status clarified, we had a great evening that ended with us making plans to meet at the Museum of Natural History the next day.

Over the next week, Cameron and I tried to see as much of each other as possible. Besides the museum, we walked around Central Park, ate lunch together at the office, and made dinner at his apartment. I was giddy when I was not dealing with the separation from Mike or our planned trip to Phoenix for my friend Tate's wedding. While I could not forbid Mike from going, I hoped that he would decide not to go and even informed Tate that he might have a "work commitment." I left for work on Friday with Mike still undecided. At 1:00 p.m., he called to say that he would meet me at the airport at four o'clock. To say that I was disappointed is an understatement.

My friend Natalie had counseled me not to tell Tate or Helen, another friend getting married that fall, about my split with Mike. She felt that it would upset them unnecessarily before their weddings. Meanwhile, Mike thought that a weekend together in the desert might get me to change my mind. He was not ready to give up, and I got the sense that he did not believe (or want to believe) that I was serious about moving out. I suppose he thought that a big party with friends would remind me how much fun we had together. And truth be told, Mike and I were at our best in these situations. We loved spending time with friends and dancing, and we could socialize independently of each other. We were the consummate frat-boy–sorority-girl couple, and Tate's wedding was shaping up to be a grown-up version of a formal. I could understand why he wanted to go; I just was not happy about it. I knew that I was not changing my mind and did not want the burden of faking a happy marriage all weekend, especially because I was not a good actor.

It did not take long for one of my more perceptive friends to notice that I seemed unhappy, and in a private moment one afternoon, she asked what was wrong. I revealed what was happening. It felt good to be honest and hear her words of support. Afterward, I walked slowly back to my room to get ready for the ceremony and find the resolve that I needed to pretend for another twenty-four hours. Thankfully, Mike and I did not need to speak much to each other since there were enough friends and acquaintances from college at the wedding to keep each of us occupied. Still, it was difficult to relax. Even dancing to old favorites did not help. I was relieved when the weekend was over, and I started moving my things to Natalie's the week I got home.

That same week, Mike and I began marriage counseling. I made my lack of interest in working things out obvious, but Mike insisted that we continue the weekly sessions. After one meeting, I met my best friend Lauren for dinner to bring her up to speed on what was going on. She listened, and although she and her husband liked Mike, she was supportive of my decision and excited to hear about Cameron. Lauren is an amazing friend. She is there to share good times and bad and is supportive, even if she does not always agree with you. What would transpire between Tate and me over the next few months would serve to remind me of the importance of friends like Lauren.

I began splitting my time between Cameron's apartment and Natalie's. For several weeks after she arrived home from her honeymoon, I tried to reach Tate by phone to tell her about the separation. My calls were not returned, and I finally blurted out what was happening, over voice mail, hoping that would get her to call me back. I was hurt, and I did not understand why she was not making time to talk. Tate was one of my closest friends; at least I thought she was. I had always suspected that I considered her a better friend than she considered me, but I had pushed the idea away anytime it crossed my mind because I did not want to believe it. But this situation forced me to see more clearly where I fell on the friend spectrum, and this made her unresponsiveness hurt even more.

When I finally saw Tate at Helen's bachelorette dinner, she asked me a few questions, and I realized that rather than speaking to me, she had contacted Natalie to get information. She had also decided that the reason I was leaving Mike was that I had met someone else. Angry and looking for an escape from the situation, after dinner, instead of going to Natalie's, I grabbed a cab across town to Cameron's. As Natalie later shared, Tate felt that my action only confirmed her belief that there was another man in the picture.

I expected acquaintances to judge me in one way or another for leaving Mike, but I assumed that my friends would be supportive. I had not considered that this might not be the case; so I was mortified that a friend questioned my integrity and furious that she had labeled me guilty without the chance to prove my innocence. At least my grandfather gave me the chance to explain the situation when he asked if I had been cheating on Mike. Yes, my grandfather wanted to know if I cheated. I wanted to crawl under a rock. As the first and only girl grandchild, I had always had a close relationship with my Poppy.

"Janey, did you start dating Cameron while you were still married to Mike?" he asked one night over the phone.

The question felt like a punch in the stomach, and it was definitely not one of the moments I would choose for my life's highlight reel.

"No, Mike and I had agreed to separate before I started dating Cameron," I answered quietly.

"Okay. That's what I thought. Carol thought you might have taken up with him beforehand, and that was why you were leaving Mike," he said.

Carol was my grandfather's girlfriend. I silently thanked her for embarrassing me and stirring the pot. While I was licking my emotional wounds, the thought did cross my mind that my grandfather's question and its source were a little ironic. Carol was my grandfather's steady girlfriend, but he was neither a widower nor a divorcee. He was still married to my grandmother, who was suffering from Alzheimer's in a nursing home. The irony was not lost on my mother, who did not approve of the girlfriend or my grandfather's behavior. Regardless, I saw the conversation with my grandfather and Tate's comments as confirmation of what I perceived as others' judgment of me. I had to be honest with myself. Although I knew that my marriage to Mike had always been a mistake and that I had wanted to leave for many reasons, others did not. Meeting Cameron was a coincidence of great impact and bad timing— one that I understood could easily give the impression of impropriety, especially to people that felt a divorce needed to be accompanied by an appropriately long mourning period or easily summed-up explanation. But since I did not intend to reconcile with Mike, I did not see a reason to be a nun. I was caught up in a whirlwind of emotions, and my behavior was being dictated by my heart, leading to relationship decisions that would probably give a divorce lawyer heartburn.

While my grandfather was otherwise supportive, Tate did not appear to be. Her nonresponse to my calls stung, but her reaction when I saw her hurt more. I had hoped for the opportunity to talk to her one-on-one to explain how Mike and I had gotten to this point, but I never got that chance. I was devastated by her actions and confused by what appeared to be her lack of support. The more unavailable Tate was to me, the more I pulled back, shutting her out. The situation climaxed at Natalie's thirtieth birthday, when Tate's sister approached me and proceeded to read me the riot act about what was and was not appropriate behavior for a married woman, while I watched Tate sit in a corner and gossip about me.

"Hi Dena," I said, greeting Tate's sister.

"What are you doing?" Dena asked rhetorically. "I mean, who do you think you are? Leaving your husband for someone else is no way for a married woman to behave!"

I was dumbfounded. I remember wanting to open my mouth to say something, but no words came out.

"When you're married and you have problems, you try to work things out," she continued. "You don't just leave and run off with the first guy you're attracted to. A marriage isn't like some random boyfriend that you can just ditch. Go to counseling. Don't just walk away. You should be ashamed of yourself!"

As she spoke, I could feel my face flush and tears start to well in my eyes. I bit my tongue so that I would not cry. After her verbal assault, all I wanted to do was leave, but I knew that I needed to stay until we sang Natalie "Happy Birthday." I wound my way through the crowd, hoping to find a place to hide among some acquaintances or other friends.

The incident took me to my emotional low point. Being publicly berated by someone who did not know the facts was one of the most demoralizing experiences. What I did not know at the time was that this experience would prove to be one of the most valuable lessons I ever learned.

As someone that had enjoyed gossiping with friends, I never took much stock in the idiom: "Don't judge a book by its cover." When a friend observed, while sharing some "juicy news," "I know we shouldn't judge, but life is so much more fun when you do," I agreed.

Standing as the one being judged, and in public no less, I rethought my judgmental nature. Having learned firsthand what it feels like to be on the other side of others' judgments, I decided to retire to a more boring position. In the years that have followed, I have often found myself saying, "There are two sides to every story," or encouraging others to try to see other possibilities. That does not mean that I am a saint—far from it—but I have taken the experience to heart and have tried not to do to others what was done to me. Divorce can make you angry, bitter, and sad. It can also make you a better person.

I saw Tate one last time on New Year's Day 2001, when she made it clear that she did not approve of Cameron not being Jewish. Twelve years later, I still regret that our friendship died, but I recognize that I am as much responsible for its death as Tate. Wanting to leave my old life behind as quickly as possible, along with any painful feelings associated with it, I turned away rather than force a discussion. Five years ago, in an effort to extend an olive branch, I admitted my responsibility and apologized for the rift, doing so in a letter that I hoped would encourage Tate to make amends also. I know a letter was not the most courageous way to ask for forgiveness, but based on what had transpired, I feared hearing rejection over the phone. I received no response, but I feel better knowing that I tried.

Mike and I stopped counseling sessions after four weeks, when the therapist said she felt I had no interest in resolving our issues and did not believe that it was worthwhile to continue. At the same time, I was spending more and more time with Cameron, even missing Yom Kippur services that October to go to Vermont for a long weekend. The trip was fun, but I could not help but think that if there were ever a year that I might not be inscribed in the Book of Life, it was this one. Sensing that I was at risk of exclusion, I made a promise to work extra hard to do the right thing the rest of the year in order to absolve my holiday sins. As I thought about the year ahead, I started to realize that as Cameron and I became more serious, I was going to have to confront the fact that he was not Jewish—something I was conveniently ignoring.

Often, Cameron and I would engage in discussions that would challenge me to think differently—whether it was about books, politics, or business. Our conversations about religion were no different, with the exception that they often took place on long runs in Central Park. There is nothing like a fifteen- or twenty-mile run to get you in the mood to talk about God. Cameron would present his argument that to maintain order in ancient times, men created religion. The concept of an omnipotent being that could levy harsh punishments over individuals and entire nations was smart politics. Once the idea of an all-powerful, omnipresent, omniscient God was established, laymen could write a code of laws and ethics and say that they were the word of God, which made getting acceptance from the public easier. Cameron often held up the laws of kashrut as an example. He would share his view at the time that the dietary restrictions were really about public health.

"When people mixed milk and meat or ate pork or shellfish, they got sick, and the lay leaders needed a way to prevent disease," he said. "After they established the idea of God, they just said, 'God said, "no can do."'"

"Do you believe in God?" I would ask, sometimes during and sometimes after these discussions.

"I believe there is something else, but I'm not sure what that something else is," he would reply.

Cameron's views were not new to me. I had heard Jews and non-Jews rationalize religion before, and it could be a very logical and appealing argument, especially when you were trying to find a way to make religion a nonissue in order to make an interfaith relationship work. My head agreed with Cameron. The Torah is a political document, but as someone who was not Jewish, there was something he was missing. He did not understand my emotional and cultural connection to Judaism. Torah as a blueprint for civil society was not enough for me to disregard the history and culture I share with other Jews. At the same time, I was not confident in my opinions because I did not feel I had studied the Torah or other Jewish texts enough to make a strong counterargument. Actually, to be honest, it was not that I had not studied enough. I had not studied at all. My knowledge consisted of a few highlights remembered from religious school, including the creation story, the Ten Commandments, and the stories of Passover and Hanukkah. Cameron often remarked that his father, who went to theology school and was a layman at his Episcopal church, knew more than I did about Judaism. It was understandable that I did not feel like I came to this discussion from a position of strength.

While Cameron and I were starting to discuss religion, I was reading *The Red Tent*, the book of historical fiction by Anita Diamant in which she tells the story of Jacob's daughter Dinah, found in Genesis chapter 34. In the Bible, her brothers tell her story; in the book, her story is told from her own perspective. I was tearing through the book and discussing it with a friend, who also read it on the train to work. I was in the thick of it on Valentine's Day, my first with Cameron. After work, Cameron and I headed to a cozy French bistro in the East Village to celebrate. During dinner, I started talking about the book, even taking it out of my bag to show him the family tree page. At some point, the conversation moved from the book to our ongoing discussion about religion and then into an argument. By the time we left the restaurant, we did not speak and rode silently back uptown in a taxi—not the Valentine's Day either of us had imagined.

I was frustrated that we were not getting anywhere in our religion discussion, and I realized that I needed to do a better job of articulating why it was important to me to have a Jewish home and children without sounding as if I were succumbing to family pressure. While my family was glad that I was out of an unhappy marriage and dating, they were concerned that I was getting serious with someone so quickly, especially someone who was not Jewish. Do not get me wrong—they liked Cameron; they just would have been more comfortable if he were a Jew. I understood their fear of this just being a rebound relationship. After I had experienced firsthand the difficulties of marriage to someone from a similar background, I appreciated that it was a good idea to minimize differences as my mother had suggested. On the other hand, I felt I had already fulfilled my role as the good girl: I had married the person who met my family's Jewish criteria. Now I wanted to pursue a relationship with someone I felt brought more to the table than the right religion.

To understand better what I believed, I decided to read the Torah. Since I had never read it from cover to cover, I figured it was a good idea to get more comfortable with my own religion before I investigated a different one. It was far more interesting than I thought—even racy in parts. But other than reaffirming my belief in one God, it did not help me clarify my position.

So, I went into research mode. As background, I am kind of a geek. I love learning. I love reading. And when a subject directly affects my life, I tend to scour the Internet and library for books and information so that I can become better informed and make knowledge-based decisions. This is probably why my actions with regard to leaving Mike and getting involved with Cameron were so surprising to some people. It just was not my typical pattern of behavior. I did no research and read no books before I plunged myself into the throes of divorce.

I read several books on interfaith relationships, Jewish family life, and Christian symbols. The interfaith books shared the different ways that couples resolved the religion issue from pursuing one faith to conversion to raising children in two religions. It even discussed how some families felt that joining the Unitarian church was a good compromise because of its liberal theology. The options that were presented were interesting, but the only one that appealed to me was a Jewish home. The problem was that I felt that by insisting on Judaism as the only religion that I was digging my heels in and not showing the ability to compromise, which at the time, I thought was more important. I was not making much progress. I cracked the book about Christian symbols, hoping that by being better informed about the other side, I could find areas where I could give. It did not work.

Part of me wanted to scream, *"Ugh! This is too hard!"* and call it quits. But I believed in Cameron and me, and I was not ready to give up. Not to mention, the idea of failing at another relationship was not so appealing either. If I had been in the practice of talking to God (I was not), now would have been a good time to appeal for some help. But since I felt that the combination of questioning my faith and my other transgressions over the past year had already earned me a black mark next to my name, I assumed that divine intervention would be asking for too much. I know now that God would not have been appalled at all since I was engaging in a very Jewish act. Since Jacob wrestled with God and man in chapter 32 of Genesis, wrestling with the idea of God has been at the core of Jewish identity.

Determined to find a solution, I began to look inward to try to define my beliefs. I realized that as convenient as it would be to disregard a belief in a higher power, I could not. As the Monkees said, "I'm a believer." I also knew that while I accepted that Jesus was an important historical figure, I did not believe that he was divine. He also scared the bejesus out of me (an issue it took me another seven years to work out—see chapter 4). Most importantly, I could not shake my Jewish peoplehood, that underlying bond that unites an individual Jew with the entire Jewish community. *Kol Yisrael arevim zeh bazeh*[2] (all Jews are responsible for one another). With that realization, I found the reason why I wanted a Jewish home: my people were counting on me. I felt that I could not let them down.

As Cameron and I continued to try to find a solution to religion in a future home with children, I finally explained myself one night at our kitchen table. As tears streamed down my face, I articulated the guilt that I felt for considering intermarriage. "After all the things the Jewish people have endured, how can I turn my back?" I said.

"I don't think anyone is asking you to turn *your* back," responded Cameron.

"Six million Jews died in the Holocaust, and we're losing more because people are marrying outside the faith and choosing not to raise their children as Jews. How can I do the same? If I don't help to carry on the religion, who will?" I continued.

Cameron did not respond as I sat in the chair crying, finally releasing all my frustration, confusion, guilt, and pressure. I never thought that I would have this conversation with a potential (not Jewish) mate, but here I was. I clearly saw that, rather than being part of the solution, I was now part of the problem I just described.

I am not sure how I knew that intermarriage and Jewish continuity were concerns of the Jewish community. I was not, as a young adult, engaged in Jewish life outside of the observance of holidays with my family. I did not read the Jewish press. Maybe I heard the disappointment and concern in the voices of the adults in my family when they spoke about my uncle and cousins who had married out. Maybe it was a friend's comment or a topic of a High Holiday sermon at my parent's synagogue. Whatever the source, I knew that intermarrying was considered wrong and bad for the Jews. Given my predilection for pleasing others, I did not want to be one of those "bad Jews" who were willing to let the future of the faith be someone else's problem. I cared too deeply about my connection to the Jewish people and my Jewish family to do that.

Now that I am actively engaged in passing on Judaism to my son and watch other interfaith parents nurture their children's Jewish identity, I see that my beliefs about intermarriage were misguided. I accepted as true what vocal Jewish leaders and academics said about intermarrieds—they lose belief, and their children are less likely to associate themselves with a religion—because I did not see any Jewishly engaged interfaith families that countered this perception. I did not know that intermarriage did not always equal abandonment of faith, but that might have turned out to be a good thing. Looking back, I think that this idea of giving up my Jewish identity and my children not having a connection to Judaism because Cameron was not Jewish subconsciously ignited my fight response, which created a determination to beat the odds. If things worked out with Cameron, my interfaith family would be different; we would prove the intermarriage naysayers wrong.

After the conversation, we again tabled the discussion of religion in the home. Then, as if God really had been watching, a brochure arrived in the mail from the Center for Religious Inquiry (CRI), an interfaith program based at St. Bartholomew's (St. Bart's) Church on Park Avenue in Midtown and directed by a rabbi. I opened it and noticed that one of the offerings was a month-long course for people in interfaith relationships, comparing and contrasting Christianity and Judaism, taught by St. Bart's rector and a rabbi. As my face lit up, my first thought was that this may be the only time in my life that I was happy my name was on a direct mail list; my second thought was that I could not wait to tell Cameron about it when he got home. When Cameron arrived, I excitedly showed him the CRI catalog. Knowing that we were approaching the one-year anniversary of our first date and discussing marriage, we agreed that this program might be just what we needed to resolve our problem of religion in our future home. I went online and registered us both for the class that summer.

The night of our first session, Cameron had something come up at work that made it difficult for him to leave, so, with a brand new spiral notebook in hand, I went to class alone. After introductions, the rector and the rabbi dove into the material. As I sat and listened, I looked at the participants. I was the youngest person in the room and the only one in an interfaith relationship. With the exception of one woman who was there just because the subject was of interest to her, all of the other people in the room were in their fifties and sixties, and they were taking the course because they had a child who was dating or married to someone of a different faith. I was both impressed and surprised: impressed that these parents would seek out something like this in order to bridge a gap or improve their relationship with their child, surprised that there were parents that actually did this kind of stuff. I do not remember either of my own parents ever pursuing any kind of adult education, and I felt quite certain that it never crossed their mind to take a course such as this one to gain some insight that might help them have a better connection with one of their children. While my parents have always been well-read, well-traveled, and engaged in many cultural activities, up to this point in time, they just were not that intellectually curious when it came to religion. I wanted to tell my classmates how amazing I thought they were just for being there and how their children were lucky to have parents that cared to do something like this.

Throughout class, I diligently took notes so that I could go over them with Cameron at dinner. I came home gushing about the class and looked forward to Cameron joining me the following week. But the second week played out like the first, with Cameron at work and me at class alone. This was not working out as I had hoped. I enjoyed the course and was learning a lot, but this was something we were supposed to be doing together so that we could learn in order to make a more informed decision about our religious home. I was disappointed and felt that time was running out. We only had two more sessions left. Cameron promised to make it to the third one. As it turns out, that was the only meeting he really needed to attend.

Call it fate, destiny, or divine intervention, but it is funny how, sometimes, things just have a way of working out. Cameron did come to the third class, and from the moment it started, it seemed like that night's discussion was tailored just to us. The rabbi told the story of his own daughter, who married a non-Jew who chose to convert before the wedding. He used the story to illustrate how choosing one faith did not prevent a family from still participating in rituals or celebrations of the other faith family, and that sometimes what we perceive as important to someone really is not as important as we believe. He talked about how his son-in-law was nervous to tell his parents that he was converting, worrying about their reaction. When he did tell them, his parents asked one question: "Will any future grandchildren be able to come to our house to celebrate Christmas?" He said yes. His parents were fine with the conversion.

The story reminded me of Cameron's family. His mother and father were deeply involved with the Episcopal Church socially and religiously. They attended services most Sundays and were active members of the vestry. Yet, they did not go to services on Christmas ("Too many Cs and Es"—Christmases and Easters, the Christian equivalent to the High Holiday Jew), nor was their home celebration religious. But Christmas was the holiday that my mother-in-law looked forward to the most. When I asked Cameron about it, he said that it had always been more about being together as a family. I was hoping that no matter what our decision was about a religion in our home, that my future in-laws, like the parents in the rabbi's story, would be happy as long as we were joining them in this tradition.

As class continued, the reverend discussed the importance of choosing one religion for a home. To make his point, he shared the example of a school child that is told to make a winter-holiday art project. As he spoke, it seemed as if Cameron and I were the only ones in the room. "Your child can make only one project," he said. "He or she must choose red and green paper to create a Christmas theme or blue and white for Hanukkah."

I felt as if he were speaking directly to us.

"What should your child do?" he asked. "It appears that this is a simple choice between colored papers, but for a child being raised in a home with two religions, with no clear religious identity, this is not a choice between red and green or blue and white, it is a choice between Mommy and Daddy. And that's a decision no child wants to make," he added.

I have no recollection of what else was said. My mind was on the example. Thinking about putting my child in the position described made me want to cry, and I did not even have a child yet! I also thought about how the books I had read on different interfaith arrangements had focused on the parents and how they chose to navigate two faiths in the home, their compromises, and their feelings. The vignettes never put forth how the parents' decision affected children or a child's perspective. The reverend's story shocked me (and I realized later, Cameron too) into thinking about our situation from a very different point of view. Six years later, we heard how this situation played out in real life.

While on summer vacation in Maine, we met an interfaith family from Westchester, New York. One afternoon, as we sat on the beach talking, our conversation turned to how we decided to handle religion in the home. "How did you guys decide what to do about religion?" the wife asked.

"We happened to be taking a class about interfaith relationships before we got engaged because we were struggling to come to an agreement on religion in the home," I said.

"The class was taught by a priest and a rabbi," added Cameron.

"The priest presented a situation that forced us to consider our decision about religion from the perspective of our future children rather than from an adult's point of view," I said. Then I recounted reverend's story.

The other couple looked at each other, and then the wife said, "That happened to us this year!" Then she told us about an incident that took place at their daughter's school.

"This past December, our daughter, Meredith, came home from school very upset one day. I asked her what was wrong, and she told me about her math class. In order to illustrate the concept of groups, the teacher asked all the students that were Christian and celebrate Christmas to stand on one side of the room and all of the Jewish students that celebrate Hanukkah to go to the other side. Since up to this point we had told our children that they were both religions and celebrated Christian and Jewish holidays, Meredith stood in the middle. She said she didn't know what to do, and that she was the only student who didn't choose a side.

"Then her teacher said, 'Meredith, please pick a group.'

"Meredith told her, 'I'm both religions. I celebrate both holidays.'

"The teacher responded, 'You can't be both; you can only be one for this exercise. Now, please pick a side.' She said she just stood there in the middle of the room paralyzed.

"Meredith told me that she was embarrassed, and that she wanted to be like everyone else; she wanted to be one religion. While I recognized that the lesson was not well-conceived, since it was possible that a student could be a religion that did not celebrate either holiday, I felt terrible that this happened to my child. The experience drove home the point that we needed to choose one religious identity for our family."

Years after our premarital class, when we had relocated to Dallas, a rabbi at our temple there would make a similar point during an Interfaith Mom's program, saying, "I'd rather you choose to raise your children as Christians than choose to do both or nothing."

After class, Cameron and I walked out with a couple that was taking the course with us because their son had married a Jewish woman. We talked about how much we were enjoying the discussions and then spent a few moments patting the other on the back for engaging in dialogue. "Atta boys!" out of the way, we said goodnight. As Cameron and I strolled uptown, trying to decide where to eat dinner, he turned to me and said, "Religion is more important to you than it is to me. I'm on board with raising our children as Jews."

"Really?" I asked, unsure if I believed what I had just heard.

"In our society you don't need to do anything to feel Christian," he added. "We could do nothing in our home, and our children would think they were Christian. There is more to being Jewish than just religion. For our children to be Jewish, they need to be taught what it means to be Jewish. I'm okay with our children being raised as Jews, but it means that we're responsible for ensuring that they learn about Judaism," he said.

I am not sure if my face registered the shock I felt from hearing these words. I was hoping that we would come to this place, but after not making much progress previously, I thought it was just as likely that we would decide that we could not agree and break up. My heart exploded with happiness and gratitude. I was so overcome with emotion that I do not recall my response. What I do remember is that we held hands as we continued our walk north into our neighborhood and to a Thai restaurant for dinner.

The following month, after a short hike to the top of a small mountain in the Berkshires, Cameron got down on his knee and fumbled in his pocket.

I said, "What are you doing?"

He replied, "Trying to ask you to marry me!"

A year later, we were married in Hawaii. We had started to plan a small ceremony and reception to take place on the property of my aunt and uncle's home in Connecticut, but I had no real interest in another traditional wedding, although I told Cameron that if he really wanted one, I would do it. Thankfully, he did not. (Cameron often mentions that one of the nice things about marrying me was that I came with a full set of china.)

Since we were paying for the event ourselves, we wanted to keep it intimate. I wanted something low-key and Cameron's one stipulation was that he wanted someone we knew to perform the ceremony rather than a "rent-a-rabbi." We thought to ask the reverend and rabbi, who taught our class if they would officiate, but they had a "no officiating" policy. Cameron then decided that he wanted his best friend's father, Mr. McCormick, who he had known since childhood and who I had met several times, to do it. Mr. McCormick was a Baptist minister. Cameron said that he would tell him that we wanted a religiously neutral ceremony—just God, no Jesus. I agreed, although the idea of a minister alone performing the vows made me uncomfortable.

A Christian officiant did not seem to fit with the decision we made about religion, even if the ceremony did lack a religious identity; and although Cameron assured me that there would be no mention of Jesus, I did not trust that would be the case. I feel silly admitting this now, especially since I have had the opportunity to spend more time with the McCormicks, and I know that Mr. McCormick would have honored our request, but at the time, I was uncertain about how our new religious commitment would play out, and I was scared of any blurring of the lines. Plus, I knew that the mention of a minister would not sit well with my mother and others in my family.

For all my concerns about who would read us our vows, that was not what sent us running to Hawaii. On our morning commute to work, Cameron and I discussed the wedding plans. The conversation turned heated as we grappled with the definition of small—immediate family only, or aunts, uncles and cousins too? How did we decide which members of Cameron's large, extended family should be invited? As we got closer to the office, the discussion became a shouting match with me blurting out, "I don't even want to have a wedding! Let's just get married on our honeymoon and forget about all this!"

We had already booked four days in Napa Valley and San Francisco, followed by a week in Maui. My emotional outburst got Cameron's attention, and he said in a calm voice, "Really? I'm game for that. Do you have the guts to tell your mother?"

Fired-up, I responded, "Yes. I'm calling her as soon as we get to the office! Do you have the guts to tell yours?"

"Sure," he said. Later he admitted that he thought I would chicken out and did not think he would need to call his parents.

When we arrived in Stamford, I marched into my office, closed the door, and called my mother with the news. The wedding was off. We were getting married when we got to Hawaii. She was welcome to join us, but it was okay if she chose not to make the trip. Neither of our families attended; instead, both chose to make receptions for us when we returned.

That is how we came to find ourselves standing on the beach at sunset, listening to Mr. Spirit Wind read our vows as we stood barefoot in the sand, tears coming to his eyes as he noted the connection between the blue of the sky and ocean, our eyes, Cameron's shirt, and the ring bag. He said that he would perform a ceremony using any religion we wanted, but we requested just the basic "I do's" since a Jewish wedding ceremony performed by a non-Jew did not seem kosher. The event was brief. After ten minutes, we were officially man and wife.

From divorce to marriage, those two years were an interesting ride, filled with many bumps in the road. But in my heart, I knew the journey was well worth it, even if at the moment, I did not have any idea the role it would play in shaping us as a family and a couple or what challenges and joys lay ahead.

THREE

TOO JEWISH FOR MY JEWISH FAMILY

We became too Jewish for my family a few years after Cameron and I married. At Interfaith Moms' meetings, while other women shared the challenges they faced with family members of another religion, I discussed the issues I had with my own Jewish relatives. More than a few moms raised an eyebrow, and frankly, I was as surprised and confused as everyone else.

After Cameron and I became engaged, my family members had no problem making known their feelings about intermarriage. My brother, who would later marry a non-Jew, shared his disappointment in my choice to marry outside our faith. My stepbrother communicated his not-so-positive feelings toward non-Jews, via my mother and stepfather. My grandfather wanted to know how any children would be raised.

He asked, "Will you raise your children Jewish?"

"Yes," I said. "Cameron and I have agreed to have a Jewish home and raise our children as Jews."

"Oh, okay," my grandfather responded. "Is he going to convert?"

"No," I said.

I had not even considered asking Cameron to convert. Having a Jewish home was deeply important to me, and I wanted Cameron to help me create one, but I believed that conversion was a very personal decision and one that someone should make on his or her own, not because he or she was pressured. I also knew Cameron well enough to know that if he felt any pressure at all, he would do the exact opposite. From a win–loss perspective, I thought that I had already won. I had gotten everything I had wanted in the arrangement: a Jewish home and Jewish kids.

While Cameron, who is not observant, did not feel he sacrificed, he did agree to give up sharing a part of his identity with his children. I was appreciative and grateful for his choice. Asking him to go the additional step and become a Jew felt greedy and came with the risk that he would change his mind. I felt there was too much to lose to go down that path.

"Maybe one day Cameron will decide to convert," my grandfather said.

"Maybe."

I understood my grandfather's questions and his hopes. He was the oldest son of observant Jewish immigrants from Hungary, and Judaism and its continuation were important to him. His father, my great-grandfather, was a *chazzan* (a cantor), who grew up at the Great Synagogue, also known as the Dohany Street Synagogue, in Budapest on the Pest side of the Danube. His form of Judaism was not Orthodox but Neolog. Neolog Judaism was a Reform movement that began in the late nineteenth century in mostly Hungarian-speaking regions of Europe. The Jewish Agency for Israel characterizes Neolog Judaism as traditional, falling somewhere between Conservative and Reform.[1] Other sources liken it to the more traditional wing of the US Conservative movement.

After immigrating to the United States, my great-grandfather Soma sang at Oheb Shalom Congregation, a Conservative synagogue in Newark, New Jersey, and later at Ahavath Zion, a more traditional congregation, also in Newark, at which he also served as temple president. My mother remembers going to Ahavath Zion, sitting in the upstairs pews, and watching him help lead the prayers. Music was important to my grandfather's family, and my mother often talks about the grand Passover Seders that included the families of my great-grandfather's many brothers. The brothers would have sing-offs to see which one was the loudest and best. One celebration was so big that the family had to rent a hall, and a dais was arranged at the front of the room on which the brothers sat, led the Seder, and sang.

Given how central Judaism was to my grandfather's upbringing and identity, it is not hard to understand his desire for Cameron to convert. He had watched his son, my uncle, marry a not Jewish woman as well as several of his brothers' children. With my engagement, another generation was continuing the pattern.

While my grandfather asked questions, my mother was uncharacteristically silent with her opinion. When we told her upon our engagement that our children would be raised as Jews, her only response was, "Great." I mistakenly understood my mother's silence as satisfaction with our decision. What I only learned in recent years was that she doubted that Cameron and I would live up to our commitment.

"You and Cameron really put your money where your mouth is," she said later. "I didn't think you would do anything actually, but you've done what you said you would do: create a Jewish home."

Although I was shocked at the time that she had not believed that we would make good on our promise, I should not have been surprised. My family's closest experience with an interfaith marriage was my uncle's, my mother's brother. My uncle's home had no religion but did have a tree and gifts on Christmas. In fact, my cousin found out he was "half" Jewish by accident. When he was ten years old, he made a comment about Jews in front of the family during Thanksgiving. His tone offended my mother and prompted her to break the news to him about his Jewish ancestry.

"We're Jewish; your grandfather is Jewish; and your dad is Jewish," she said.

My cousin, eyes wide and mouth open, stared at those of us in the room. "I'm not!" he said and walked out.

Understanding that my family's experience with intermarriage was not positive, Cameron and I worked to show that an interfaith home could have a religious identity. While living in Connecticut, after we married, we hosted a Hanukkah party for my family. It was fun, and even my uncle and his family attended. Shortly before GE transferred us to Cincinnati, we had started to think about joining a temple. I inquired about the openness of Greenwich area synagogues to interfaith couples. When work moved us, we joined Valley Temple in Cincinnati, a small, warm, and open synagogue with many interfaith members. Beyond its welcoming reputation, Valley is famous for being Jerry Springer's congregation. (Yes, Jerry Springer the tabloid talk show host and former mayor of Cincinnati is Jewish. He even had an aliyah on Yom Kippur. I guess with a show like his, it is probably not a bad idea to be in temple on the Day of Atonement.)

Now we not only had a religious home—and one with celebrity appeal no less!—but a way to meet people in our new city. Once a month we would race home from our office in Dayton, which was an hour drive north, in order to change and go to Friday night Shabbat services. We always enjoyed these evenings, which Cameron liked to say offered "good reminders" and would follow the socializing at the oneg (postservice reception) with dinner at a restaurant. My mother and stepfather even joined us during one of their visits. We loved our intimate congregation and were eager to show it off.

When our son, Sammy, was born, we had a bris, for which our rabbi created a beautiful and inclusive ceremony. He ensured that all of our immediate family participated—my mother, father, stepfather, brother, and Cameron's parents and sister. My father-in-law carried Sammy into the kitchen on a pillow, jokingly whispering to him that there was still time to make a getaway. Joking aside, my in-laws and sister-in-law were happy to be participants in Sammy's first Jewish lifecycle event. Cameron, who never once questioned having a bris, was as proud as I was to have our child enter into this sacred covenant with the Jewish people. The importance of this ancient ritual was not lost on me as I tried but failed to contain my emotions (and postpartum hormones) as I read my part of the service through the tears of joy that were streaming down my face.

I thought about how lucky we were to have a family that embraced our choices and to have found, through Valley, a synagogue that embraced us as well. We became regulars at Valley's Tot Shabbat services and attended the congregational Hanukkah celebration. A model for how we would celebrate various Jewish holidays also developed. Since our distance from my Jewish family in New Jersey and the timing of the celebrations often prevented us from celebrating together, I began to host the holidays. With most of our time in Cincinnati spent at the office, we did not have a large network of friends, and the ones we had were not Jewish. What we did have was an adopted Jewish family.

My stepfather had gone to law school in Cincinnati, and his best friend's ex-wife, Hannah, lived there. Her children had moved away, and she took Cameron and me under her wing, treating us like her own kids, and Hannah's parents, who were Holocaust survivors, made us their adopted grandchildren. This Cincinnati family was the one with who we shared the Jewish holidays. What I learned was that I loved orchestrating the celebrations. Freed by distance from any familial rules or constraints, I was able to enjoy the holidays my own way.

Cameron and I still remember sitting at our kitchen table during a High Holiday meal, listening to Hannah's parents tell us their story: how they were married in secret, in Germany, and then escaped to England, where they worked as household help before immigrating to the United States. We were mesmerized, and if it were possible for our admiration for them to grow, it did on that night. So far, being an interfaith family did not seem very hard. We did not have any issues with either of our families. Everything was agreeable.

While some couples experience ongoing problems related to their difference in religion, many others experience interfaith issues intermittently, sometimes triggered by a hot button—such as holiday lights or a Christmas tree—and sometimes cropping up in a more random manner. Our first brush with tension over our religious homelife left both Cameron and me scratching our heads. Our Shabbat celebration was the issue.

After two years in Cincinnati, Cameron's job moved us to Dallas. Again, we made it a priority to join a synagogue. We were fortunate to find another congregation, Temple Emanu-El, which openly welcomed interfaith families. We became active in outreach programming. I got involved in the Interfaith Moms group, and Cameron started the Interfaith Dads group. We developed friendships with families like ours and learned how to build a strong Jewish identity in our son.

At a December Dilemma program, where we discussed how to handle the issues that often creep up during the Hanukkah–Christmas season, I learned that if we wanted our children to see themselves as Jews, we should not make December the primary shaper of Jewish identity. It should be a yearlong process. One of the primary suggestions was to celebrate all Jewish holidays throughout the year, with an emphasis on weekly Shabbat observance.

Sammy and I were celebrating Shabbat during a Friday morning Mommy and Me program called Cradle Roll at the temple preschool, and we enjoyed doing the blessings and songs. I thought it would be nice to try at home and a good way to fulfill Cameron's stipulation that, if we were going to have Jewish children, we needed to teach them about Judaism. Plus, since my teenage years, I had felt that Shabbat was special.

The seeds of Shabbat's transformative power were laid when I was a teen, and I would attend the Friday night service before a friend's bar or bat mitzvah. I anticipated meeting my friends in the sanctuary, singing the prayers, and trying to avoid the stern look the rabbi gave when he caught us talking. In my early high school years, when my parents separated, I remember going to services with my mom. Services provided a comforting place to escape the tumult of my parents' situation. A few years later, when I started to attend Jersey Federation of Temple

Youth (JFTY) conclaves and during my National Federation of Temple Youth (NFTY) trip to Israel, I fell in love with the warm, campy services with song leaders playing guitar and singing Debbie Friedman melodies, which were beautiful alternatives to the traditional ones used at temple. Today, I still get excited when we use those tunes during services, and I always lean over and whisper to Sammy, "this is how we sang this song (or prayer) when Mommy was a kid." I asked Cameron if he would be okay if we started a Shabbat ritual at home.

"At the December Dilemma meeting the other night, they said it was important to celebrate Shabbat and other Jewish holidays throughout the year in order to build a clear Jewish identity," I said. "You know Sammy loves when we celebrate Shabbat on Friday mornings at Cradle Roll. What do you think about us doing Shabbat at home?"

"I don't have a problem with it," Cameron said. "It sounds like a good idea, but you need to take the lead on it."

"I will," I responded.

I wish I could say that our early experience was smooth. Since I had not celebrated Shabbat in the home growing up, I felt awkward, even nervous that I might not say the blessings correctly, or that I would look foolish in front of my family. I know this is crazy since neither my not Jewish husband nor my one-and-a-half-year-old knew differently. But since it was an important ritual, and one that I felt I should feel comfortable performing, I was scared that I might get it wrong. We muddled our way through the blessings for the candles, wine, and challah. As the weeks passed, we became more comfortable with the prayers.

I have learned through my conversations with Jewish moms, as well as various books, that my awkwardness performing Shabbat home rituals is not an uncommon feeling. The author Wendy Mogul, in her book *The Blessing of a Skinned Knee*, mentions that her family "stumbled through a blessing" when they first began a Shabbat home ritual.[2] But for many like me, who did not grow up in a ritually observant home, it is not just about trying to remember the right prayer or correct pronunciation of the Hebrew words; it is also the idea that saying a blessing before a meal feels very Christian. As a child, when I ate dinner at a Christian friend's home, grace was said. At the homes of my Jewish friends, we just ate.

Having learned, recently, that there is a blessing for almost everything in Judaism, including going to the bathroom, giving thanks for the food on our table should not have felt strange. Certainly observant Jews would raise their eyebrows at the idea that I felt as if I were adopting Christian behavior by praising God as "the creator of the fruit of the vine" and for "bringing bread forth from the earth," but when you are not accustomed to something, it can take a while to become comfortable.

During Interfaith Moms meetings, the not Jewish women often say how they "don't get" why their Jewish husbands or the Jewish moms in the group are so uncomfortable with saying a blessing—a Jewish blessing—at the dinner table. For many of us, the answer is, "it's just not what Jews do (outside of the very observant)."

My friend Sandra often mentioned that her not Jewish husband encouraged the introduction of the Shabbat prayers.

"Joe grew up in a home where grace was said every evening before dinner, and he felt that it reminded him to be appreciative for what he had," she said. "He really wanted to introduce something similar so that our boys would learn the same lesson. He could sense that I wasn't comfortable with the idea since, in my mind, grace was something Christian people said and we were raising our kids Jewish.

"He said, 'It doesn't have to be grace. It can be the Hamotzi or Shabbat blessings.' He was insistent, so we started having Shabbat dinner on Friday nights."

I imagine the apprehension that Sandra and I felt toward prayer before meals is similar to how many Jews in the mid-nineteenth century felt when the practice of a weekly sermon delivered by a rabbi, which was modeled on what was done in Protestant churches, was introduced. When the custom of a rabbinic speech first started, it was done at the end of the service so that people had the option to leave.

Slowly, we began to feel more at ease with our Shabbat ritual and began adding to our weekly celebration. First, it was *tzedakah* (charity). Sammy put money into a handmade tennis-ball-can tzedakah box before we lit the candles. We even let him select the organization that would receive the funds once a year. For several years, it was the Australian Koala Foundation because, as Sammy said, "We can help animals and the earth by planting trees."

During a Shabbat picnic, we received a booklet that included blessings for tzedakah, the group, children, and after the meal. We added these to our weekly ritual. I was eager to build our observance and make it more meaningful. I read books such as Meredith Jacob's *Modern Jewish Mom's Guide to Shabbat* and incorporated new ideas. We started asking each other, "What was your favorite part of the week?" "Right now," was often the answer from all of us. My husband and I each started to whisper something special in our son's ear after we said the blessing for male children. (Thank you, Meredith, for the suggestion!) It included telling him how much we loved him and something we were proud of him for from that week. Sammy embraced the ritual and, after a while, made it his own by designating himself as the "decider" of who gets to whisper first.

Sammy and I also started doing Shabbat-related projects. We tie-dyed a tablecloth to use on Friday nights and Jewish holidays. We baked challah, which I have learned, is more art than science. Sammy started calling himself the "master challah braider," wrapping the snakes of dough in various designs and then appraising his work and, like a true artist, explaining what each shape represented. He would ask Cameron after the Hamotzi if he liked his masterpiece.

When we started doing Shabbat, I had no idea how our home celebration would unlock the real beauty of the holiday. Now that I saw what a joyous part of our week it had become, I was eager to show my mother. Besides sharing what we thought was magic, I thought sharing Shabbat with her would demonstrate that while Cameron might not be Jewish, we clearly had a Jewish home. Celebrating together would prove our commitment to Judaism. I felt certain that my mother would be excited to celebrate with us when she visited, imagined that she would be proud, and that upon going home, she would tell my family and her friends about it. At times, I am still a little girl, looking for my mother's approval, and yes, I felt as if I had something to prove. I felt I needed to show how Jewish we were. It is a feeling that anyone who has ever wanted to be accepted as a full-fledged member of a club can relate.

I imagined her saying to my brother, "Your sister and Cameron are really Jewish. You should see the Shabbat dinner we had."

Or to her friends, "You'd have no idea that Cameron isn't Jewish. You should hear him say the blessings in Hebrew. You would have no clue that this is an interfaith home."

Instead of the pat on the back or stamp of approval that I thought I would get when I mentioned that we would have Shabbat dinner at home on Friday night, she said that we should go out for dinner.

"Why are you making things difficult for yourself? I'm here to make your life easier by taking you out to dinner. I'm relieving you from the burden of cook-ing," she said.

I just looked at her. I was completely confused. Had I implied that making Shabbat dinner was a burden? I do not remember complaining about it. I thought I had spoken enthusiastically about celebrating Shabbat.

"Uh, I appreciate your offer, but I enjoy making Shabbat, and we like celebrating together at home," I responded, trying to be polite and appreciative while hiding my disappointment.

My mother repeated this refrain every time she visited for the next two years, and each time, I explained that Shabbat was not a burden, but a joy. I confided to Cameron that I just did not get it. I thought that our Shabbat observance would be viewed as a good thing.

As our comfort level with Jewish home rituals grew, so did our holiday observance. When Sammy was three, we decided to have a sukkah. A sukkah is a temporary structure (it looks like a trellis with covered sides and vines or branches across the top) that symbolizes the tents that Jews lived in during the forty years in which they wandered the desert. We had (and continue to have) a large organic vegetable garden, and we thought that it would be a nice way to connect our gardening efforts to Judaism and give them a deeper meaning. My mother happened to be visiting when we were making decorations for the sukkah. While cutting out leaves and fruit from construction paper, my mother again asked, "Why are you going to all this trouble? You have so many other things to do."

"It's fun for Sammy," I responded. "He is really looking forward to having a sukkah, eating in it, and having his friends over for a Sukkot party. Plus, it's a good opportunity to be thankful for everything we've grown in the garden."

Looking back, maybe I should have explained to her the importance of year-long engagement with Jewish holidays as a way for interfaith families to build Jewish identity. Yet, I believe that would have only implied that we were implementing these home rituals because we felt we needed to, not because we wanted to.

Again, I talked to Cameron about how confused and hurt I was by my mother's response.

"When I thought about the possible challenges we could confront as an interfaith family, I never considered that resistance to the observance of Jewish rituals in the home by my Jewish family would be one of them," I said. "I expected a more positive response because we were doing what we promised to do: create a Jewish home and raise our son Jewish."

"Honey, I don't know what to tell you," Cameron said. "It's weird. You would assume the family with the issues would be the one whose traditions are not observed."

"I get the sense that my mom and Joel (my step-father) feel that we've gone too far," I added. "I thought we'd gotten it right. Instead, I feel as though there is a game-show announcer saying, 'You've made the wrong choice again!'

"If I hadn't been so sure that how we've incorporated the practice of Judaism into our home was going to be a home run, maybe I wouldn't feel so disappointed."

The next chance I had, I shared my confusion with one of our rabbis. He said, "She does want your family to be Jewish, but she wants you to be Jewish the way that *she* is Jewish."

This framed the issue in a relational context rather than a religious one. Psychologists frequently mention the difficulty parents have letting their children go and watching grown children become parents—*parents who do things differently from them*. What I saw as a choice based on the different dynamics in my home—a home with parents of different religions—she saw as a rejection of her parenting model. After my conversation with my rabbi, the more I thought about my mother's reaction, the more I realized that it did not matter what I was doing differently. The fact that I was doing it differently was one of the issues.

What I learned is that what we often perceive as issues unique to interfaith families are frequently the same tensions most parents and their adult children face: parental control, independence, and boundaries, to name a few. In a study supported by the National Institutes of Health and published in 2009 in *Psychology and Aging*, nearly all parents and their adult children (94 percent) said that they experience some tension in their relationships.[3] While some of the issues inter-faith families confront often appear to be religious in nature, when examined more closely, they are really the same challenges we all face with our parents, regardless of faith or cultural differences.

The well-known psychoanalyst and social psychologist Erich Fromm said, "The mother–child relationship is paradoxical and, in a sense tragic. It requires the most intense love on the mother's side, yet this very love must help the child grow away from the mother, and to become fully independent."[4]

Being independent often results in doing things differently from our parents. Yet, I also think that my mother's reaction to our level of observance was, in part, due to her need for affirmation that what she did to build my Jewish identity was right. It is understandable why she might feel insecure about this subject. I did choose to marry outside the faith, and it is common for parents of children who intermarry to feel rejected by their child's choice and ask, "What if I had done more to build a strong Jewish identity in my child?" In a way, our home rituals were perceived as another rejection and an answer to the question, "Could I have done more?" From this perspective, my actions said, "Yes, you could have done more to prevent this from happening."

There was also the element of parent–child competition that is common be-tween mothers and daughters—even those with strong connections. I saw my actions as building a religious identity for my family; she thought they were an attempt by me to prove that I was a better Jewish homemaker than she was. This was not my intent.

I had no idea our observance of Jewish rituals could trigger such thoughts. I do not feel my parents are to blame for my marrying a non-Jew. I just fell in love. Cameron's religion and my mother's parenting had little to do with the decision. I do not even like using the word *blame* because it implies fault or responsibility for a bad result. I do not see my marriage as a negative outcome. On the contrary: after a failed attempt, I see my happy, loving marriage as a success, regardless of religious differences. From my perspective, my mom should congratulate herself on a job well done. It is because of the strong Jewish identity that I developed through Jewish education, involvement in youth group, and a trip to Israel that our interfaith family is engaged with Judaism.

I also looked at my mother's response through the lens of assimilation. Born in 1945, as part of the Baby Boom generation and to a father who was a first-generation American, my mother grew up straddling both the new and old world. Her father's family was observant and practiced the traditional rituals they brought with them from Eastern Europe. My mother recalls watching my great-grandmother Jessie koshering her kitchen and rendering schmaltz (chicken fat). Her mother's family was assimilated, belonging to a Conservative synagogue and celebrating Christmas. Interestingly, she points out that regardless of background or level of observance, both sides of the family came together to celebrate all holidays, including Christmas.

"Everyone participated, and everyone was included," she said.

While my mother was exposed to traditional Judaic practices, her experience was more liberal. She grew up at Congregation Ahavath Achim, a Conservative synagogue in Belleville, New Jersey, which her parents helped found. High Holiday meals, as well as Hanukkah, and later Passover, when my grandfather's family no longer hosted the big Seders, were observed in her home with traditions created by her mother, not her paternal grandmother. Shabbat, Sukkot, and Simchat Torah were celebrated at temple.

"We never had a sukkah at home. We went to temple to decorate the sukkah, and I remember marching around the sanctuary on Simchat Torah," she said. "When we did celebrate Shabbat, it was at temple. I remember my mother and me going together."

"Did Nana incorporate Mum-Mum's more observant rituals?" I asked.

"No. My mother made her own, just like all families create their own traditions," she added.

Just like all families create their own traditions. The irony of this comment was not lost on me.

My Jewish upbringing largely mirrored my mother's. My father, who also grew up in a Conservative home and whose father was also a founding member of a synagogue, Beth Shalom in Livingston, New Jersey, initially wanted our family to affiliate Conservative when I was ready for religious school, which we did. But we quickly moved to a Reform congregation. The denominational change did not seem like a big deal and made us similar to many other Americans. According to a 2009 survey conducted by the Pew Center's Religion & Public Life Project, "roughly half of the US adult population has changed religion at some point in their life." Included in this figure are those that change within their religious tradition.[5] Like many of the respondents to the Pew survey, my parents changed because there were aspects of the synagogue and its practices that they did not like.

Like their parents, my parents were active in our temple, serving on many lay committees. In 1987, my mother was sworn in as sisterhood president on the twenty-fifth anniversary of her mother assuming the same position at a different synagogue. On the same day, my father became brotherhood president, and I became youth group president. (We were quite the force at Temple Sholom that year.) But while we were very involved in our congregation, our religious celebrations were limited to the High Holidays, Passover Seders, and Hanukkah. Why these? Rosh Hashanah, Yom Kippur, and Passover have great significance in the Jewish religion because the Torah commands us to observe them. The same can be said for Sukkot and Shavuot, but many American Jews do not celebrate these two holidays as regularly. Hanukkah, a minor holiday celebrated at home, only took on increased significance as Jews living in predominately Christian societies elevated the celebration due to its proximity to Christmas. I do not recall participating in other Jewish holidays, except for what was done during religious school.

As far as the practice of home rituals, Passover and Hanukkah were the only two occasions when we said blessings over candles or food at home. The message was that religion was practiced in temple. Shabbat was something that happened in synagogue (no wonder I was nervous the first time we lit candles; I had no model for home observance), as were prayers to God. God was not discussed at home, and Torah stories were not used to drive home good lessons. While I do not remember it ever being explicitly stated, it was implied that people who prayed at home or talked about God were either very religious or fanatics.

This was conveyed through my parents' actions. There was no talk about God, religion, or spirituality outside of what was deemed an appropriate time (i.e., holiday ritual) or place (temple); and we had no visible Judaica inside the home. Jewish ritual objects, such as menorahs and Seder plates, can be quite beautiful and real works of art. It is common to see them displayed. Displaying these pieces is a way to show that a house is a Jewish home. Ours were stored neatly in a cabinet. Jewish life was something that was taken out a few times a year and then returned to storage until the next occasion. My impression of my family's Judaism was that it was shallow. We went through the motions of practicing specific rituals, but our actions and engagement lacked any deeper meaning or connection. Therefore, I was surprised when my mom mentioned in recent years that she saw herself as a spiritual person.

"I consider myself to be very spiritual," she said.

"Really?" I responded with some surprise in my voice.

"I do. I may not observe all the rituals, but I feel very spiritually connected."

"What do you mean by that?" I asked.

"I mean that I have a belief in God."

I know that my childhood home was similar to the homes of many second-, third-, and fourth-generation Jews who were easily integrated into American life. Deborah Dash Moore writes about the Jewish homes of Baby Boomers in "Assimilation in the United States: Twentieth Century," for Jewish Women's Archive, a nonprofit organization devoted to telling the stories, struggles, and achievements of Jewish women in North America. She discusses how Jewish home observance was "centered almost exclusively around holidays," especially Passover and Hanukkah, which were home-based rather than synagogue-based.[6] Moore notes that it was during these celebrations that Jewish cuisine appeared.

Sociologist Will Herberg pointed out in his late 1950s piece, *Protestant-Catholic-Jew: An Essay in American Religious Sociology*, that the "great mobility of American society encouraged" assimilation. "As the second generation prospered economically and culturally, and moved upward in the social scale, assimilation was speeded."[7] Foreign language and culture, outward signs of difference, were shed first. Religion was impacted, but not as fully since it could be, in a sense, hidden. Still, many children of immigrants, said Herberg, "developed an uneasy relation to the faith of their fathers."[8] He noted that sometimes this discomfort manifested itself as indifference, and sometimes it meant the adoption of a denomination that was perceived as more "American." However, Herberg states that, in many instances, the ties to the family faith were never completely severed.

My mother is a second-generation Jewish American, and our migration to Reform Judaism and less observant home practices, from my grandparents' Conservatism, and great-grandparents' Orthodoxy, follows what Herberg observed. Findings from the 2008 Brandeis University Steinhardt Social Research Institute's study, *It's Not Just Who Stands under the Chuppah: Intermarriage and Engagement*, support the effect that assimilation has had on ritual observance by non-Orthodox Jews, especially adults raised in the Reform movement. It states that children in many liberal Jewish households, whether wholly Jewish or interfaith, practice Judaism episodically, with most observance centered on the High

Holidays, Passover, and Hanukkah. It says, "week to week, children being raised in these homes encounter few family rituals and traditions to remind them of their Jewish identity."[9]

Subsequently, my return to a more outwardly Jewish lifestyle fits with what historian Marcus L. Hansen called the "principle of third-generation interest" in his 1938 work, *The Problem of the Third Generation Immigrant*. He states, "What the son wishes to forget, the grandson wishes to remember."[10]

As a third-generation American Jew, I have economic and cultural parity with many in the non-Jewish American majority and no issues of foreignness. Herberg observes that, for members of the third generation, assimilation made self-identification an issue. He says that for people like me, the family religion, with some Americanization, could provide a source of identification. It could define our "place in American society," without compromising our "Americanness," and connect us to our ancestors, who we "no longer" have "any reason to reject," but want "to remember for the preservation of heritage and history."[11]

Understanding the relational and historical context for my mother's discomfort with our home observance helped me appreciate her response. Still, what seemed to be missing was an understanding that my home is different from her home and her childhood home. The approach to building Jewish identity that my mother is comfortable with can pass in a home where both parents are Jewish (although there is much debate about Jewish engagement among inmarrieds as well), but an interfaith home needs to be more thoughtful. Interfaith couples need to spend more time practicing Jewish rituals and engaging in a dialogue about what it means to be Jewish and what you want to impart to your children if Judaism is the family's choice.

According to the Steinhardt Social Research Institute study, "Jewish socialization in the form of Jewish education, experience of home ritual, and social networks plays a far more important role than having intermarried parents, in determining

Jewish identity, behavior, or connections."[12] Living Jewishly, Jewish education, and Jewish friends are better predictors of future Jewish engagement than the faith of a parent. The findings show that the limited personal experience with these things is a bigger factor than intermarriage in the substantial number of young adults disengaged from Jewish life.

As Cameron often says, "The world around us—at least in the United States—is mostly Christian. You don't need to do much to have a child believe he's Christian too. If you want your child to be Jewish, you need to teach him what it means to be Jewish and how to be Jewish."

I have heard this thought echoed by many not Jewish parents raising Jewish children in my Jewish-living classes and outreach discussions. It is also discussed in the Steinhardt study: "It is childhood upbringing and socialization that primarily account for the differences seen in adult attitudes and identity, not whether both parents were Jewish."[13]

This is why we do things such as "talk Torah" during Shabbat, do Jewish crafts, celebrate Tu B'shvat in the home, and make our temple one of the focal points of our social life. We consciously work to build Sammy's Jewish identity. The result is that Sammy thinks being Jewish is cool.

"I love being Jewish!" he said after being told that we were going to a family Shabbat service and dinner on a Friday night. "I can't wait to go to temple tonight!"

And if his love for Judaism is measured by the frequency with which he sings Jewish songs, then his love is large as he can often be heard humming or quietly singing something in Hebrew while he builds with his Legos or gets dressed. I hope this affection will carry through to the challenging teen years. I understand that it is common for young children to think their faith is cool, but my hope is that by continually giving him positive Jewish experiences, even during his teens, that he will retain that lovin' feeling.

At some point, my mom became resigned to Shabbat at home on Friday night when she came to visit. I never confronted her about the confusion or hurt that I felt because of her reaction. By the time I reached my late thirties, I knew that trying to discuss something like this with my mother was difficult. She can get defensive and angry. My memory of the time in my early twenties when she stopped speaking to me after I tried to share with her my feelings about some of her behavior toward me was still fresh. Instead, I chose to speak with my actions.

I stood my ground about celebrating Shabbat in our home, and after a while, she stopped suggesting that we go out to dinner. On the rare occasion that she does, Sammy reminds her of the plan.

"Nanny, it's Shabbat. We eat at home on Shabbat."

My mother good-naturedly replies, "Uh! I forgot."

After an especially enjoyable Shabbat together, my mom even asked to take home a few of my Shabbat prayer booklets. If we are visiting her on a Friday night, she will make Shabbat dinner at her home. I did not ask her to do this and have expressed our appreciation. I choose to believe that my decision to use actions rather than words was a good one, and that my mother's gesture is a sign of acceptance of our observance. It also means more to me than any words of approval that I could have conjured up in my head.

While my mother's discomfort with some of our Jewish choices occasionally appears, my religious involvement has driven a wedge into my already distant relationship with my brother, Alan. His comment about being disappointed in my choice of a not Jewish marriage partner lingers. When he became engaged to my Christian sister-in-law, Lisa, my mother, in a show of support, reminded him of what he had said to me and encouraged him to apologize.

She asked, "Do you remember what you told Jane about marrying outside the faith when she and Cameron became engaged?"

"Yeah, I know; I know what I said," he responded.

"Maybe you owe her an apology."

"Yeah," said Alan.

I did not get one, and I never expected to. When you voice your opposition to something and then adopt the very policy you were opposed to, it can be embarrassing to acknowledge your choice. I also understand that his comment was his way of conforming to the commonly held opinion on intermarriage and not necessarily his own view. In an opinionated family, where there is talk about one another at the dinner table, it is easier to follow along with the majority than to cast one's lot with the person being dissected.

While I resisted pointing out my brother's apparent change of heart toward intermarriage, Cameron used the opportunity to needle Alan. During a visit to my mother's, Cameron said, "Alan, there's only room in the family for one Goy, and I've already taken that spot."

We all laughed, except Alan. He did not find the comment very funny.

I saw Alan and Lisa's engagement as an opportunity to try to bridge the distance in my relationship with him. I am five years older than Alan, and we were not close growing up. Alan graduated from college three weeks before my wedding to Mike. We very rarely did things together, did not have much in common, or have much to talk about with each other. When he decided to marry Lisa, it was the first time that we were ever in a similar situation at the same time. In my mind, we were finally going to have something in common—intermarriage— and I had hoped that it would help break the ice between us.

When I called to congratulate him, we probably had one of our longest phone conversations ever. I shared the names of the books that I read and information on the Center for Religious Inquiry. I strongly encouraged him to find a class similar to that one Cameron and I took, or, at least, find a counselor to speak with—one who worked with interfaith couples—to help them determine how they wanted to handle religion in their home. I knew there would be pressure from my mother to have a Jewish home, and while I blazed the trail for him by being the first to marry outside the faith in our immediate family, in another way I made it harder for Alan. Cameron and I may have become too Jewish for my Jewish family in some respects, but we also raised expectations of how an interfaith family can embrace Judaism. No longer was it assumed that intermarriage equaled a home with no religious identity; there was now a more hopeful model that my family could look to that showed that an interfaith family could be Jewish.

Under pressure from my mother during the wedding planning to make a decision on a religious home, Alan and Lisa stated that they would raise their children as Jews. This was important to Alan, but as Lisa later revealed to my stepmother, she was willing to say anything to get my mother off her back and keep the wedding plans on track. The situation drove home how lucky Cameron and I were to come across the class we took, and how the time we put into coming to a decision on our own, without familial pressure, no matter how frustrating it was at times, was well worth it.

Like Cameron, Lisa grew up as an Episcopal. Religion is important to her mother, but she was turned off in her twenties by what she felt was hypocrisy in all faith. It was clear when she met my brother that all religion made her uncomfortable. She was okay with attending holiday meals at relatives' homes because, mostly, with the exception of Passover, they did not have a big religious component, and she was okay with my brother lighting Hanukkah candles. But other religious observance was off-limits. She accompanied Alan to Rosh Hashanah services once before they got married and was so upset that, through tears, she proclaimed that she could not sit through all that "mumbo jumbo" again, and that she would, therefore, no longer go to High Holiday services but would not prevent Alan from attending. Lisa had her own issues with religion, Jewish or otherwise, to work out.

During this same period, I was part of the leadership team responsible for the Interfaith Moms group. When we would have a program, I would grab an extra copy of any handouts so I could send them to my brother and Lisa. I believed that I was being thoughtful, and that information from these programs would be helpful to them too. I knew that there had been heat around the issue of religion, and that they had, at times, a frustrating experience with my family during their engagement, as they worked to resolve how they would raise their children. For these reasons, I mailed them some articles distributed at a discussion on dealing with parents and in-laws. I thought that they would appreciate the materials. So, I was not prepared for the phone call that I received from my brother one evening.

"Jane? It's Alan," he said in an agitated voice that indicated that he was upset with me about something.

"Hey, Alan. What's up?"

"We got the material you sent us," he said.

"Great, there are some good suggestions in it," I responded.

"You've upset Lisa very much. She doesn't like that you send us this stuff—this propaganda," he added angrily. "Stop sending it; I don't want you to upset her like this!"

"I'm sorry," I said apologetically. "My intent was not to upset her. I just thought that since you are in the same situation as Cameron and me that you might find it interesting, helpful."

"She doesn't want it. Stop trying to convert her!" he growled.

I was silent. What was he talking about?

I could feel my anger rise as a result of their response and accusation, and I could not refrain from pointing out what seemed obvious. I responded in a hard voice that rose in volume. "Alan, don't you think that if I wanted to try to convert someone it would be my own husband! Wouldn't it be easier for me to proselytize in my own home rather than in someone else's?"

Silence.

"Just stop sending us stuff," he said and hung up.

Cameron, who was standing nearby, saw that I was annoyed and asked, "What was that about?"

"Lisa thinks I'm trying to convert her because I sent her and Alan articles from some Interfaith Moms meetings," I said.

"What?" Cameron said with raised eyebrows.

"So much for trying to build a connection with Alan," I responded. "I really did not intend to upset either of them. The handouts I sent didn't even have to do with religion. They were about setting boundaries and communicating with your parents and in-laws!"

Never in my wildest dreams did I think that a few photocopies would generate such a reaction, but the experience provided one of many lessons I have learned along this interfaith journey. It highlighted for me the emotional response that religion can create and, because of that, the sensitivity that we need to bring to our actions and the conversations related to it.

While we were experiencing some challenges with my family, we encountered no resistance from Cameron's parents. I still remember being enveloped in a warm embrace by my mother-in-law when I first met her. We entered the house through the kitchen, and Pam and Jack were there to greet Cameron and me.

"Mom, Dad, this is Jane," Cameron said by way of introduction.

Pam wrapped me in a big hug and replied, "It is so nice to meet you!"

My father-in-law welcomed me with equal enthusiasm. I was surprised and moved by their kindness toward and acceptance of me. In my mind, I did not exactly fit the profile of the kind of girl I assumed that they had hoped Cameron would bring home. Not only did I practice a different religion, but also, I was a soon-to-be divorcee—not the resume I imagined that they had in mind for a prospective daughter-in-law. Yet, somehow, those things never seemed to be a problem.

Whenever I have asked Cameron if his parents expressed any doubts or concerns about me being Jewish or our choice to raise Jewish children, he would respond no.

"Did your parents ever say that they had issues with me being Jewish or our decision to have a Jewish home at any time when we were dating or during our engagement or even after our wedding?"

"No. In fact, they think it's interesting," he said. "They said, 'Oh, Jane's Jewish? How neat.'"

After twelve years, I know when Cameron's response indicates that he actually had a conversation with his parents about something and when he has not and is just telling me how he imagines the discussion would have proceeded. So, I called my mother-in-law to ask her myself.

I asked Pam, "Did you ever have any concerns related to me being Jewish or to our decision to raise Jewish children?"

"No, none whatsoever," Pam replied. "I was disappointed when I realized that Sammy would not be baptized in our parish church, like Cam, Mary, and Eric (Mary's son). But as someone that grew up in a spiritual home, I felt it was more important that Sammy have some sort of spiritual life—regardless of religious denomination—rather than none at all, so that really outweighed any disappointment that I felt."

This mindset, coupled with a focus on our religions' similar beliefs and values, has played out in my in-laws' involvement, in our Jewish life. They have always been interested in engaging in conversations about religion, sharing ideas on outreach and membership at religious institutions, participating in lifecycles, Shabbat, grandparents' day at Sammy's Jewish preschool and day school, and answering Sammy's questions about the Torah (remember, my father-in-law went to theology school). Pam and Jack have made a conscious decision to be involved in our spiritual life.

They have made efforts to educate themselves about Judaism too. I have spotted *The Complete Idiot's Guide to Understanding Judaism* tucked into their packed bookshelves, and they have discussed articles they have read. All of these actions have indicated an honest desire to learn and be engaged with their son's Jewish family. We have even had opportunities to learn together, such as when Pam shared the book *The Faith Club* with me. Once I was done reading it, we were able to discuss it with each other.

I always assumed that my in-laws did these things because they loved Cameron, wanted to be a part of their grandson's life, and were just happy that there was some faith in the home that could reinforce the values we wanted to instill in Sammy. But over the years, I have realized that it is not just out of love that they do what they do but because it is just who they are. Pam and Jack are Christians in the best sense of the word, embodying the values of their faith; yet through their actions, they live more "Jewishly" than many Jews I know.

In Judaism, more emphasis is placed on deed than creed. Describing a difference between Judaism and Christianity, Rabbi Joseph Telushkin writes in *Jewish*

Literacy that Judaism has always stressed the performance of commandments, unlike Christianity, which placed a much greater emphasis on faith.[14] Rabbi Sharon G. Forman states in *Honest Answers to Your Child's Jewish Questions* that it is expected that Jews will "do good deeds and follow some of the commandments" regardless of their belief in God.[15] In Judaism, helping to make the world a better place is more important than accepting a specific divine concept.

Looking at my in-laws from this perspective, they are wonderful Jewish role models. I recently pulled out of my file cabinet a sheet with a mitzvah list from our Interfaith Moms' "What Is a Mitzvah?" program. Rereading the list, I realized that my in-laws fulfilled most of the mitzvot listed: preserving the environment, check; visiting the sick, check; caring for the elderly, check; being hospitable, check; and the list goes on. But of the many good deeds they do, several stand out to me: caring for the elderly, feeding the hungry, tzedakah, and welcoming the stranger.

Years after purchasing a travel agency from a woman in Burlington, Vermont, my in-laws not only stayed in touch with her as she aged but helped care for her. Among other things, when she was ready to go to Florida for the winter, Jack would drive her south and would fly down to make the return trip in the spring. As for feeding the hungry, he coordinates for his church the Ecumenical Lunch Bunch program, which provides summer lunch for children and families in need in the Burlington area. Jack and Pam's charitable giving (or tzedakah) is not just limited to the financial support that they give to their favorite charities, but it also includes spontaneous fundraising efforts for those in need of help. For example, Pam organized a fund drive to help a nearby town deal with the devastation from the August 2011 flooding that ravaged the state. Rather than make an individual contribution, she cooked dinner for her neighborhood. For a donation, neighbors could take the night off from cooking and pick up one of Pam's meals. The effort raised over one thousand dollars. Pam's work with the Lost Boys of Sudan, the young men who fled their war-torn country and resettled in the United States, many in Vermont, illustrates how we can truly welcome the stranger in our community.

When I first met my future mother-in-law, she was a volunteer working with the Vermont Refugee Resettlement Program, helping to settle these men in their new home.

Beyond connecting our beliefs in *Tikkun Olam*, repairing the world, we have expanded Rabbi Forman's statement, "doing good deeds is more important than believing whether a certain idea about God is true for you,"[16] to mean that interfaith families like ours should focus on religious similarities rather than the differences in our specific belief in God. The brand of Episcopal that my in-laws practice is theologically and politically liberal, in line with other mainline Protestant churches, and shares a similar point of view on social justice and religious issues as like-minded Jews. By focusing on what unites rather than divides us, it has been easy to create an inclusive environment. I asked Pam how she and Jack feel about their involvement in our Jewish family life.

"How has it been for you and Jack, participating in our various Jewish activities? Has it ever been too much? Have you ever felt left out?"

"It has all been positive; we have always felt welcomed at the synagogue, the bris, grandparents' events," she answered. "Your temple friends and anyone else we've met there have always been so nice, and I do enjoy the music at the services and the cantor's voice.

"I've always liked learning new things and making connections. When I looked through your temple's prayer book (*Mishkan T'filah*), I noticed how similar it is in a sense to our Episcopal prayer book. There are similar prayers and liturgies for the different types of services."

We do not just share similar views on religion and our need to make the world a better place; we also share a carrot cake recipe. Judeo-Christian Carrot Cake is one of the most delicious carrot cakes I have ever tasted. The cake got its name because of its Jewish and Christian roots. It originated with the sisterhood of Ohavi Zedek, Vermont's oldest and largest Jewish congregation, and was then passed to the women of St. James Episcopal Church in Essex Junction, Vermont. It has now been shared with me, the Outreach Chair at Temple Emanu-El in Dallas. Members of my committee who have enjoyed leftovers during a planning meeting gave it "five forks."

I believe that my in-laws' comfort with our religious observance stems from the fact that, in many ways, it is similar to their own, now and during their childhood. There is not that same difficulty caused by us doing things differently because, while the specific rituals may be different, the engagement in home ritual and creation of a home rich in faith is not. I also think that guilt, or the lack thereof, plays a part. As part of the Christian majority, they are not continuously reminded of the imminent danger of disappearance their religion faces because of intermarriage and, therefore, do not carry the same feelings of blame that many Jewish parents do when their children marry a non-Jew. There is no asking of the question, "What if I had done more?"

I know that I am tremendously lucky to have in-laws like Pam and Jack. Even when similar values are being taught and lived in a home or talked about in a chapel, many parents of children in interfaith marriages spend time and energy focused on the differences, rather than honoring what makes them the same. It is easy to see how. Religion is more emotional than rational for many, and the sometimes fiery rhetoric from the pulpit can add fuel to the fire, causing us to lose sight of what unites us and what we really desire, which is to be involved in a positive way in the lives of our children and grandchildren.

My mom said one day, "You are lucky. Jack and Pam have accepted your choice and are involved in your Jewish family. I'm not sure I would be able to do the same if I were in a similar position. I hope I would be able to."

"I know how lucky I am," I replied. "I am very grateful for all they do."

If someone asked me what challenges I anticipated encountering as an interfaith couple, issues with my Jewish family over my Jewishness would not have been on the list, especially in light of our commitment to a Jewish home. After being labeled a disappointment for intermarrying, I never could have imagined adding super Jew and proselytizer to my list of titles. But as is true in all aspects of life, we cannot always predict what will happen.

Former US Secretary of State Condoleezza Rice has said, "Life is full of surprises…Being open to unexpected turns in the road is an important part of success. If you try to plan every step, you may miss those wonderful twists and turns."[17] Soon, I would learn firsthand the folly of trying to plan every step and find myself learning to embrace the teachable moments we find in the twists and turns of interfaith family life.

MY DECEMBER DISASTER

I have always been a good student and conscientious about following directions, finding comfort in knowing that I could expect a certain outcome by studying hard or doing as I was told by an authority figure that I respected. Maybe it is because my childhood homelife could be volatile that I prefer the predictability of structure. When I explained to Sammy why we celebrated Christmas, I ran into the limits of following instructions.

It was like using directions from early iterations of MapQuest: the directions said turn right, but to get to the destination, it was a left turn that was needed. What I thought was going to be a simple conversation about being Jewish and our Christmas celebration became a lesson in "how not to tell your child that their father is not Jewish," throwing me headfirst into the twists and turns to which Condoleezza Rice referred. She called them wonderful; at the time, I did not think they were as great as she suggested. It took some reflection to see the positive aspect.

When Sammy was four, I broke the news that Cameron was not Jewish. I did not set out to have this conversation. In fact, all I was doing was reminding him that Christmas is not a Jewish holiday. Period. The end. No tears, no drama. No luck. Before I knew it, I had dug myself a big hole, and the more I talked, the deeper it got.

Before I share my December disaster, it is helpful to understand something about Sammy's personality. Excuse me if it sounds like bragging; I am a Jewish mother. Sammy is a sweet, warm, good-natured, and loving child. He is sensitive and compassionate. He listens carefully to not miss any information that is being offered.

From a young age, he has had a voracious curiosity about all things, constantly asking questions. When he learns some new information, he is quick to say, "Really? I didn't know that." As his former kindergarten teacher says, "Sammy is not just a collector of facts; he also wants to understand how and why things work."

He has had an insatiable thirst for knowledge since he was a baby and is an enthusiastic learner who delights in discovery and "aha moments," making connections between material previously learned and new information. His scientifically oriented mind enables him to see concepts and complex relationships, often making him seem wise beyond his years.

When he saw me crying after finding out that a relative died, he said, "Mommy, when a person dies, it is just like when a star dies. A person goes into the ground and creates the material for new life, just like when a star explodes, and it leaves behind the material that makes new stars." Conversations with him are often detailed, informative, and challenging.

One early December afternoon, Sammy and I were leaving the mall after seeing a model train exhibit. He looked at the Christmas decorations and mentioned that he was excited for the holiday. Feeling that this was a good opportunity to explain the concept of an anthropological Christmas, I reminded Sammy that we are Jewish, and Christmas is not a Jewish holiday.

"We don't celebrate Christmas," I said. "We help Amah and Papa (my in-laws) celebrate."

This discussion did not surprise me as he had started to ask about Christmas. He was attending a Jewish preschool and was learning about the holidays all the time. Recently, he had begun choosing his book that my stepsister sent him, *A Child's First Book of Jewish Holidays*, to read before bed. One night after we finished reading, he said that the author had made a mistake.

"Mommy, there is a mistake in the book," he said.

"Really?" I asked. "Where?"

"They forgot Christmas!" he said in that how-silly-is-that kind of way.

"No, they didn't," I answered. "Christmas is not a Jewish holiday."

Then I held my breath and thought, *Oh, God, what is next? I do not want to have to explain Christianity and Jesus and why Jews do not believe in Jesus to a four-year-old.*

"Really?" he asked. "Huh. I didn't know that."

The next night, after reading the book again, Sammy brought up Christmas a second time. "Christmas isn't in here because it's not a Jewish holiday," he said.

"Right," I responded.

"What kind of holiday is it then?" he asked.

Seriously, I thought, *God must be testing me.*

"It's a Christian holiday," I said, bracing myself for the follow-up question and reminding myself to do what his teachers said: "Just answer the question he asks; don't elaborate."

"Oh," he said.

He wanted to read the book again the next night. This time, toward the end of the story, Cameron came in to say goodnight. Sammy said, "Daddy, you know what? Christmas isn't in this book. Do you know why?"

"Why?" Cameron replied.

"Because Christmas is *not* a Jewish holiday!" Sammy said eagerly, sharing this new information as if he were telling Cameron something that he might never have heard before. "It's a Christmas holiday."

"You mean Christian," replied Cameron.

"Yeah, Christian," said Sammy. "Isn't that interesting?"

"Interesting, buddy."

Then Sammy changed the subject, much to my relief. At this point, I think I had beads of sweat forming on my face from the stress of the conversation. I did not intend to discuss Cameron's religious identity. Up until this point, Sammy believed that Earth's entire human population was Jewish, with the exception of his grandparents in Vermont. Sammy never linked Cameron's religion to his parents and did not ask any questions. To be honest, I was perfectly happy letting Sammy think that his father was Jewish because I was not prepared to have the discussion.

I did not know what to say, and my resource for interfaith parenting talking points—Interfaith Moms—had not had a program about the subject. I would have had to wing it. It would be much easier to wait and continue to pretend that Cameron was a Jew. Somewhere deep inside I thought that if we pretended long enough, it would be true; Cameron would convert, and we would not need to have the discussion at all.

I know I said that I did not consider asking Cameron to convert and felt that if he chose to do so it would need to be a personal decision. I really believed that. But, I cannot lie; by the time Sammy was four, Christmas had gone from fun and carefree to stressful. Pretending was turning out not to be such a good strategy.

After sharing Sammy's questions with a Jewish friend, she asked, "Why are you avoiding the conversation about Cameron's religion?"

"Why are you avoiding telling your daughter her great-grandmother died or having the conversation about where babies come from?" I responded.

The fact is that I am not alone in avoiding the discussion of complicated, complex topics that make us uncomfortable. Most parents have confronted this discomfort before. There are many topics we wish we did not have to discuss with our kids, including death, religion, and sex. Part of the reluctance to having these conversations comes from being unsure of our own beliefs, our past actions, our own limited knowledge, and fear of our children's reactions. We wonder: What if I confuse him? What if I upset her? What if I scare him? What if she realizes that I do not have all the answers? Will I cause him to question his own identity? How will she judge me? Will she think I am a bad parent? Will I put bad thoughts in his head? Will I give her ideas about "bad" behavior?

These are just a few of the things we, as parents, worry about when faced with discussing a challenging subject. After realizing her religious school parents, who spoke eloquently with their children about adoption and war, were tongue-tied when it came to answering their Jewish questions, Rabbi Sharon G. Forman wrote *Honest Answers to Your Child's Jewish Questions: A Rabbi's Insights*. In the Preface, she says that the phone calls she received from parents during her time as a religious school director were typically not about Hebrew homework but rather about how to answer their children's Jewish questions in a developmentally appropriate and honest way. She notes that parents struggled to provide answers because their Jewish knowledge was fragmented, and their own backgrounds often did not prepare them to offer anything more than the "traditional party line...about God, prayer, Jewish holidays, and customs."[1]

Like Forman's parents, I was not prepared for this discussion. As my conversation with Sammy played out, some of my fears of a negative reaction were realized.

The irony of the situation at the mall was that I also celebrated Christmas as a child. My paternal grandmother was not Jewish, and she would come to visit during the holiday. We would put up a tree and a wreath. I even remember writing a note to Santa with my dad's help and putting out cookies. The celebration was not limited to a tree and gifts in my house. Christmas Eve was spent with my dad's family and included dinner and presents—but no holiday decorations. My mother's side always got together on Christmas Day to exchange gifts because my out-of-town relatives had the day off and could come to New Jersey to participate, and because outside of going to a movie and for Chinese food, there were not a whole lot of other things to do. Somewhere between the ages of seven and nine, we stopped having a tree and wreath because my brother thought only Jewish people did those things, but the Christmas Eve and the Christmas Day celebration with my extended family continued.

In theory, I should have been comfortable having a tree and Santa Claus. In fact, how I celebrated Christmas since marrying Cameron was not very different (with the exception of stockings and a nonreligious grace before lunch at my in-laws) from how my Jewish family celebrated. So why had the holiday become so emotionally stressful?

For one, there was this fear that Sammy might like celebrating Christmas better than Hanukkah or the other Jewish holidays and decide that he wanted to be Christian. I call this my "Fear of the Christmas Tree Theory," and I believe that it is one thing that drives some Jews to oppose, adamantly, having a tree, wreath, or lights in any Jewish home—inmarried or intermarried. As Steven Colbert and Jon Stewart portrayed in the skit "Can I Interest You in Hannukah?" from a Colbert Christmas special, Christmas is merry, cheery, jolly, and fun; why would a child not love celebrating it?[2]

We know they do, and Sammy did and still does. But as I reflected on my feelings, and as the conversation played out, I realized where my holiday stress came from. I did not want to shatter the vision of our happy Jewish home by revealing Cameron's religious identity (I recognize the contradictions: not

Jewish husband, image of a Jewish home, Hanukkah, a Christmas tree) and my own discomfort with Jesus.

Why, if these things were an issue did I marry someone who was not Jewish? Well, when I became engaged, I did not have a crystal ball. It was impossible to know what things would bother me four, five, or ten years in the future. Something that was easy to accept in the beginning took on new significance later, and issues that were long buried or not thought about emerged. Regardless of religion or type of relationship, we all face these challenges in life. What helps us move forward is the intellectual curiosity to learn, the ability to reflect, self-examination, talking about our feelings, and in the case of a marriage, a supportive spouse with whom you have a common goal or vision. I believe that the last piece is critical to the success of any interfaith couple. If Cameron and I had not made a clear commitment to a religious identity for our home early on, it would have been difficult for me to work through my issues.

At the mall Sammy responded to my reminder about Christmas not being a Jewish holiday with, "Mommy, I know Christmas is not a Jewish holiday, but we celebrate it, and we're Jewish."

I heard myself say, "Well, Daddy isn't Jewish. He's Christian, like Amah and Papa." After I said it, I knew it was a mistake.

Sammy dropped to the floor in tears. I scooped him up and told him that I was sorry he was upset. "Daddy loves us very much, and because of his love he does everything Jewish, even though he's not," I said. "He helps us celebrate all of our holidays and participates in all Jewish events. We are so lucky."

"I'm not lucky," Sammy said tearfully. "I don't want to be different from Daddy. I want to be the same."

Feeling that I was quickly losing control of the situation and feeling hurt by Sammy's comment, I decided to use the suggestions from the December

Dilemma discussions I had participated in. I assumed that if I explained that our participation in Christmas was like our participation in the birthday of a friend that I would be able to regain control of the situation and calm Sammy. There was no reason to think that this would not work since this was what the experts recommended. I still have the copy of *The December Dilemma—Tips to Survive the Holiday Season* that was originally published by the Union of Reform Judaism's (URJ) "Project Welcome" that I received at one of these December programs and that the facilitating rabbi suggested following.

It said that, by age six, "most children understand that celebrating Christmas at" grandparents' is similar to celebrating a friend's birthday. They partake in the food and activities, "give a gift and accept a party favor, but" then "the celebration is over because it's not" their birthday.[3] Maybe four was too young for this discussion, and that is why it went wrong so fast, but I was not sure what else to do.

"I'm sorry you feel that way," I answered. "When we help people we love celebrate, it makes them feel good. It's like going to a birthday party. It's not our birthday, but we go to the party, have fun, and get a thank-you gift."

"I don't want to be a helper. I want to be like Daddy," he sobbed and continued to repeat and sob the entire twenty-minute drive home.

When we got to our house, I let Sammy watch the PBS show Super Why. The tears had stopped, and he was quiet. As I watched from the kitchen, I thought that the worst had passed, and that we could have a calmer discussion that evening. Ironically, the episode he watched was about how the character Pig was different from his friends. He was an animal, and his friends were humans. Sammy turned around from the family room couch and said, "I have the same problem. I'm different, just like Pig."

My face scrunched into a pained look, and I said to myself, "I have created a mess of this situation!"

The story went on to teach that being different could be special and how to feel good about one's self. As the show ended, Sammy turned to me again and said, "The difference between Pig and me is that he likes being different. I don't."

It felt like the knife on my cutting board had just been plunged into my heart. With tears in my eyes, I walked out of the room and headed to Cameron's home office where he was working. On my way upstairs, I thought about how hard Cameron and I had worked to build Sammy's Jewish identity. He attended Jewish preschool; we celebrated many Jewish holidays in our home, and participated in temple events. All of our Dallas friends were Jewish or interfaith, raising Jewish children. Our synagogue and Jewish community was the center of our life. I was upset and emotional. I believed that my fear that Sammy wanted to be Christian rather than Jewish was being realized.

When I got to Cameron's office, he could see that I was crying.

"What's the matter?" he asked, concerned.

I shared the afternoon's events. Cameron pointed out that the Christmas piece of the discussion was only a part of Sammy's reaction.

He said, "Sammy thinks that being a helper is second rate, and that he's not part of the celebration. When I think about the Jewish holidays, I don't think of myself as 'helping,' I think of myself as an equal participant. We celebrate holidays and special occasions together as a family. While Christmas is not part of Judaism, my family's Christmas celebration focuses on family. Maybe it's sufficient that Sammy knows that I'm not Jewish, and that Christmas is not a Jewish holiday but a holiday we celebrate as part of our family. There will be plenty of time for Sammy to learn why Christmas isn't a Jewish holiday and its religious significance to Christians."

I went downstairs and tried to talk to Sammy.

"Sammy, honey?" I said.

"Yeah?" he responded.

"I want to tell you that you're right. Even though Christmas is not our holiday, we celebrate it with Daddy," I said. I was really stuck on driving home the point that Christmas is not a Jewish holiday.

"No, it is my holiday! I don't want to be different. I don't want to be a helper!" he said angrily.

Okay, so I did not get it. Well, it was not that I did not get it. I was scared to say, "Yes, Christmas is like all the other holidays we celebrate as a family." If I said that, I felt as if I would be a failure as a Jewish parent. Saying it would be like admitting that we celebrated Jesus.

"Hey, what's going on? Why is Sammy upset?" Cameron asked when he came into the kitchen.

"I don't want to be a helper! I want to celebrate Christmas just like you!" Sammy shouted.

Cameron looked at me with eyes that said, *Didn't we just talk about this?* "Sammy, we do all celebrate Christmas," he said.

"No, Sammy and I help celebrate Christmas. We're Jewish," I responded stubbornly.

With bulging eyes, Cameron replied, "Enough! Let's just eat dinner and talk about this later."

After dinner, while Sammy was in the bath, Cameron pulled me aside.

"Honey, I know it's really important for Sammy to know he's Jewish, and he does know that he's Jewish. This has nothing to do with him not wanting to be Jewish. This is about being a full participant in a family tradition. You've got to calm down and trust me on this one," he said.

I took a deep breath. Exhausted from the day, I tried Cameron's approach when I went in to Sammy's room to say goodnight.

"You're right," I said softly. "We are all 'celebrators.' Even though we're Jewish and Daddy is not, we do celebrate all holidays as a family."

With a big smile on his face, Sammy said, "See Mommy, I told you we're not helpers."

I went to sleep emotionally exhausted but woke with a feeling of relief. It felt good that Sammy now knew that Cameron was Christian. While Cameron's religious identity was not a secret, not sharing it openly with Sammy made it start to feel like one. I was glad that it was in the open; Christmas was more enjoyable for me. The revelation removed some of the stress and allowed me to enjoy the holiday more.

As I reflected on the situation, I realized that I needed to rely less on the "professional" advice on how to handle interfaith discussions. Up to this point, I assumed that if I read it in a book about interfaith parenting or received the information during an interfaith program that it must work. I did not take into account that often the sources of this material, while passionate about interfaith issues and knowledgeable because of work with interfaith couples, do not have personal experience with intermarriage. While it is true that you do not have to have personal experience with something to give good counsel, it does provide more perspective and insight. I realized that it is important to listen to, receive, and factor this type of information into a conversation, but that not all guidance fits every situation. Sometimes I needed to adjust my approach based on my own circumstances, my child's age, and my instinct about what will work for my family. I needed to be less rigid about following the "rules of the road" for interfaith families and more confident in my own ability to navigate these issues, using the decision Cameron and I made about how we wanted Sammy raised as the foundation.

If I had been in a calmer state of mind during my conversation with Sammy, I might have connected his reluctance to being a helper to the joy and importance young children place on being the leader. At the time, in preschool, there was much focus on teaching the children responsibility, using a job chart. While there were many jobs, the only two Sammy spoke of were the "caboose," or the last in line, and the leader. The "caboose" was responsible for ensuring that no one was left behind. Being last in line also meant that the next day he would be the leader. The "caboose" was only mentioned in the context of the anticipation and excitement Sammy felt for the job that was on the horizon. Being the leader was considered the most important responsibility, and Sammy would remind us first thing in the morning when it was his turn. The other helper assignments were never as exciting or viewed as equal.

I was also reminded that timing is everything. Four o'clock in the afternoon in a mall full of holiday cheer was not the time to discuss Christmas or Cameron's religion. Had the conversation with Sammy not struck an emotional cord and had I been thinking rationally, I would have responded, "You're right, we do," to his statement that we are Jewish, and we celebrate Christmas. Then I would have revisited the subject later, maybe even in January, after the excitement of the holiday was over. We cannot always control when a topic will come up, but we can control when and how it is discussed. We can also recognize and admit our mistakes. When we are caught off guard or have an emotional reaction, we do not always respond in the way we would like. None of us get it right all the time, but hopefully we can learn from the moments that go awry.

This conversation replayed in my mind when, a year ago, Sammy asked questions about reproduction. I said, "These are good questions. I would like to think about the answers and then get back to you."

"Okay," Sammy said.

How different things might have been if I said, "You're right we do. I'd like to talk about why we celebrate Christmas, but right now let's get home to see Daddy and have dinner."

I might also have considered likening Sammy's role as a Christmas helper to the shammash, which is the helper candle that is used to light the other Hanukkah candles. It is often elevated or placed to the side on the menorah in order to differentiate it. As the helper, the shammash has an important role: without it, the Hanukkah lights would not glow. Without Sammy's help, the Larkin Christmas would not be as special. As I think about this analogy now, I see how it could have been useful at the time. I wish I had come up with it five years ago.

Another thing I learned from this experience was not to worry about sharing all information at once. Simply understanding that Christmas is a Christian holiday and Daddy is Christian was enough for a four-year-old. A more detailed discussion of religious differences could have happened over time as Sammy had questions or as situations presented themselves. Opportunity did knock about seven months later, when Sammy summed everything up with one question.

"Mommy, what's the difference between Christmas and Jewish people?" Sammy asked.

"Do you mean Christians?" I asked.

"I meant Christians," Sammy replied.

"Well, Christians and Jews are similar in some ways. We both believe in one God—the same God," I said. "But Christian's believe that Jesus is God's son and is godlike."

"Do Jewish people believe in Jesus?" he asked.

"Jewish people believe that Jesus was a man, a regular person just like the rest of us, who did many good things, such as take care of the sick and poor. We believe that he was a good person; we just don't believe that he was special or divine," I said. "When you say that someone is divine, you are saying that they are like God. Jewish people do not think Jesus was like God; we think he was more like Moses."

"Okay, I get it," he said.

Once Sammy learned that Cameron was not Jewish, he wanted to know who was Jewish and who was not. Every day for about a month, usually on the way home from school, he would ask who was and was not Jewish among people we knew.

"Mommy, who else besides Daddy and Amah and Papa is not Jewish, that I know?" he would ask.

"Well, Aunt Mary and your cousin Eric," I said, naming Cameron's sister and her son.

"*Besides* family," Sammy responded.

"Actually, many of your friends have a daddy or mommy that isn't Jewish," I said.

"Really?" Sammy replied in amazement. "Like who?"

"Ellen's daddy, Mr. Jay; Jon and Emily's dad, Chase's dad, Rebecca's dad, Michael's mommy, Eve and Ellie's mommy, Charlotte's daddy, Cole's daddy, Audrey's daddy, Lucy's mommy, and Jordan's mommy," I responded, listing many of his preschool friends who had interfaith parents and were being raised Jewish.

"Wow! So a lot my friends are just like me," he said, seeming to like that he was not the only one.

"Exactly," I replied.

"So there are a lot of people that are Christian. But still, most people are Jewish," he said.

"Well," I said pausing, "most people in *our* life are Jewish."

I wanted to put an emphasis on our life so that he did not think that Jews were a majority. I knew that while he was at the age where he was beginning to recognize and understand differences, sameness still gave him comfort. At the same time, I understood that it was normal for preschoolers to assume that everyone was the same, especially if most people in their immediate world were similar. I knew that, in time, Sammy would learn and understand that Jews were a minority. Two years later, while he was attending kindergarten at a Jewish day school, that day came.

"Did you know that most people are *not* Jewish?" he said one night at dinner.

"I did know that," I replied. "Where did you learn that?"

"At school today," he said.

I felt glad that I had not engaged him in this discussion two years earlier and had let him learn this fact on his own.

A month after the "Daddy isn't Jewish" discussion, Sammy questioned me about Cameron's religious identity.

"Mommy are you sure Daddy's not Jewish?" he asked.

"Yes."

"I'm not so sure," he responded. "He does *everything* Jewish."

"I'm sure," I answered. "We're very lucky to have him."

"It's okay to say you don't know if you don't know," Sammy replied.

Smiling as I listened to my child reassure me that it was okay to admit when I did not know an answer, I said, "You're right; it is okay to admit that you don't know something. But, I know that Daddy isn't Jewish, and I also know that he loves his Jewish family very much."

"You never know, Mommy," he said and walked off to play.

I understand that for a four-year-old, knowing that his mommy and daddy are the same as he is comforting. Preschool-age children are still in the process of developing a clear understanding of who they are and how they fit into the world. They feel secure when their perception of reality is confirmed, and they understand where they belong. For Sammy, learning that what he perceived to be true about Cameron was actually false shook his worldview. He wanted his idea of his family to be real.

I also recognize that Cameron's appearance as a Jew in a Christian's body can lead to questions about the authenticity of the not Jewish claim. Cameron participates equally in all Jewish rituals and life, including reciting blessing in Hebrew and does not engage in non-Jewish religious observance outside the exchange of gifts on Christmas. Frankly, his actions logically lead to the question why someone who is so involved in Jewish life does not convert, but that is a discussion for another time.

Cameron's behavior does not confuse Sammy about his own Jewish identity. He knows no other religion and is deeply engaged in Jewish life. If asked, he will say, "I'm Jewish, and my mom is Jewish; my dad is Christian." Cameron's Christianity is just something he accepts. Now, at age nine, Sammy recognizes that his dad is special. He knows Cameron must love us a lot to give so much of himself to a religion that is not his own.

I believe my own Jesus issues helped to fuel my stress and anxiety about Christmas. The less-than-smooth handling of the discussion with Sammy made me realize that it was time to examine my discomfort. Two things helped me as I worked through my thoughts on the subject: an Interfaith Moms program, titled "How to Talk to Your Children about God," and reading *The Faith Club*, the *New York Times* best seller about three women's—a Christian, Jew, and Muslim's—quest to find faith and understand one another's religion.

By the time the talking-to-your-kids-about-God program came along, Sammy had already asked about God. Wanting him to have a more caring view of God than I did as a child, I told him that God lived inside all of our hearts, and that he was loving and kind. This image was one I had only started to embrace as my ritual practice increased and as I began exploring my own Judaism through our temple programming. Into my early thirties, I still held remnants of my childhood idea of God as powerful, judgmental, omniscient, and something to be feared.

Somehow learning about Jesus, going to a church service with a friend, or even listening to a dinner table grace that mentioned Jesus felt sacrilegious. I remember thinking as a child that God was watching these things and was very disappointed that I was engaging with "the other side." I recall going to a friend's first communion, sitting in the pews of Our Lady of the Lake, looking at the Stations of the Cross hanging on the walls, feeling uncomfortable, and asking God not to be mad at me, to forgive me for being in a church and hearing a priest talk about Jesus. For at least a week after the service, I wondered if God would punish me and hoped that he would not.

Out of fear of punishment, I never shared these feelings with anyone and carried them with me into adulthood. It was not until I read *The Faith Club* that I realized that I was not the only Jew who had a hard time with Jesus. In "The Crucifixion Crisis" chapter, Priscilla, the Jewish author, has an emotional reaction to a story about the crucifixion, written by Suzanne, the Christian author. She identifies the long history of anti-Semitism and persecution—often directed by the church—that Jews have faced as one of the main reasons for her reaction, but she identifies other contributing factors too. She writes how she realized that deep-seated apprehensions and concerns had been agitated in her.[4] She goes on to discuss how, as a child, she felt excluded and isolated among Christian neighbors. She learned, at a young age, that Jews needed to stick together and to be wary of those who were not Jewish. She says she recognized the power of the majority and sensed that learning about Jesus was somehow impermissible for a Jew.[5]

As I read this chapter after our Christmas debacle, I kept repeating, "Yes, yes, yes" to myself. I had no idea that others felt this way also. Priscilla gave voice to all the emotions I felt myself. She decided to face her fears of Jesus and get to know him better. After learning more about his life, she found that he no longer scared her, and she did not feel "like a bad Jew for finding his words and deeds fascinating to hear and something to learn from."[6] Her actions inspired me to do the same, and I hoped by doing so that, like Sammy, I could feel like a full participant in my family's Christmas celebration.

So, I set out to learn about Jesus. By chance, Cameron's childhood friend had sent him a video about the future of Christianity. When it first arrived, I felt threatened by it. What was this friend, who Cameron claimed was an atheist, trying to do? Had he undergone some religious rebirth? Was this evangelical, born-again material? After looking at the DVD on the coffee table for several weeks, curiosity finally pushed us to watch it. It was fascinating, and it was not at all what I expected. The video did not preach or espouse that Christianity was the only path to God; rather, it explored how to create a deeper spirituality in greater alignment with the modern world, using the concepts of contemplative prayer and integral psychology. It was definitely new age-y, yet interesting, and I found myself drawing parallels to Judaism. While it did not exactly help me get to know Jesus better, it exposed me to a side of Christianity that I was unaware of—a side that was a lot less threatening than the exclusionary rhetoric we sometimes hear from Christian leaders in the media or neighbors, classmates, or coworkers.

Shortly afterward, I came across the PBS Frontline series "From Jesus to Christ: The First Christians" while channel surfing one night. I sat on the floor in the family room, guarding the TV clicker so that Cameron would not try to change the station. I was mesmerized and not only learned about Jesus from leading scholars but learned about the evolution of Christianity. I did not feel threatened anymore.

We frequently fear what we do not know or have only limited knowledge of or experience with. When we confront our fears through learning or interaction, we can overcome our discomfort. *A wise man is strong; a man of knowledge increaseth strength* (Proverbs 24:5).[7]

My new information and perspective, coupled with our everyday Jewish choices and year-round practice of Judaism's rituals and holidays, enabled me to take away the power I had given to Christmas. I no longer worried that having a tree or enjoying our family's holiday celebration would result in me being less of a Jew or my child running out to join the church. Our tree became just a tree.

With its Star of David ornaments, art projects from Sammy's infant and pre-school years, as well as objects collected on trips or in the first years of our marriage, it is, if anything, a reflection of our family, including our Jewish identity. Because of all the Judaic symbols, a friend has suggested that our tree is more of a Hanukkah bush. While it could be mistaken for that, our intention has never been to create something to help Hanukkah compete with Christmas. It just happens that the tree is a great place to display Sammy's many creations. In fact, we work to ensure that Hanukkah is not presented as the Jewish equivalent of Christmas.

The year after I made my peace with Christmas, I was a facilitator at my temple's December Dilemma discussion. After the breakout sessions, the rabbi leading the program brought the group back together to wrap up. During these final thoughts, he strongly discouraged those in attendance from having a tree. From my perspective in the audience, I felt that the tone of his comments on this topic went from being advisory to judgmental. What I heard was that to have a Christmas tree or lights was bad for interfaith couples that were choosing to create Jewish homes. I did not like the idea of assigning good and bad Jew status to any Jewish person, let alone to couples that we wanted to encourage to make Jewish choices. These "you are bad"–type statements, whether explicitly or implicitly stated, are what drove interfaith couples away from choosing Judaism. I decided to speak up, not only as vice-chair of the outreach committee but also as someone who was being lumped into the "bad Jew" category. I raised my hand, and the rabbi called on me.

"Jane, you have a comment," he said.

"Yes." I said. "We are an interfaith family. We have a Jewish home. We celebrate Shabbat every Friday; my son goes to preschool here at Temple; and we are actively engaged here and in the Jewish community. We also have a Christmas tree. It is the only thing that my husband, who does everything Jewish, asks to do. He has embraced a Jewish life, and I feel it is important for the relationship for me to compromise on this point. It is a way for me to honor him, just as he honors me by doing all things Jewish. And because we live 'Jewishly' all year long, the presence of a tree does not detract from our son's Jewish identity. If you ask him, he will tell you that he is Jewish; his dad is not. He walks around singing Jewish songs all the time. Sammy knows he is a Jew."

"Well, sounds as if it works for you," the rabbi responded, with an annoyed edge to his voice.

I found myself being annoyed at his annoyed response. I was not suggesting that every Jew run out and get a Christmas tree. I was trying to make the point that what you do all year matters more than a tree that goes up once a year, and that if your home has a clear Jewish identity twelve months of the year, you can find room to respect and honor another tradition. Compromise does not make a "bad Jew," nor do separate but mingled celebrations.

Interfaith family religious homelife is filled with contradictions. Even families with one clear religious identity find themselves in paradoxical and ironic situations as they strive to find a balance that works for them. Some are conscious decisions, and others flow from the natural evolution of family life or are created by the calendar. My Christmas stocking at my in-laws in Vermont is one example. It is white wool, knit with blue Jewish stars.

When it was presented to me at my first Christmas with the Larkins, when Cameron and I were dating, I was touched rather than offended by the blending of the two symbols. I saw the stocking as an effort on the part of my future mother-in-law to recognize and honor my religious identity, while making me feel a part of their holiday celebration.

I feel much the same way about our Christmas tree. It is clear from the decorations that we are Jewish, yet the smell, color, and feel of the evergreen in our living room allows my husband to enjoy a symbol that conjures wonderful memories of a family celebration and make new ones with his Jewish family.

We have lit the menorah in front of the tree and have had Shabbat dinner on Christmas Eve while gazing at its lights. When Hanukkah has fallen during Christmas, we have lit the candles with my in-laws, adding the glow of the flames to that of the tree lights. Sammy even asked my mother-in-law to crochet him a new batch of kippot as a Christmas gift.

While some may be against such blending, I find beauty in the acceptance, respect, honor, and inclusiveness of it all. Yet, I do not want my words or actions to be misinterpreted as a stamp of approval for having a tree or lights or a wreath. For some families that have not fully embraced one religion, the different symbols may be confusing for children or touch a nerve with one partner.

My rabbi's comments came from this point of view. If he had said, "Wow, Jane, that is great," it could have undermined his argument for interfaith couples to pick one religion for their home.

I recognize that not all families are making the choices Cameron and I are, and I can see how it can be difficult for a rabbi to put himself or herself in a public position that appears to sanction a Christmas tree in a Jewish home. Privately, clergy or other Jewish professionals have more leeway in discussing individual solutions or arrangements with families, based on their particular situation. From my perspective, this is the real dilemma in December Dilemma discussions.

I define Jewish interfaith families as those actively engaged in creating a Jewish home and making Jewish choices, such as temple membership and involvement, Jewish preschool or day school, religious school, and regular holiday and ritual practice. Often these couples are bothered by what they feel is the judgment of them as "bad Jews" for any acknowledgment of Christmas in their home. Jewish leadership, given the high rate of intermarriage and the desire to have these families make Jewish choices, discourages dual holiday symbols as a way to solidify an interfaith family's Jewish identity. With, at most, one program a year, most congregations are focused on the latter. This is what makes forums such as interfaith moms, dads, parents, or couples groups and Interfaithfamily.com an important part of outreach efforts. These avenues provide for the intimate sharing of stories in a nonjudgmental environment, learning by listening and nuanced counseling on approaches to interfaith challenges.

When I took over the position of chair of the outreach committee at Temple Emanu-El, my desire for a new approach to the December conversation was strong. We had taken a hiatus from offering the program, and the committee was eager to bring it back in some way. Concurrently, we hired a new associate rabbi, who, as part of her duties, became our committee's clergy liaison. The committee felt that the time off and new rabbi gave us an opportunity to rei-magine the December Dilemma discussion.

As is always the case with any conversation around the December holidays, the committee members had many strong opinions about the subject, many born from personal experience as an interfaith family or Jews by Choice or by their experience as a Jew living in the heart of the Bible Belt. After a particularly high-spirited discussion at one of our meetings, we identified a few things we wanted our December program to accomplish: We wanted to broaden the conversation to include a discussion of issues faced by all congregants, not just interfaith ones; we wanted to be positive—after all, the season is supposed to be celebratory; and we wanted to emphasize the importance of year-round observance as a way to strengthen identity and remove the power ceded to December-specific holiday symbols.

With a road map defined by the larger committee in hand, the program and committee chairs, along with our rabbi and staff liaison, were able to formulate a program to achieve these goals. First, we created a new title. We agreed that the word *dilemma* in the old headline created a negative vibe that set a disagreeable tone. As a participant in five previous December Dilemma programs, I knew firsthand that some participants left feeling angry, frustrated, or without what they believed were reasonable suggestions to address their concerns. We all felt strongly that we wanted attendees of the new program to leave with a positive feeling.

"How about calling it December Celebrations: Experiencing the Joys and Oys of the Holidays," said Taylor, the program's cochair.

"I love it!" the rest of us said in unison.

The new title was positive and reminded us that the season was about celebrating, yet it acknowledged that there were stressors, and that we can experience both emotions simultaneously. The Yiddish "oy" not only rhymed but also was uniquely Jewish and injected some lightheartedness into the discussion. Laughter can be a potent tool for coping with the stress of life, and while we did not want to minimize the seriousness of people's issues, we did agree that it would be helpful to lighten the mood a bit.

Title in place, we moved on to the meat of the program. Our rabbi would open with a discussion of symbols. My first thought was that this sounded very much like the "Ghost of December Dilemmas Past." But Kara's presentation was different. Gone were the emotionally charged images typically associated with the December holidays. In their place were symbols from sacred life that illustrated the point that Jews and Gentiles have been blending and integrating symbols since antiquity.

For example, the zodiac appears in a prominent mosaic in Beit Alpha, the ancient Byzantine-era synagogue located in northeastern Israel. This sign, which was definitely not considered kosher by the prophets, was widely used as decoration in churches and synagogues of the period. The Israeli Ministry of Foreign Affairs describes the mosaic as having, "the twelve signs…arranged in a circle" with "their Hebrew names" surrounding "the sun god Helios…seated in a chariot drawn by four horses. The four seasons appear in the corners…in the form of busts of winged women wearing jewels; they are inscribed with the Hebrew months initiating each season…"[8]

Another symbol used was the hexagram—or what Jews identify as the Star of David. Kara taught that Hindus, Buddhists, Christians, and Muslims used the star, and that it was not until the seventeenth century in Vienna that the symbol became a general identifier of the Jewish community. When she came to the dreidel, the only December symbol represented, she discussed how this top, spun with the fingers, that was used in ancient Greece and Rome, had also been found in countries such as Japan, Germany, Poland, France, Korea, and Scotland, with a cubed top and letters on each of the sides. Letters varied by culture but often included *P*, *N*, and *H*, three of the four letters found on Jewish dreidels. (The Hebrew letter *pei* is used on dreidels in Israel instead of *shin*, which is used outside of Israel. This is because the letters of the dreidel are an acronym for the saying *Nes Gadol Hayah Poh, a great miracle happened here* or *Nes Gadol Hayah Sham, a great miracle happened there*.)

This discussion of symbols set a less confrontational tone for the smaller, more intimate breakout discussions that sought to give participants tools to deal with the holiday season. Topics included: being confident in our choices—responding to the judgment of others; dealing with insensitivity in the workplace, school, or community; how to identify the cause of your "oy" and what you can do about it; expressing creativity and creating new traditions; and navigating family issues.

I had the privilege of facilitating the navigating family issues group. I had several people who were about to complete the conversion process and who were struggling to figure how to handle Christmas with their not Jewish families. One wanted to boycott her family's celebration. I suggested to her that she think about her long-term relationships and consider other ways to demonstrate her new religious identity without alienating her family. I pointed out that since Hanukkah and Christmas fell together that year, it was an opportunity to celebrate both. She could join her family for their celebration and bring a menorah. She could ask them to light the candles with her at the end of the day and show her family that she was choosing a new religion, not a new family. Her action would demonstrate to her family that they could be included in her new traditions too.

Another participant was troubled by the fact that she was told that she needed to give up her Christmas tree now that she was becoming Jewish. At issue was that her tree and celebration, which were nonreligious, were some of the few tangible connections that she and her siblings had to their deceased mother. I proposed that rather than give up the tree, she make it a reflection of her now Jewish home. Jewish symbols could be added to the decorations, and when the opportunity presented itself, she and her siblings could celebrate Hanukkah at the same time. Other breakout groups emphasized building one's Jewish identity through Jewish culture, study, and year-round ritual observance as a means of building confidence, creating new traditions, and volunteering on Christmas day.

This more nuanced approach to the traditional December Dilemma conversation created a safe space for attendees to explore solutions to their challenges and find tools to reclaim the joy of the season. The feedback we received from participants was overwhelmingly positive. They felt that we provided a warm, nurturing community for them to discuss many types of situations. As an outreach volunteer, it was gratifying to know that we made a difference.

As I write the final words of this chapter, I am sitting in my living room in front of our tree. It is late. *"Not a creature is stirring, not even a mouse."*[9] The smell of evergreen is fresh. I love the fragrance of a real tree. It reminds me of the summer resort we go to in Maine. As I gaze at the ornaments illuminated by small white lights, I see my family and friends.

The giant, laminated dreidel that Sammy and I made when he was one at a Mommy and Me class reminds me of my friend, Nina, and her daughter, Ellen, who we met in the class shortly after moving to Texas. They were our first friends and have since become our Dallas family who we share holidays with. The horse and jockey from Keeneland, the thoroughbred racing facility in Kentucky that hosts one of the premier races leading up to the Kentucky Derby, was one that we bought when Cameron and I went to the event with my cousin when I was three months pregnant with Sammy. The beautiful wooden hamsa my mother brought me from Israel. My mother-in-law's crocheted Star of David that she gave to us from her ornament collection. The garbage from the year Sammy decided we needed to incorporate the three *R*s—reduce, reuse, and recycle—into our tree trimming. He rummaged through the recycling bin and found items to add to our decorations, spilling the contents of the bin all over the kitchen in the process. The Jewish star garland made for us by a friend as a thank you for inviting her daughter to spend Hanukkah with us when she was away on business. A picture of Sammy at his desk, in a kippah, during kindergarten at his Jewish day school, surrounded by a frame that he decorated with Pam during Grandparents Day. Our newest ornament, a snowman made in 2012 by Sammy at a bone marrow drive for a child with whom he went to preschool. The boy was fighting leukemia, and Cameron and I had our cheeks swabbed in order to become part of the national bone marrow registry. This Frosty look-alike is a reminder that, in the season of giving, we may at some point have the opportunity to give the ultimate gift—the gift of life.

As I replay each ornament's story in my mind, I also think about how my family's holiday traditions mirror those of many Jews that have gone before us. For the Jewish elite of Western Europe, holiday symbols (such as the tree) signified secular inclusion in society. In his article "Jews & Christmas" on My Jewish Learning, the leading transdenominational website of Jewish information and education, Rabbi Joshua E. Plaut writes about how wealthy German Jews posed for family portraits in front of decorated Christmas trees, and that following in the footsteps of the Viennese Jewish socialite Fanny Arnstein, many had trees in their homes. Theodor Herzl, "the father of modern Zionism," was among those that engaged in this tradition.[10]

Plaut also points out that in the late 1800s, as Christmas became a more secular holiday in the United States, Jews in major cities incorporated many Christmas traditions into their own Hanukkah celebrations. But while many Jews adopted Christmas traditions as a means to assimilate, it did not mean that they abandoned Jewish ritual observance. In his discussion of Herzl in *Jewish Literacy*, Joseph Telushkin notes that the Zionist was not totally assimilated. "He attended services quite regularly at the liberal synagogue in Budapest, and throughout his life adhered to the traditional practice of asking his parents for a blessing before he undertook major projects."[11] Plaut believes that when Hanukkah was being promoted as the Jewish alternative to Christmas in the 1950s and 1960s, it actually elevated the status of this minor holiday. He states that Christmas did not destroy Jewish identity but rather provided an occasion for Jews to reaffirm their Jewishness through ritual observance and the performance of Christmas mitzvot.[12]

The debate about whether to have a tree or not has been waging for a long time. Many Jews, past and present, have come down on the side of the tree, and the Jewish people have managed to survive. If we remind ourselves of this, then Christmas does not need to be feared. For families that attend to the construction of their religious identity during the other eleven months of the year, a tree will not make them less Jewish (just as the lighting of a menorah will not make an otherwise Christian interfaith family less Christian). If we observe our chosen religion year-round, what happens in December stays in December. One season or one month does not need to define us.

For Jews, it is more likely that the debate among denominations and in Israel over who is a Jew will be what shakes a family's Jewish identity. I never thought much about the various views on Jewish descent until I became involved in outreach work and realized how my own family secrets could affect my very acceptance as a member of the tribe. The often-heated discussions over the best way to maintain Jewish continuity—genealogical purity versus egalitarian acceptance—have the potential to rupture Judaism far more than a tree.

FIVE

MY GENEALOGICAL CLOSET

The debate over who is a Jew is a contentious one, pitting Jew against Jew and creating tension between denominations. At the center of the fight is Jewish law or *halakha*, specifically the area of the law that states how one's Jewish identity is determined. According to halakha, Jewishness descends from the mother. All denominations from the most Orthodox to the most liberal accept this definition. At issue is that the Reform and Reconstructionist movements recognize as Jews children born to Jewish fathers and not Jewish mothers too. The Orthodox and Conservative movements do not. The different definitions of who is a Jew complicate things such as marriage between Jews (Conservative and Orthodox rabbis only officiate at marriages between matrilineal Jews), synagogue affiliation (only matrilineal Jews can affiliate at some Conservative and many Orthodox shuls), and Jewish day school attendance (patrilineal Jews are sometimes asked to convert before being accepted to a Conservative or Orthodox institution). The issue also creates problems with Israel, which uses matrilineal descent to determine which rights a Jewish citizen is accorded.

As one can imagine, these conflicting boundaries of inclusion in and exclusion from the Jewish people cause problems for denominational leaders and negative feelings and animosity toward Judaism among followers. But while some hold fast to the strict interpretation of Jewish law, there is biblical and historical precedent for the acceptance of patrilineal descent. Jon Entine writes, in *Abraham's Children: Race, Identity and the DNA of the Chosen People*, that Jewish female lineage has never been pure, and that in the early biblical period, Jewish men often took wives from the local population because women were viewed as property and, therefore, marriage an acquisitive transaction. He notes that the Bible does not discuss the Israelites' marriage customs from their time in Egypt, and that some sections suggest that intermarriage was widespread, since during this period, the tribe was a mix of "Semitic and...other lineages..."[1]

Entine points out that a variety of tribes leave Egypt with Moses, and that God allows the Jews to keep as a reward all virgins, following their defeat of the Midianites. God makes a similar allowance in Deuteronomy, which notes that beautiful women can be possessed as long as they follow specific rituals and prohibitions. This is stated in the same book that forbids the taking of non-Hebrew wives. As Entine says, the "debate over the racial purity of the early Hebrews seems a bit ridiculous as there was an endless supply of Gentile virgins around for the picking."[2]

It was not until Jewish leaders became alarmed by the spread of Islam and the high rate of intermarriage among Jews living in Babylonia between 200 BCE and 500 CE that a process for the passage of Jewish DNA was established. While many historians believe that matrilineal descent—only someone born to a Jewish mother is a Jew—was established in the fifth century BCE by Ezra, Entine cites the Harvard professor Shaye Cohen's position that it originated earlier with Roman traditions that Jews adopted. He says that the Mishnah, or Jewish Oral Law, codified and recorded around 200 CE, mirrored Roman law, which said that the status of children from marriages of citizens of Rome and noncitizens was determined through the maternal line.[3] He notes that it was only with the rapid adoption of Islam that many Jewish communities embraced matrilineal descent, the definition of Jewishness advocated for by rabbis in the Talmud (rabbinic commentaries on the Mishnah).

Yet even after matrilineal descent was adopted, Entine shows through genetic research that the Jewish people's family tree was not pure along the female branch. He notes that as Jews dispersed throughout Europe and Asia, they usually coupled with local women rather than bringing wives along.[4] Often, these women did not formally convert. They simply adopted Jewish rituals and customs and raised Jewish children. Up until this point, the concept of Jewishness passing solely through matrilineal descent was aspirational—our purity relative. Yet the genetic data shows that, after the initial mixing of Jews and non-Jews,

Jews mostly inmarried, in large part due to their segregation and isolation from Gentile society.

The social revolutions that swept through areas of Western Europe in the nine-teenth century changed this trajectory. Emancipation of the Jews enabled them to become more acculturated than they were, and acculturation led to a rise in intermarriage. Egon Mayer writes in *Love & Tradition: Marriage between Jews and Christians* that "intermarriages between free-thinking Jews and Christians fol-lowed on the heels of emancipation," and he notes that the rate of intermarriage increased into the double digits in Switzerland, Hungary, Germany, and France.[5] In Germany, by 1933, the intermarriage rate was around 44 percent.

This data shows that many Jews began to choose easier entrance into main-stream society through marriage to Gentiles over adherence to the deep-rooted Jewish norm, compelling Jews to marry other Jews.[6] This desire to gain near-equal status within society-at-large led some intermarried Jews to convert to Christianity, while others never lost their sense of Jewishness. The newly formed Reform movement was a way for some to integrate their more assimilated and Jewish lives. Others remained culturally and ethnically Jewish.

At the same time this transformation of Jewish life in Western Europe was tak-ing place, the life of Eastern European Jews, who accounted for about half of the world's Jewish population at the time, remained relatively static. According to Mayer, in the 1880s, Eastern European Jews lived in much the same way as they did in the Middle Ages.[7] Inmarriage was the norm until they began to migrate in mass to the West—in particular, to the United States—during and after the Russian pogroms of 1881.

Like the statistics Mayer cites from the earlier modern era in Europe, ones for Jewish intermarriage in the early days of America also are at best imprecise, but some do exist. Historian Malcolm H. Stern studied Jewish marriage re-cords after the Revolutionary War and found that 29 percent were marriages between a Christian and a Jew. This is understandable since, at the time, the

Jewish population of the United States was only about one-quarter of 1 percent. Clearly, there were few Jewish bachelors and bachelorettes. The influx of nearly three million, mainly Eastern European Jews between 1881 and 1923 changed the makeup of American Jewry. No longer were the mostly westernized German Jews the majority. The new Jewish immigrants created a kind of ghettoized social life, often centered in densely populated Jewish areas, such as the Lower East Side in New York. They carried with them the powerful social norm of inmarriage. It is estimated that initially the rate of intermarriage was low— less than 2 percent. But issues regarding interfaith relationships quickly arose.

Immigrant parents and children worrying about the temptations of interdating and intermarriage wrote to the editor of the *Jewish Daily Forward*, the preeminent Yiddish newspaper in America, with their concerns.[8] Some spoke of their promise to parents in the old country that they would walk a righteous path, but now they found themselves in love with a Gentile. Others shared how Jewish friends or family shunned them upon the disclosure of their interest in someone who was not Jewish. Good statistics on actual intermarriages during this period are scarce, but Julius Drachsler, a graduate student at Columbia University, published, in 1921, a study of intermarriage in New York City that gives us some perspective. Among Jews, he found the rate to be around 2 percent.[9] Drachsler used information from marriage licenses, but given the relaxed legalities and ability of immigrants to Americanize names or revise their own history—intermarriage was so taboo, what incentive was there to be honest?— it can be assumed that the real rate of intermarriage was higher. Drachsler acknowledges as much in his explanation of his source data.

> Only those cases were recorded where there was absolutely no doubt as to the intermarriage. This naturally would make the intermarriage ratio lower than it probably is in actuality; for, numerous Jews and Jewesses who intermarry drop their original Jewish names and adopt non-Jewish names. Moreover, in intermarriages between Jews and non-Jews it is very frequent not to have a clergyman of either faith perform the ceremony, thus accentuating the lack of religious affiliation of the parties...[10]

The rate of intermarriage among American Jews steadily increased from Drachsler's early twentieth-century estimates with the largest jumps happening in the 1960s, '70s, and '80s. It was during this period of rapid growth in interfaith families (some in the Jewish establishment might call it alarmingly rapid) that the most progressive branches of Judaism began to acknowledge the need for change and greater acceptance of intermarrieds within the Jewish community. This approach was suggested in an effort to stop what many Jewish academics saw as the path to Judaism's extinction. In 1968, the Reconstruction movement became the first to accept patrilineal, as well as matrilineal, descent. Ten years later, Alexander Schindler, the outspoken and pioneering leader of the Union of American Hebrew Congregations, the predecessor of the Union of Reform Judaism (URJ), called for Reform Jews to engage in outreach to interfaith families, saying that outreach was an affirmation of Judaism. Even after this bold charge, it took the Reform movement several more years to embrace patrilineal descent. It was not until 1983—the year of my bat mitzvah—that the Reform movement in which I was being raised acknowledged as Jews children born to Jewish fathers and not Jewish mothers if they were raised in the Jewish religion. Today, Conservative and Orthodox Judaism and the State of Israel still do not recognize patrilineal Jews as actually being Jewish. Change is slow.

I provide this brief history to show that the Jewish community has been sounding alarms about intermarriage for thousands of years. It does not matter whether in ancient Israel or twenty-first-century America, the refrain has been the same: those that marry out are weakening the faith and will cause Jews to vanish. Yet, it appears that the efforts to prevent this calamity and establish perfection in our religious DNA have failed. The rate of intermarriage in the United States, which is home to the largest Jewish population outside of Israel, has remained in the mid-40 percent range for about thirty years. Even with almost half of American Jews marrying outside the faith for approximately three decades, Judaism still stands.

Are those that predict the Jews' demise wrong? Is it possible that there is more to our survival as a people and religion than genealogy and endogamy? For me, what we know about our ancestors' mating habits from biblical times and data from recent genetics research, as well as our more modern history of integration into Western societies, gives credence to the idea that Judaism has survived not because of our bloodlines, which are linear, but because of something deeper, something covenantal. It was not until the Jews offered up their offspring, not their marriage partners, as the guarantors that they would observe the Torah that God agreed to give the Torah to the Israelites (Midrash Shir HaShirim 1:4).[11] Judaism has continued because of this promise to pass on our shared beliefs to our children through the retelling of Jewish history.

From my perspective, our values, education, and observance have sustained the Jewish people, not DNA. Others recognize this as well. Yehuda Bar Shalom, an Israeli professor and author of *Educating Israel: Educational Entrepreneurship in Israel's Multicultural Society*, pointed out at a retreat that I attended that Jews are united by shared values, not genetics.[12] Lawrence Schiffman, the vice provost for under-graduate education at Yeshiva University, commented on the results of genetic research in *Abraham's Children* while serving as the chair of the department of Hebrew and Judaic studies at New York University. He said that the research showed that the "spiritual and educational heritage of the Jewish people" had "been maintained throughout the ages" and will "play a role in how Jews define themselves" but will "challenge some long-held academic and personal religious views."[13]

If we acknowledge that our DNA is imperfect and that Jewish spiritual practice and education have continued through the generations despite intermixing with other faiths, then it is possible that more interfaith couples than we believe have passed on some form of Jewish identity to their children. In her book *Still Jewish: A History of Women and Intermarriage in America*, gender historian Dr. Keren R. McGinity shows that Jewish women who intermarried in the twentieth century were not entirely lost to the Jewish community; most retained some connection to their Judaism, including some who became more engaged in the faith. She notes that most of the women she studied who intermarried in the twentieth century maintained their Jewish identity, and she suggests that, when looked at over time, it is possible that intermarriage is not as "bad for the Jews" as some people think.[14]

McGinity writes that, for those who married out in later years, it was likely that they would raise their children with strong ties to Judaism. While her work focuses on Jewish women who intermarried, I believe that her point can be applied to men too. The reason I feel this way is that if we accept as fact the assumption that intermarried Jewish men and women dropped their identity as Jews and did not raise Jewish children, then based on what we know about mating from Entine's genetic research and studies on intermarriage over time, Judaism might already be extinct. Since the Jews are still standing, it is clear that some connection to the Jewish people was passed on through the years.

This point raises the question: Is intermarriage just a convenient scapegoat for those who seek to explain loosening Jewish engagement but who refuse to acknowledge that Judaism has failed to make itself relevant to many of its practitioners during various periods in history? McGinity writes how the idea that Jewish identity could remain important to intermarrieds, or that it could become important over time, "was persistently beyond the comprehension of those who wrote about the issue."[15]

I use this information to not only point out that intermarriage has not been as terrible for the Jewish religion as some like to believe but also to offer some perspective on my own family's background and provide context for our experience. As far as I am concerned, I am the product of a Jewish mother and Jewish father. But what most people, including my closest friends, do not know is that, technically, I am not Jewish.

I mentioned previously that *my paternal grandmother was not Jewish*, which means technically that my father is not either. But as Jewish law states that Jewish identity is determined matrilineally, that does not change my status as a Jew. What does change my position as a Jew is the inconvenient fact that *one of my maternal great-grandmothers was not Jewish*—my maternal grandmother's mother, the female relative from which, according to halakha, my religious DNA descends. If we follow this branch of my family tree, what we find is an entire family that, for four generations, has lived and practiced as Jews, but who is not considered Jewish by traditional Jewish law.

My great-grandmother Mildred was born to German immigrants and raised Catholic. (A cousin told me that there was suspicion among some family members that her father was part Jewish. He was raised in Bonn during the emancipation, but I found no records that indicated that he might have been a Jew.) While Mildred and her siblings grew up Catholic, in adulthood each moved away from Catholicism and practiced a different religion due to the various faiths and ethnicities introduced to them through marriage. My mother and her cousin describe my great-grandmother's family as the United Nations and agreed that the diversity never was a problem. All newcomers were accepted, regardless of creed or ethnic origin.

Mildred married her first husband, a Christian, in 1918. My maternal grandmother, Dorothea, was born to them in 1919. The marriage ended in divorce in 1920. Like other independent, free-spirited woman of the 1920s, my great-grandmother initiated the dissolution of the marriage. Her first husband played no role in my grandmother's life going forward. According to my cousin, this was my great-grandmother's choice; she wanted a clean break.

While the 1920s saw divorce become more socially acceptable, it was still seen as unacceptable by the Catholic Church. Intermarriage was also frowned upon. Disregarding religious norms, Mildred married my Jewish great-grandfather in 1921. My cousin said, "I think after the divorce, Mil figured that, in the eyes of the church, she was already going to hell in a hand basket, so marrying a Jew didn't matter."

Still, the choice of a Jewish partner in 1921 was interesting, given that the 1920s saw a rising tide of anti-Semitism directed at Jews and Catholics. Famed automaker, Henry Ford Sr. used his newspaper, *The Dearborn Independent,* and publishing company to print attacks on Jews, starting in May 1920, and the Ku Klux Klan and legislators across the country were active in trying to stop what they perceived as a Catholic takeover of America. Under these circumstances, my great-grandmother could have chosen to marry a Protestant who could have helped her to escape religious intolerance, but instead, she chose to align herself and her child with the Jewish people.

The coupling is interesting from my great-grandfather's perspective as well. Eddie was the grandson of a rabbi, but like many second-generation Jews, he grew up in a home that was less religiously observant. He did not have a bar mitzvah, and his connection to Judaism was more social and cultural. Eddie married Mildred at a time when intermarriage was increasing, despite religious prohibitions against it and the assertions by Jewish community leaders and academics "that those who intermarried ceased to be a Jew."[16] In the case of my great-grandfather, intermarriage did not alter his connection to Judaism. He and my great-grandmother chose to have a Jewish home and raise Jewish children (they had a son together in 1922).

Like other non-Jewish women throughout history, my great-grandmother did not convert. This decision and our belief that her children never formally converted to Judaism meant that, *technically, my maternal grandmother, Dorothea, was not Jewish.* To be considered Jewish by Jewish law, my grandmother and great-uncle would have had to go through conversion. Halakhically, an adopted child needs to be converted, unless it is known that the birth mother is a Jew. What further complicates my maternal grandmother's Jewish identity is that it is our understanding that my great-grandfather never formally adopted her (no adoption records have been found). My grandmother just assumed my great-grandfather's name and religion, which means that technically, my grandmother was not even considered Jewish through patrilineal descent.

These details of my family's Jewish lineage raise the question: How did they hide that they were intermarried from the Jewish community? It was likely that, because of their name, no one suspected that the Weiss family had any interfaith secrets. They were members of Oheb Shalom in Newark, New Jersey, a large and well-regarded Conservative congregation and a charter member of the organization that would become the United Synagogue of Conservative Judaism. Its rabbi from 1906 to 1940 was the prominent Conservative leader Charles I. Hoffman, who was known as a Jewish community activist. While he was described as someone who personified Conservatism, David Schechner, the congregation's historian, described the shul as "to the left of the Conservative movement," and "ahead of its time on issues like civil rights, women's rights, and social justice."[17]

It is possible that my great-grandparents knew that this progressive synagogue would be a safe place to hide. It is also possible that, at a time when finding acceptance within the Jewish community for an interfaith family would have been difficult, Hoffman was willing to look the other way because of his more progressive leanings, concern that the young and unaffiliated were leaving Judaism, and knowledge of the destruction of Jewish life caused by the Russian pogroms.

Hoffman's successor, Dr. Louis M. Levitsky, an established rabbi, teacher, and author, continued Oheb Shalom's progressive agenda and furthered its culture of hospitality. He was also the clergyman who married my maternal grandparents, who met as young adults on the steps of the synagogue during Rosh Hashanah. It is conceivable that if Levitsky had been told of my great-grandmother's (and therefore, my grandmother's) true religious identity, he might not have performed the wedding. It is also possible that he saw that there was more to be gained by accepting this family as part of the Jewish community than there was in strict adherence to Jewish law or denominational doctrine.

It may have also been a favor for my grandfather's father, who was a cantor at an Orthodox shul in the area. However, I do not believe this was the reason. Under the circumstances, asking Levitsky to perform this marriage as a favor would have been equivalent to asking him to break a basic Jewish tenet. Given my great-grandfather's position within the Jewish community and his deep respect for the faith, I know he would not have made such a request. This last point raises the question of how my grandfather's observant parents felt about my grandmother's religious DNA. Since my grandfather suffers from dementia, I spoke to his younger brother Ralph. According to my Uncle Ralph, the family knew that my great-grandmother was not a Jew, and they were well aware of the implications this had on my grandmother's and any future children's status as Jews.

"Do you think it bothered Soma and Jessie that Dorothea wasn't technically Jewish? Did they have a problem with it?" I asked.

"Not that I remember. I do recall that when my cousin Gail married a non-Jew, my father was very upset about it, and she wasn't even his daughter," Ralph said. "So maybe my parents had a problem with it early on, but it was something they got over."

"Was my grandmother's religious identity a secret or something that was openly known?"

"It was a secret," my uncle replied. "I'm sure my parents didn't even tell their siblings."

"Did Mum-Mum or Pop-Pop treat my grandmother differently because of her mother's religious background?"

"No, they accepted her as their daughter-in-law and a Jew. They thought a lot of her," said Uncle Ralph. "If there were any issues in the beginning, time healed all wounds."

What amazes me about this piece of my family's Jewish history is not only that they found a place for themselves within the Jewish community as early as the 1920s but also the response to intermarriage by my grandfather's observant parents. While many Jewish parents during this period sat *shiva* (the seven-day period of mourning Jews observe when a parent, sibling, child, or spouse dies) for their children who intermarried and cut them off from family life, my great-grandparents chose to accept the union and worked to maintain their son's relationship to the family and Judaism. Their choice may have been made easier by the fact that my grandmother was raised as a Jew, but the troublesome issue of her mother's religion would have still needed to be suppressed. Yet, somehow my mum-mum and pop-pop were able to see that there was more to be gained from relaxing the standard of a pure Jewish womb than there was from strict adherence to a social norm. Sammy is proof that they made a wise choice.

My Jewish Family Tree

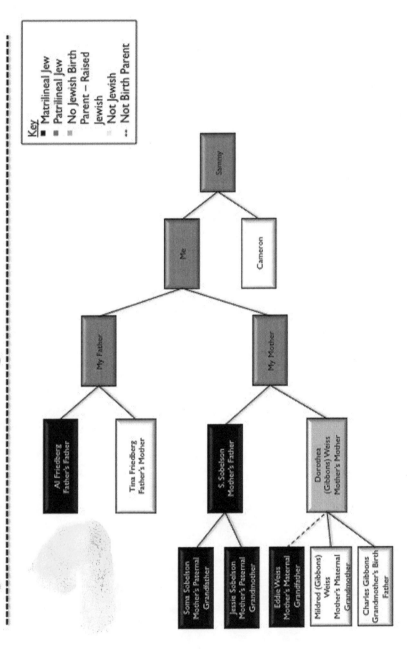

Key
- ■ Matrilineal Jew
- ▨ Patrilineal Jew
- ▨ No Jewish Birth Parent – Raised Jewish
- ▨ Not Jewish
- -- Not Birth Parent

Sammy

Me

Cameron

My Father

My Mother

Al Friedberg
Father's Father

Tina Friedberg
Father's Mother

S. Sobelson
Mother's Father

Dorothea (Gibbons) Weiss
Mother's Mother

Soma Sobelson
Mother's Paternal Grandfather

Jessie Sobelson
Mother's Paternal Grandmother

Eddie Weiss
Mother's Maternal Grandfather

Mildred (Gibbons) Weiss
Mother's Maternal Grandmother

Charles Gibbons
Grandmother's Birth Father

The issue of non-Jewish female DNA appears on my father's side of the family as well. *My paternal grandmother was Lutheran,* and like my maternal great-grandmother, she chose to marry a Jew. My father's parents were married in 1940 by a judge, with Jewish friends as witnesses. My dad thinks that these friends knew that Tina was not Jewish, but he is not sure if anyone at Beth Shalom, the Conservative temple my grandfather literally helped to build (his building supply company donated the construction materials), knew my grandmother's secret. At the time of their wedding, intermarriage was receiving much mass media coverage, although the attention was focused on Catholic–Protestant unions. Interestingly, between 1936 and 1940, 46 percent of Lutherans married someone of another religious denomination. Most of the marriages were to Catholics and unaffiliated Christians. My grandmother was one of those in the small bucket that married a Jew.

When my father was born in 1941, he was raised in the Conservative movement. Yet, at this time, interfaith unions were not part of Conservative Judaism's public discourse. (The Rabbinical Assembly, which is the international association of Conservative rabbis, did not discuss intermarriage at its annual convention until 1964.) But while the Conservative establishment was not discussing it, by the late 1940s, when my father started his religious education, marriage between Christians and Jews was gaining more widespread media attention. Jewish activists were calling mixed marriages a threat to Jewish survival, and their alarm was increased by the pope's December 1949 Christmas address in which he invited non-Catholics to be part of the Catholic Church.

Yet, my grandmother's religious identity did not stop my father's rabbi from welcoming the family into the community and treating my father the same as those considered Jews by Jewish law. One indication of this is that my father was called to the Torah for his bar mitzvah in 1954. Some might say that the rabbi did not know that my grandmother was not Jewish. But there is also a chance that he did know or had suspicions. If that was the case, then his decision to look the other way and embrace my dad's interfaith family was radical since few rabbis from any Jewish denomination in the 1940s and 1950s recognized as Jews children who were born to not Jewish mothers.

But why would he do it? Was it a business decision made because of my grandfather's donation? Was he a more left-leaning Conservative whose caring and inclusive attitude was more in line with the Reform rabbinate? (While Reform Judaism officially discouraged intermarriage, some rabbis did suggest in 1937 that if an interfaith match could not be prevented, the couple should be welcomed.[18]) Was it a reaction to the pope's address, rising anti-Semitism, or the huge loss of Jewish life during the Holocaust? Was it an assumption that a last name like Friedberg would allow the family to pass as Jews, and therefore, no one would question my father's Jewishness? My mother claims that she was surprised to learn that my Nana Tina was not Jewish.

"When your father and I were dating, we were out to dinner with Poppy Al and Tina," she said. "During the meal, Poppy Al leaned over to me and said, 'You know, Tina isn't Jewish.' I was shocked."

"Why? Hadn't Daddy mentioned that to you before?" I asked.

"No, your father had not mentioned it, and what I saw was a Jewish home. Tina made all the Jewish holidays; she did everything; there was no reason to think she wasn't a Jew."

This revelation did not stop my parents from getting married either. Rabbi Levitsky, the same Conservative leader who married my mother's parents, officiated. If he knew the interfaith stories of these two families, it did not stop him from uniting my parents under a chuppah, even though, according to traditional Jewish law, it was a marriage between two non-Jews.

We do not know why my father's rabbi included and accepted him as a Jew, but his actions enabled my dad to develop a strong Jewish identity and pass on his faith. Judaism was a part of him, and he shared that with his children by modeling the importance of involvement in temple lay leadership. He served as the president of our synagogue's brotherhood and on the youth group committee. He also was chair of the temple directory. Regardless of the Christmas tree that was put up when my paternal grandmother came to visit during the winter holidays, there was no question that we were Jewish. My parents saw themselves as Jews.

Learning about my family's religious history has been fascinating but has left me with many unanswered questions. I wish that I could speak to my relatives and their rabbis to understand their decisions and experiences. I could listen to their narratives and compare and contrast their interfaith experiences with mine. I could learn why they made Jewish choices. I could ask their rabbis what they knew about my relatives' mixed marriages and why they accepted them. I could find out if they thought about how their decision to embrace these families as Jews could affect the Jewish identity of future generations or if they believed that the families' real religious makeup would remain a secret. I could learn what drove these individual clergymen to dissent from the accepted principle of matrilineal descent. I could ask if they would make the same choice today. Unfortunately, I am left to guess at the answers to my many questions.

Because of the choices that my maternal and paternal families made, I stand by my belief that even with my mixed blood, I am a Jew, and, therefore, Sammy is a Jew. Given what we know about Jewish mating in biblical times, as well as the Diaspora, I believe that if people dug into their genealogical closets, many would find a non-Jew or two buried in them. Some may be hidden deep in the past and others not that far below the surface. My guess is that, like me, there are others who have interfaith secrets and a tradition of Jewish observance—but not conversion—in their past. Whether it is a twig or a branch that is impacted by these revelations, it is clear that our family trees are not as simple as they may appear. I wonder how many other Jews like me, from all denominational backgrounds, sit in synagogue pews. A close Jewish friend recently shared her surprise about learning that she has Irish Catholic blood on her Jewish father's side of the family. The only hint of this lineage is in his middle name, which is Macklin.

Do these interfaith secrets make those of us who hold them less Jewish? Should our Jewishness be stripped because of the choices made by family and clergy before we were born? As one of the people who falls into this category, I can say that regardless of my religious genetics, when I think about identity questions such as who I am, what I am, and where I belong, Judaism is a key part of how I define myself. From my point of view, the answer to "From whom do I come?" is what makes my Jewish story interesting. Straight, clean lines provide order and may even offer comfort to those that prefer that things, including our lineage, follow predetermined rules, but it is the zigzags of our family histories that give the story of the Jewish people richness, depth, and diversity.

As I have explored my own Judaism more deeply, have engaged in work with interfaith families as a result of my own marriage, and have built Sammy's Jewish identity, I have found myself thinking about what my religious family tree means for our Jewishness. I know my family's religious DNA makes it seem that intermarriage is a regular theme, but what is also clear is that the retention of one's Jewish identity and the decision to pass Judaism on to the next generation also is a consistent characteristic of my ancestors' mixed unions. I am thankful that Sammy and I can declare a place among the Jewish people because of my grandparents' decisions and the actions of a few rabbis. And as I look at my choices, I realize that I am carrying on my family's tradition of creating a Jewish home within the context of an interfaith relationship, and it makes me proud that, by and large, my family is defying conventional Jewish wisdom regarding intermarriage.

Yet the fact remains that we derive our Jewishness solely through two men: my maternal and paternal grandfathers. With the exception of my maternal grandfather's mother, there is technically no female Jewish blood on either side of my family. While my mother believes that it is meaningless to discuss our family's religious lineage since my not Jewish grandmothers participated in passing on Judaism and lived their lives as Jews, I feel the need to contemplate what our religious genes mean to my identity. Part of me agrees with my mom that what is important is that both sides of my family invested in Judaism's future by engaging in ritual practice and community and, later on, by aligning themselves with spiritual leaders and congregations where they were accepted. Another part of me wonders about the consequences my ancestral background will have for Sammy and thinks about how my family's story relates to the broader discussion of intermarriage within Judaism today.

For my mom, who is in her late sixties, the religion of her mother and grand-mother is irrelevant. She was raised as a Jew; she raised her children as Reform Jews, and she continues to practice in that movement. With the acknowledgment of patrilineal descent by Reform Judaism, her mother's religious DNA does not affect her acceptance as a Jew. She believes that she could, if need be, find a haven in Israel. But given the religious freedom enjoyed by Americans, she has no plans to make *aliyah* (immigrate to Israel). For her, her religious genealogy has no consequences. In fact, she is steadfast in her view of herself and her family as wholly Jewish.

This was made clear during one of her visits to Dallas. While we were driving, she asked me about my friend Nina.

Nina is one of my closest friends, and we celebrate most holidays with her and her extended family. Her husband is not Jewish, but, like Cameron and me, they are raising Jewish children. An interesting piece of Nina's story is that she is the daughter of an interfaith couple. Nina's father is Jewish, and her mother is a practicing Catholic. Nina and her brother were raised Jewish, and she often says that she got her Judaism from her mother. Much like my grandmother and great-grandmother did, Nina's mom did and continues to do everything to ensure that Judaism is carried into the next generation. What I find so admirable about this is that religion is most often passed on by the mother, and Nina's mom, like many others past and present, has passed on a faith that is not her own.

"Interesting," my mom said. "So, Nina isn't really Jewish."

"Yes, she is," I responded.

"No, she isn't," my mother replied. "Her mother isn't Jewish, so neither is she."

"Yes, she is," I said defensively. "Her father is Jewish; she was raised Jewish; she considers herself a Jew and practices Judaism. In Reform Judaism, she's a Jew!" I said, my voice rising.

"But technically, she's not a Jew," my mother said matter-of-factly.

As my emotional temperature rose, I thought, *Is she kidding me? How can she be saying this? Did she forget about the skeletons in our own genealogical closet? Why is she trying to diminish someone who not only means a lot to me, but who has shown nothing but kindness and generosity to my family, including my mother.* Recognizing the people-in-glass-houses-shouldn't-throw-stones moment, I responded, "Technically, neither are we!"

"Oh, God, Jane," she said, rolling her eyes. "Are you still on that? You really need to get over it!"

Did I need to get over the truth? Was I superior in my Jewishness because my mother and maternal grandmother identified with and practiced Judaism? What excluded Nina from belonging to the Chosen People but included me?

I am as steadfast as my mother in my belief that I am a Jew, but the fact remains that we are only Jews in the eyes of liberal Judaism and, therefore, in no position to be judging the Jewishness of others. According to halakha, neither Nina nor I are Jews. Too upset to engage in the discussion further, I did not respond. When I calmed down, I recognized that my mother's comments had more to do with her feelings about Cameron and me living far away than they had to do with Nina's Jewish lineage.

My relationship with Nina, and especially the time we spend together during holidays, is a reminder to my mom that I am not celebrating with her, that I have moved away, and that I have built a life separate from hers. I know that whatever sense of loss, sadness, disappointment, or envy she feels is wrapped up in her words. I realize that when we feel threatened or vulnerable, we can say hurtful things as a way to try to make ourselves feel better. Still, understanding where the comments came from does not make them feel any less personal.

As someone who is intermarried and engages regularly with other interfaith families, I have heard these types of statements from others on many occasions. Maybe because of the historical exclusion Jews have faced, it feels good to be the excluders. Maybe by claiming to be more authentically Jewish, it makes some feel less guilty about their less than rigorous practice or engagement with Judaism. Whatever the reason, I know there are others, even within liberal Judaism, who share my mom's thinking. Many people have negative thoughts about interfaith couples and feel the need to share these feelings directly with people touched by intermarriage. It feels good to them to negate the Jewish identity of others. Rabbi Arthur Hertzberg warns against this type of sanctimony in his 1979 book *Being Jewish in America: The Modern Experience*, "believing people must…not rob anyone of his essential place in the world."[19]

Yet while some within the Jewish community do not consider Jews like me, or Nina, truly Jewish, I believe that I am Jewish to the core, regardless from which gender I inherit my Jewishness. Judaism is my spiritual foundation and its values my moral compass. Its beliefs and rituals are woven into my life and inform my actions. It is my connection to faith and God. When the congregation stands on Friday night and sings the Shema, a warm feeling rushes over me as I feel one with Jews everywhere. Since childhood, the image of Jews around the world singing this prayer in unison has appeared in my mind when *"Shema Yisrael"* leaves my mouth. Although I have sung HaTikvah more times than I can count, I still get goose bumps when I hear the beautiful melody of the Israeli national anthem and think of all the things the Jewish people, *my people*, have accomplished. I have a deep connection to the Jewish state that is not diminished by my disagreement with some of Israel's government policies. Like many of the women in McGinity's study, my interfaith lineage coexists with my identification as a Jew; and it is precisely because of my family background and own experience with intermarriage that I believe I am obligated to defend a place for interfaith families within Judaism.

My commitment to work to change the generally accepted opinion about the dire effect intermarriage has for the Jewish people and to advocate for intermarried outreach has grown out of my family's experience. I have seen how the acceptance of mixed-blood Jews like me can encourage the embrace of a Jewish life. Given the rate of intermarriage, it is time that interfaith couples are welcomed and the "righteous strangers" among us acknowledged by more than just the progressive denominations. A "righteous stranger" is a non-Jew who lives among Jews, adopts Jewish beliefs and practices, but who does not go through the formal conversion process. In the eyes of the Jewish community, they are special, yet we do not always treat them or their children who are raised as Jews as the wonderful people we say we believe them to be. We are repeatedly told in the Torah "to love the stranger as you were strangers in Egypt." But many find it difficult to love the strangers that they view as diluting the gene pool.

Still, Cameron's experience as a non-Jew living a Jewish life differs from that of my grandmothers'. Rather than having to hide his faith, today in progressive Judaism, people like Cameron are being publicly recognized for their contribution to a Jewish future. For example, the Reform rabbi Janet Marder wrote a moving sermon called *Blessing for Non-Jewish Spouses—Yom Kippur Morning*, which congregations across the country use. It acknowledges not Jewish partners involved in Jewish life, including those that live Jewishly in most ways, those committed to another faith, and those that do not define themselves as religious. She thanks them for choosing to align themselves with the Jewish people and for raising Jewish children. She movingly points out that, as a minority religion, our continuity depends on our children and thanks these not Jewish spouses for "making the ultimate gift to the Jewish people."[20] It will be wonderful when more interfaith couples hear these words from parents, siblings, clergy, and the larger Jewish community.

I share this part of my story in order to demonstrate that Judaism can pass from generation to generation, even in an intermarried household. Cameron and I will further the investment in the Jewish faith by interfaith parents when, in three years, we pass the Torah scrolls that contain the sacred beliefs, values, and rituals of the Jewish people to Sammy at his bar mitzvah. Before then, it is incumbent on us as Jewish parents to nurture Sammy's Jewishness so that he feels a deep commitment to the faith and is secure in his place within the Jewish community when someone questions his authenticity as a Jew.

When I started this chapter, Sammy and I were on a plane en route to New Jersey to visit my family. He glanced at my computer while I was writing. I tried to shield the screen, but he read the part of this chapter where I state that technically we are not Jews.

"Mommy, why did you write that we aren't Jewish?" he asked nervously.

"Well, some of Mommy's relatives aren't Jewish, and that makes some people think that we're not Jewish. But I want you to know that we are Jewish, especially in the eyes of Reform Judaism," I said reassuringly.

Sammy sighed, "Good. You scared me for a minute because I don't want to be anything else."

"I'm sorry; I didn't mean to do that. We are Jewish, and don't let anyone tell you otherwise."

Some within our ranks might suggest that mixed-breed Jews like Sammy and me technically are not Jewish, but given the rate of intermarriage, it is Jews like us that are key to Judaism's survival as more than a cultural identity.

SIX

IT'S NOT WHO STANDS UNDER THE CHUPPAH

Sammy's connection to Judaism did not just happen; it is the result of conscious choices made, based on our decision to raise him as a Jew. Cameron's words from the evening he agreed to a Jewish home prior to our engagement, "We need to teach [our children] what it means to be Jewish," inform our actions and are a large part of why he has never once made it difficult to engage with the Jewish faith or community.

In homes where parents share the same faith, it can be easy to assume that religious identity and engagement is passed on through osmosis, but it is important to note that there is evidence to the contrary. As I mentioned in chapter 3, a key message in the data from the 2008 Steinhardt Social Research Institute study, *It's Not Just Who Stands under the Chuppah: Intermarriage and Engagement*, is that many liberal Jews raised in homes with two born-Jewish parents lack experience with Judaism's rituals and traditions. The report states that many young people receive the message from their parents "that Jewish life is something to be taken out on a few occasions throughout the year but set back in storage the rest of the time."[1] It says that this lack of involvement coupled with Jewish education that ends at the bar or bat mitzvah is leading to substantial disengagement from Jewish life by the time these young adults get to college.

For some Jews, passing on Judaism to the next generation consists of teaching their children to enjoy bagels and lox, Chinese food on Sunday, and Woody Allen movies. This is cultural Judaism, not engaging in Judaism. While no one will deny the importance of Jewish culture in helping to shape and strengthen

Jewish identity, leaders of the progressive Jewish denominations acknowledge that attention needs to be given to connecting and reconnecting people with Jewish community and practice. This is supported by the findings of the Pew Research Center's Religion & Public Life Project 2013 study of American Jews, which says that Jews who describe themselves as secular or culturally Jewish are less religious, have fewer connections to Jewish organizations, and are not as likely to raise their children Jewish—regardless of the faith of their marriage partner.

And according to the Union for Reform Judaism (URJ), approximately 80 percent of children who become b'nei mitzvah will be completely disengaged from the Jewish community by the time they finish high school. The issue is enough of a concern that the URJ launched the Campaign for Youth Engagement at its 2011 Biennial. The program's goal is to "improve the ability of Reform institutions to involve young people in meaningful Jewish life."[2]

While engagement is the issue of the moment, it is not a new one. We can look at Judaism's response to social, political, and cultural change in the eighteenth, nineteenth, and twentieth centuries and see that we have grappled with this challenge before.

These periods saw the creation of denominations of varying observance levels in an attempt to keep Jews engaged with their faith. The Reform movement helped to maintain the Jewish connection of those who sought greater integration into secular society during European emancipation, and some US clergy championed Conservatism as a more contemporary approach to religious observance when they saw young Eastern European immigrants and first-generation American Jews breaking away from traditional Jewish life. The idea was to prevent these people from forsaking Jewish practice altogether or joining the "radical" Reform. My family's rabbi, Charles I. Hoffman, was one of the Conservative leaders who advocated for youth engagement in the first half of the twentieth century so that the young were not completely lost to Judaism. Sound familiar?

Yet if Judaism is genetic, as some argue in the "who is a Jew" debate, then these efforts, current and historical, are unnecessary. Jewish leaders can rest easy, knowing that our DNA will ensure continuity. But genes are heritage, not faith. Clergy and lay leaders across the denominational spectrum, from Orthodox to liberal Judaism, and at various times in our history, recognize that the right genetics are not enough, and that ritual observance and community are what will sustain our faith, along with education (see chapter 7) and culture. Our concerns about religious engagement, both past and present, acknowledge that Judaism lives more in our hearts and our deeds than in our genetic code, and that continuity depends in large part on maintaining Jewish involvement. Dr. Sylvia Barack Fishman makes a similar point in her book *The Way into the Varieties of Jewishness*, saying that maintaining the boundaries between who is and is not a Jew will not be enough to transmit Judaism to future generations. She says, "Contemporary American culture makes strict boundary maintenance distasteful to most American Jews...instead...it is the nucleus of Jewish life—values and behaviors"[3] that are more important.

Ahad Ha'am, a journalist and early advocate for a Jewish state, captures this same idea in his statement, "More than the Jewish people have kept Shabbat, Shabbat has kept the Jewish people."[4] And Rabbi Milton Steinberg, in his book *Basic Judaism*, suggests that ritual and the integration of Judaism into everyday life are critical to the survival of the faith. He says that ritual serves to protect Judaism from the influence of other faiths and cultures, and he questions whether Judaism can survive if its delicate "inner parts and the spirit that informs them"[5] are stripped away.

Jewish scholars and writers, past and present, and of varying denominations, seem to agree that regardless of whether we view rituals as divine commandments or social customs, they provide us with the means by which to transmit our heritage, beliefs, and values to future generations. Ironically, in the circles I travel in, often the interfaith families are setting the example in this area. It is one of the blessings of intermarriage—families that cannot take for granted their Jewish identity. If our choice is to be Jewish, then we are forced to think consciously about what that means and what makes a Jewish home. It is easy for a child from an intermarried family to believe he or she is "both" religions or "half" of each. That may work for families who choose that path, but for those like us who want one faith for their children, a conscious effort needs to be made to create religious connection. This is why interfaith families that choose Judaism are, in some cases, more observant or engaged than inmarrieds.

Our insider-outsider status offers us freedom to experiment, and the outsiders among us bring a fresh perspective to observance, enabling them to meld their past with Judaism, adding diversity to and enriching our traditions. Contrary to popular belief, many interfaith families take the idea that we must teach our children well seriously, and they live a life that is as Jewish, and sometimes more Jewish, than inmarried families. The woman in my adult education class with the most interesting suggestions for celebrating the holidays and the most eager for Jewish experiences is a non-Jew raising Jewish kids.

My anecdotal evidence showing that interfaith families actively engage in Jewish religious practices is supported by the work of researcher Keren R. McGinity. In her article "Gender Matters: Jewish Identity, Intermarriage and Parenthood" in the Winter 2012 issue of *Contact*, the journal of the Steinhardt Foundation for Jewish Life, McGinity discusses the effect of intermarriage and parenthood on the Jewish identity and observance levels of Jewish women and men who marry outside the faith. She notes that her research finds that, often, women who intermarried between 1980 and 2000 became more conscious of their Jewish identity and about Judaism. She says, "Participants described intensified Jewish identities, increased religious practices or both."[6]

McGinity uses a woman named Bonnie as an example of someone who became increasingly religious after intermarriage and parenthood, noting that while this pattern is typical among American Jews, "the extent of her change over time suggests that the paradox created by her marriage to a non-Jew significantly fostered the development of her Jewish identity."[7] McGinity notes that being Jewish and intermarried made women such as Bonnie more conscious of their

Jewishness. This heightened awareness led them to be "proactive" about Jewish observance and education and to create Jewish networks.

My experience is certainly reflected in McGinity's findings, yet, like many people, I assumed my experience was relatively uncommon until I read her work. It feels good to know that many other intermarried Jewish women outside my circle in Dallas are engaging in Jewish life. McGinity also points out that Jewish men that intermarry sometimes experience a similar reawakening of their Jewish identity and engagement, which explains why the interfaith families I know, where the Jewish partner is the dad, are similarly involved with Judaism. Yet, she notes that children of intermarried Jewish men are less Jewishly identified because the woman is still primarily responsible for the kids' religious upbringing. With the man's role as a parent often still secondary to professional pursuits, the responsibility for imparting Jewish identity falls to the mom, who is not Jewish and does not know how to go about raising a Jewish family. McGinity says that even the men who are highly invested in trying to balance work and parenthood find it difficult to be as involved in homelife as they want to be because of the strength of traditional gender roles. She writes that in many cases, "men continue to be the main breadwinners while women continue to be the information gatherers and social organizers, and as such maintain greater influence over children's ethnic and religious upbringing."[8]

While McGinity's observations may be more common, there are women like my friends Beth and Tracy, Christians married to Jewish men, who are the primary drivers of their families' Jewish engagement and ritual practice and facilitators of their children's emerging Jewish identity and spirituality. Why are some Jewish male–not Jewish female partnerships more likely to engage in Judaism than others? Is the non-Jew's willingness to make a Jewish home a result of how she feels about her own religion? I think this can be a factor, but I do not think it is the most critical one. I say this because I know women of faith who actively practice their own religion even while they eagerly facilitate Jewish engagement for their spouse and children, and I know women of little faith who have no interest in supporting their Jewish husbands in creating a Jewish home.

I believe that who the marriage partner is (curiosity and openness to new experiences are important qualities) and the strength of the Jewish partner's religious convictions are better indicators of whether or not and to what degree a home will be Jewish. Is the female spouse open to learning about Judaism? Is she willing to seek out Jewish learning opportunities, such as The Mother's Circle and interfaith parenting or couples groups? How actively will she support religious engagement? Does the Jewish male partner have strong feelings about having Jewish children? Is he willing to voice his desire and emphasize its importance? Does he have the strength to stand firm if he should face resistance? Is he willing to assume a proactive and significant role in the children's Jewish upbringing? The answers to such questions can be a good indicator of whether or not an interfaith home will be Jewish, and I believe it can apply to same-sex and Jewish female–non-Jewish male couples as well. Beth and Tracy are examples of my point.

Beth was one of the founders of my synagogue's Interfaith Moms group because she not only needed education but because she wanted to find support and connection with others in a similar situation. Her husband felt strongly that they have a Jewish home, but he was not sure how to make one. As Beth learned more and encouraged Jewish practice, her husband's involvement in Jewish family and community life also increased.

Tracy is one of the current cochairs of Interfaith Families (as the moms' group is now known). She also is hungry for Jewish knowledge and actively participates in adult education and seeks out ritual engagement opportunities for her family. At times, she can be so knowledgeable and speak so eloquently about Judaism that you think she has converted. She has not. Her enthusiasm for and embracing of the Jewish religion have helped her husband reconnect with his faith. When they married, he was agnostic about religion. Now he teaches religious school. Beth and Tracy are not the only examples I know; there are many similar not Jewish women at my synagogue.

While I primarily initiate our family's Jewish engagement, I by no means do it alone. Cameron is quite open about how he feels about how our choice to make a Jewish home will contribute to Judaism's future. It is he who recognized from the beginning the difference between being Jewish and knowing what it means to be Jewish and acting accordingly. This idea of understanding what it means to be a Jew has led us to use our home and family life to foster a deep connection to Judaism. We see the positive impact on Sammy's Jewish identity of our regular Shabbat and holiday observance. Our practice adds meaning to our everyday life and is an opportunity to teach Sammy what it means to live Jewishly and be a mensch (a decent, honest, trustworthy human being). On the other hand, my extended family sees our practice as old-fashioned customs, piousness, and tedious obligation. We have used this perspective and our own childhood religious experiences as a basis for creating a different relationship with faith for Sammy. When we see Sammy rush our rabbis to give them hugs, Cameron and I often contrast Sammy's relationship with the clergy to ours as children. Cameron recalls that kids did not approach the priest, and I remember how my childhood rabbi was revered and feared. This formality is not what we had in mind for Sammy, yet we recognize the importance of respect for and participation in formal traditions and ritual observance.

The challenge for us has been to figure out how to make Sammy's interaction with faith enjoyable rather than an onerous obligation. The key has been moving the focus from fulfilling adult spiritual needs to cultivating a child's spirituality. What we have discovered along the way is that the two approaches are not mutually exclusive. Both are achievable through child-centered observance. In fact, Cameron and I find ourselves more religiously connected as we see faith and God through Sammy's eyes. As Sammy shares his ideas about God, prayer, the Torah, and repairing the world, we often feel God's presence in our life. The performance of important Jewish rituals as a family has also helped us feel more connected to the Jewish people. Along the way, Judaism has become more integrated into our everyday life.

Several years ago my friend Susan commented that we "inspire her to live more Jewishly." At the time, I thought that it was just a very kind, but somewhat ironic, compliment since my home was interfaith and hers, wholly Jewish. But upon reflection during a text study in which Ha'am's statement about Shabbat and Steinberg's reasons for ritual observance were discussed, I recognized just how much Judaism had become entwined in our life, making me appreciate Susan's observation. What was behind Susan's remark was how we connect Jewish rituals and holidays to nonreligious parts of our life. For example, we used Sukkot and Tu B'shvat to reinforce our commitment to caring for the environment, as environmental stewardship and healthy living are high on our list of causes that we support both financially and through our actions. I never paid much attention to these holidays as a young adult or child, as my family did not participate in celebrating them; rather, their significance was a more recent discovery.

When Sammy was born, we knew we wanted him to grow up having a fruit and vegetable garden. I had one as a child, and Cameron had fond memories of his grandfather's. Beyond wonderful childhood remembrances, we saw a garden as a way to challenge ourselves to create healthy organic food that was good for us and good for the planet. We were a little slow to make the connection between a garden and Judaism and Sukkot, in particular. But after our second year gardening, it occurred to me that we should be celebrating the results of our hard work and giving thanks for our harvest. Sukkot provided the perfect opportunity.

Our initial Sukkot celebration was basic and did not even include a Sukkah. We simply said the blessings before dinner, using a lulav Sammy made in preschool and a lemon posing as the etrog—a small step for an interfaith family muddling its way through a holiday we had never before celebrated in the home. We decided our imperfect celebration deserved an *A* for effort. But as our garden grew, so did our celebration. We graduated from our rudimentary observance to a campy one; our Sukkah was a four-person tent with a table and chairs. If the weather did not permit us to set up our tent-Sukkah outside, we relocated it to Sammy's playroom, where he "camped out." Recently, Sammy took creative Sukkah design to new heights and built one using his plastic straws and connectors. When it rained, he camped out in his artistic hut under a pretend sky.

Living in Dallas, several things in our backyard are still producing during the fall harvest holiday. It is also the time we are preparing our winter vegetable garden, making it easy to connect with Sukkot's agricultural origin. Sammy sees firsthand how the holiday applies in his own life, and it is a way for Cameron to connect to Judaism as well. Cameron does the hard labor in creating the garden; he cuts the beds, mixes the soil, and turns the compost. Sammy and I plant, weed, and pick. Sukkot gives us the chance to honor Cameron's hard work.

Beyond the ritual of observing the harvest holiday, I see our garden as a way for us to carry Jewish values into our everyday life. We see ourselves as *Shomrei Adamah*, guardians of the earth. We use sustainable growing practices including crop rotation, organic, chemical-free pesticides, and fertilizers and composting—all things that are Earth-friendly. We use a rain gauge to determine how much water we receive from Mother Nature, so we conserve what we use from the tap.

Being able to link our larger environmental actions to Judaism has enabled us to find deeper meaning in the holiday and our everyday practices. We have extended our celebration to include a discussion about the importance of supporting local farmers, and I highlight the regionally grown produce, meat, and fish I buy at the grocery store. While we talk about this throughout the year, Sukkot provides the perfect opportunity to reinforce our belief in the need for sustainable community agriculture.

We also donate a portion of our garden's vegetables to a local food pantry. We donate to this location at other times of the year, but during Sukkot, we emphasize to Sammy how fortunate we are to have access to fresh food so that we can make healthy food choices. We talk about food poverty. In order to provide as much produce as possible to those in need, we created "Share the Harvest," in which we invite Sammy's class at school to participate in our Sukkot mitzvah. Each year we are able to increase the amount of fruit and vegetables we give and provide others the opportunity to participate in our small act of social justice.

Another way we use Jewish ritual to reinforce how we live our life is by helping Sammy to see the connection between prayers we recite and what we think of as secular beliefs and actions but, which are, actually, Judeo-Christian values. When we say the Blessing for Boys and the Priestly Blessing over all children (people) on Shabbat, we remind him of the hopes that we have for him, and that all people are loved in the eyes of God. These prayers give us the opportunity to reinforce the message of love, support, and acceptance. The Priestly Blessing, which is used in Christianity and Judaism, helps to connect our interfaith family, demonstrating some of our shared principles. These blessings are also subtle reminders for Sammy about how we expect him to treat others. When he says these blessings at school during Friday morning Shabbat services, he joins the other kids in putting his hands on others' heads. The arms of the children are so tangled that it looks like a game of Twister. Sammy and his friends do this because it is fun, but in the absence of parents (not all moms or dads stay for the service), it also ensures that no one is left out if they do not have an adult to touch their head. Whether Sammy and his friends realize it or not, their action shows that they are part of a community.

The ideas communicated in these blessings also carry over into other parts of our life. Sammy and I volunteer one Saturday a month at a school in an economically disadvantaged area of Dallas. We play with the children while their parents take parenting classes. We started to do this because we want to instill in Sammy at a young age a sense of responsibility to society. We want him to know that volunteering is not just something that you do to fulfill a school or bar mitzvah requirement. What we learned on the drive home one Saturday was that besides teaching the importance of giving back to the community, in a quiet way, we were helping Sammy understand the message that we were all God's children. We were all included in the Priestly Blessing.

"Mommy, I had so much fun playing sports with the kids," said Sammy. "I can't wait to do it again."

"I'm so glad you had fun. I did too," I responded.

"You know, those kids are just kids," Sammy added. "They're just like everybody else. They enjoy the same things as kids like me. We're the same, even though they don't have as much."

"You're right," I said. "We are all the same."

Growing up, no one ever connected volunteerism to the Jewish concept of *Tikkun Olam*, repairing the world, or talked to me about how it differed from *tzedakah*, charity, or how doing these things was anything other than a nice thing to do. I was never told about the importance Judaism places on these concepts. Nor were these values connected to my faith or the messages I heard in prayers.

While you do not need to be a member of any religion to hold these values close or act in accordance with them, we feel that discussing them with Sammy in the context of being Jewish gives his actions additional meaning. He sees that a certain responsibility comes with being a Jew, making being Jewish an important trait. Connecting these values and our daily actions to Judaism has helped us to build Sammy's Jewish identity and strengthen his connection to all people.

While we have easily bridged holidays such as Sukkot and Tu B'shvat, and prayers such as the Priestly Blessing to our secular life, helping to add more purpose to our actions, finding deeper connection in things like worship has proved more challenging. I am not talking about individual blessings or Shabbat home rituals; I am talking about structured worship services. This aspect of Jewish engagement has been more problematic because Cameron, Sammy, and I are interested in different aspects of the service, touched by different things, or have competing agendas on Friday night. This can make Shabbat evening worship at temple neither fun nor transformative. Instead, it can feel like we are just going through the motions so that we can check a box on a to-do list. We know that it is good for us, and that we should do it, but it is not particularly enjoyable–until one day it is. As a runner, this analogy is familiar to me, and maybe that is why worship reminds me a lot of running.

For the most part, I enjoy running. It clears my head and feels good physically. But there are days, sometimes many consecutive ones, when I slog through the miles, legs feeling like cement. The best thing I can say about these runs is that however unsatisfying, at least it is exercise, which is something I value. Then there are days that are truly euphoric, almost magical. I feel light as a feather and could run all day without getting fatigued. I achieve that much-sought-after runner's high, that endorphin rush that floods the brain with good vibrations. The problem is that I never know when I will have this mood-altering experience. If I do not discipline myself to run, then I will miss the chance to experience this sometimes-elusive magic. If I only run when I think the stars are aligned for runner's heaven, I might not run very often.

Our Shabbat worship experience is no different. Some Friday nights are amazing and others less so. When Sammy was younger and we went to services, we would sit as a family. Sammy sat on either my lap or Cameron's, and we would sing the prayers together. Cameron had his own business, so he had the flexibility to get to temple on time. At these times, I felt that no matter what was going on outside, all was right in the world.

Now Sammy is older, and he is often more interested in sitting with his friends than with us. Cameron is working for a corporation and often does not get to services until the end. After Sammy moves to sit with a pal, I am either alone or with an acquaintance. Rather than focusing deeply on the moment, I spend a lot of time scanning the sanctuary in order to keep an eye on Sammy's whereabouts. Every so often, he will do a "drive by" to check in with me or to say a prayer. Before I know it, the service is over, and it has not been even close to the warm, mood-lifting experience I hoped for at the end of the week. Yet, we continue to go to services in hopes of finding our runner's high.

Along the way, we have learned that even in these imperfect moments there is sometimes magic to be found. At a recent Friday night service, Sammy and I sat together for about fifteen minutes before his close friend came to join us. I was thrilled to have our spot be the designated gathering place. Another friend arrived, and there were not enough seats, so the boys were off to sit in an undisclosed location. I hoped it was in the sanctuary, but it was just as likely in the hallway of the temple's preschool. I looked for Sammy when we sang Hashkivenu to see if he would come to sit with me just for that prayer as it is "our" song. It is special because we sing it every night before he goes to sleep. No luck. Then when we started to sing Shehecheyanu, Sammy reappeared and climbed into my lap.

"I wanted to come be with you for this song," he said. "I really love this one and wanted to sing it with you and give you a hug."

"I'm so glad you did," I said with a big smile on my face. I wrapped my arms around him and snuggled him tightly as we sang, "Shehecheyanu v'kiy'manu v'higi'anu, laz'man hazeh, ah, ah, ah, ah, ah, ah, ah, ah, ah, ah, ah-mein."

Sammy turned his face to me and said, "I love you, Mommy," and gave me a kiss.

"I love you too, Bug," I said, and I kissed his cheek.

It was perfect. I could not think of anywhere I would rather be, and I realized how appropriate it was that we were thanking God for bringing us to that moment. After the blessing ended, Sammy said, "I'm going to go back and sit with my friends now. I'll be back for Hashkivenu."

"We already did Hashkivenu earlier in the service."

"Oh," Sammy replied. "Well, we can still do our own tonight when I go to bed."

"We can definitely do that," I said.

"Okay, I'll find you after the service," he said and ran off to find his friends.

If we stopped going to services because of our hectic schedule, work, less than ideal seating arrangements, and distractions, then we might miss the "Shehecheyanu" moments. The only way for us to experience them is to keep showing up. Just as the only way to get that runner's high is to keep moving. Our many imperfect experiences make us truly appreciate the perfect ones.

Another thing we have learned through our less than ideal interaction with worship is that sometimes we all find spiritual connection together, but more often, we find it separately. The challenge is in accepting and supporting our differences. I enjoy communal prayer and music because they help me recall positive memories. Cameron finds connection in nature, and Sammy finds it through revisiting special places. I am sure that one reason I enjoy communal services is because that is how I experienced Judaism as a child. But beyond just feeling comfortable in this environment, there is something about a congregation singing together, regardless of the setting, which feels like a warm embrace to me; and the music is often a reminder of my early Jewish experiences. For instance, the Dan Klepper and Dan Freelander version of "Shalom Rav" reminds me of my days as a temple youth grouper. I love this particular melody so much that I walked down the aisle to it at my first wedding. Yet, when I sing it today I do not associate it with my failed first marriage but rather with sitting with my arms around friends, swaying as we sang the prayer during Shabbat services at youth group retreats.

Cameron gets little enjoyment from group worship (although he will admit to enjoying some of the music), and he comes to Shabbat evening services at temple grudgingly. One exception to his aversion to formal communal worship is when the service is outdoors, and if it involves a campfire, he is even happier. His favorite part of a recent family weekend spent at a Jewish camp in Texas was the Friday evening Shabbat service and song session held by a fire. Maybe it is the Vermonter in him, but you would hear no complaints if services were regularly held around a fire pit. I do not blame him; there is something special about being outside, especially by a fire. Sammy likes it too because it reminds him of camp.

Sammy finds spiritual connection walking through our temple's preschool, which he attended as a toddler. It does not matter if the halls are dark or the lights are on; he enjoys looking at the children's work and visiting his old class-rooms. If he goes missing during a service, it is a good bet that this is where he is. He has incredible memories of his preschool years and teachers, and it is here that he developed his connection to our synagogue. If you ask him why he likes to visit the space when it is empty, he says, "I don't know. I just like to. It makes me happy." We have come to appreciate that this is his special place and have learned to let him go.

I know there are some people who may not agree with this approach to develop-ing a child's spirituality or connection to Judaism. Maybe for them, participation in our formal rituals is sacrosanct, and nontraditional engagement is viewed as diluting the faith. I concede that it is difficult to maintain unfamiliar traditions, but I do not believe that there is only one way to learn rituals, or that knowledge of ritual practice is the single most important predictor of future involvement. Maybe our imperfect worship experience makes me want to think this way, but I really do not believe that there is a one-size-fits-all model for spirituality. I grew up in a home with little ritual, and because of this, I developed a sense that find-ing one's faith or spirituality is only done in a sanctuary.

It was only as a teenager that I was exposed to other approaches, through my attendance at youth group events. I was raised practicing religion in a way that enabled me to recite by heart certain prayers, but it also made me a functional il-literate about many aspects of Judaism and embarrassingly uncomfortable with ritual observance under my own roof. Frankly, it was only in the last nine years that I have found the ability to connect with the spiritual side of Judaism out-side of "approved religious" environments.

I want Sammy to have a different experience. I want him to know that God, meaning, and connection can be found in many places and in many ways, and that there are other aspects of religious practice, such as community, that are as important as being able to recite a blessing in a sanctuary. I recently discussed this idea with a friend, whose daughter goes to school with Sammy, after a Friday evening service.

"I have a problem with these Shabbat-lite services," said Naomi. "I understand wanting to try new things to engage families that don't otherwise participate, but it bothers me that key prayers are omitted. For example, Sara is working hard to learn the Amidah at school; it would be nice for her to practice saying it in synagogue on Friday night.

"But it's not just the liturgy that I take issue with, it's the location of the service. When services aren't in the sanctuary, it is hard for me to keep Sara focused. All she wants to do is talk to her friends. What do you think?"

"Sammy definitely has more ants in his pants when the service is not in the sanctuary, but I like the creative service. It is a nice change," I responded. "I try to remember that because Sammy is in day school, by Friday night he has already prayed five times during the week and has had plenty of opportunities to practice the prayers. I feel it is unrealistic to expect a child, with raging boy energy, to be focused for a sixth service and second of the day. The fact that he is excited to come to temple on a Friday night is enough for me," I said.

"I hadn't thought about it from that perspective."

"I think the connections Sammy is building with his Jewish friends when he's hanging out in the aisle or walking the halls are as important as reciting a prayer. It's the community aspect of coming to temple that often makes Sammy want to show up," I said. "Plus, I think that he's still learning, regardless of his level of focus. He's learning that there is more than one way to approach spirituality. He sees that you don't always need to sit in a pew or recite a standard prayer to find God in a temple. He hears the melodies and words as background music and observes from afar the rituals. It is absolutely a more passive form of learning, but I still think he is observing others practicing and witnessing their commitment to communal prayer."

The idea that you need to sit in a decorous manner during a service in order to pray and be spiritual is a classic Reform perspective. Reform services are modeled on the quiet, dignified ones of Protestants, in which congregants move and pray together. Yet, anyone who has attended a Reform service as a child or teen knows how difficult it can be to adhere to these rules. I got the "evil eye" from the rabbi many times when he caught me talking with a friend. And like Sammy, I used the excuse of having to use the restroom in order to get out of my seat and move around.

Cameron and I empathize with Sammy, and that is part of why we allow freedom of movement during services. The other reason we have relaxed our insistence on quietly sitting in a service is that we recognize the importance of community. In one respect, we have borrowed a page from the Orthodox (how ironic for an interfaith family), for whom community is very important. It is likely to find very Orthodox children playing with friends during formal worship instead of participating in the service. Of course, Orthodox Jewish life is different from Reform (interfaith) Jewish life, but still we have chosen to come down on the side of creating positive experiences rather than forced participation. Only time will tell if this approach works, but our gut says that it is the right decision now.

Sylvia Barack Fishman emphasizes the importance of communal activities, including connections built through worship to Jewish continuity. She says that the activities that have the greatest potential for creating Jewish connection are Shabbat and holiday home rituals, regular communal worship, "experiences with Jewish peoplehood," and interaction with groups representative of Judaism's diversity.[9] I cannot overstate the significant role community has played in nurturing our family's Jewish engagement and how it has made incorporating Judaism and its practices into our life easier. Sharing Shabbat dinner and holidays with friends and taking part in family Havdalah picnics, mitzvah projects, and retreats have helped us grow as a Jewish family and expand our practice.

Our attention to building community has been driven by our interfaith status, living far from our extended family, and my own experience as a child. As intermarrieds, we have sought out others like us who can understand the joys and challenges of creating a Jewish home in the context of intermarriage and with whom we can share ideas. Our interfaith connections also show Sammy that there are many Jewish children with one not Jewish parent. As far as being without family, we only need to remember our days in Cincinnati—when Cameron and I spent most of our time together—to see how much richer our life is here in Dallas because of the large community we have built.

My own childhood has also influenced our (my) desire for Jewish community. As a kid, I lived in a town with few Jews and attended a YMCA overnight camp. I had a few Jewish friends from day camp and later from youth group, but, for the most part, the people I spent time with were not Jewish. This is not bad as my best friend is not Jewish. But it did often make me feel like an outsider or on the periphery of my friendship circles. I was different, and it affected my confidence. It can be hard always being the one that is not like the others. I did not want Sammy to have the same experience. So I have sought out as many opportunities as possible to build a Jewish community for him (and our family). This has contributed to Sammy's confidence, which allows him to go easily into environments where he knows no one or is the only or one of very few Jews. Frankly, it has strengthened my religious confidence as well.

One thing we have done to deepen our relationships with our Jewish connections is to host a Jewish New Year's party. Several years ago, we decided to expand our Rosh Hashanah observance. Since we had moved to Dallas, we had celebrated the holiday in the same way each year—a holiday dinner with friends, followed by going to services at our temple the next day. While this routine was enjoyable, I felt that it was time to get more creative with our New Year celebration. So, in addition to the usual, we started to observe the second day of Rosh Hashanah. This was a first for all of us. Reform Jews do not traditionally celebrate a second day. Since acknowledging an additional day was almost antitradition in itself, it seemed perfectly okay to have a nontraditional celebration.

When I was young, the High Holy Days meant three things: new clothes, long mornings at synagogue, and family dinners. As a young adult, when I told my mother that I was going to celebrate Rosh Hashanah with a boyfriend and his family, and that I would spend Yom Kippur with her, she complained, "Why don't I get you for the joyous holiday?" I remember thinking that I recalled learning that the Jewish New Year was supposed to be the more joyful holiday, but I never actually thought of it that way because nothing really made it stand apart from Yom Kippur—one exception being that you did not need to fast. In addition, I had a solemn image of Rosh Hashanah, partly derived from the concept of the Book of Life. As a child, I thought there was a real book, and I feared that I was in danger of not being inscribed for another year. This belief made the High Holidays somewhat stressful. Even as a teen, when I knew that the book was a metaphor, I still feared that I might be left out. I did not want Sammy to grow up feeling the same way.

As I matured, my appreciation and understanding of the holidays changed. I came to view Rosh Hashanah in much the same way as I viewed the secular New Year: a time to celebrate a new beginning but also a time to reflect on the past year and make resolutions about things I would like to change, do more of, or improve upon. One difference I saw between the two New Year celebrations was that the secular New Year seemed to have equal, if not more, emphasis on the celebratory aspect of the holiday. This idea of the similarities between Rosh Hashanah and New Year's made me think about our holiday plans. Why not truly celebrate the joyous aspect of the holiday by hosting a Jewish New Year's party in addition to our traditional observance? After thinking about how I wanted Sammy to view Judaism, I decided to propose the idea of a Jewish New Year's party to Cameron. I wanted the event to be carnival-like, including games and holiday crafts for the kids and apple and honey-themed treats for all. I was not sure how Cameron would respond to adding more religious celebration to our life, but I remembered that, in the past, he shared that his childhood memories of church were much the same as mine were of temple—more serious than fun. I made my proposal.

"I have an idea for Rosh Hashanah this year," I said. "Rather than hosting a second dinner after services, how about we go to *Tashlich* and then host a Jewish New Year's party on the second day of the holiday?"

"What's Tashlich?" Cameron asked.

"Tashlich is a time of reflection. It is the ceremony where you write things you are sorry for from the past year on a piece of paper and then throw the paper and pieces of bread into water. It symbolizes the washing away of sin so that you can start the New Year with a clean slate," I responded.

"Sounds good. I guess you have a long list of things you're sorry for, huh?" said Cameron with a smile on his face.

"Very funny. What about the party?"

"I'm fine with doing it," he said. After a moment, Cameron added, "You know; Sammy is lucky. No one was trying to make religion fun when I was a kid."

Cameron and I share the feeling that it is important to make the holidays and Judaism fun so that Sammy develops a strong connection to the Jewish faith. I only need to look at my own extended family to see what a lack of positive religious experiences can do to a person's desire to continue to practice when they reach adulthood. My Jewish stepbrother, who is married to a Jew, observes the holidays out of obligation and not because he derives any fulfillment from the experience, and my Jewish uncle has a home that is absent of religion. This religious scarcity is mostly due to my uncle's experience as a child. Growing up as the grandson of a cantor came with many expectations. My mother recalls how the rabbi at their temple was hard on my uncle because of his lineage, holding him to higher standards than the other children. The effect was to turn off my uncle from religious engagement once his bar mitzvah was complete.

Examples like these are part of why we believe that adding fun to the holidays now can make the celebrations more memorable than they would be otherwise, without diminishing their significance. This can be especially important for an interfaith family. By creating positive Jewish experiences year-round, we can avoid feeling the need to pack a full year's worth of Jewish identity building into one December holiday. With that in mind, I decided to share our Rosh Hashanah observance and our nontraditional acknowledgment of the holiday's second day in an essay on InterfaithFamily.com. I hoped that our plans would encourage others to explore different ways to celebrate the holiday, especially those intermarrieds who are less comfortable than others with traditional practice. While most readers of my essay liked our party idea, one did not agree with our approach and accused me in his post of practicing inauthentic Judaism.

> Can you spell syncretism? Happy New Year. Enjoy the bubbly. But aren't you a few months early? Judaism, unlike virtually all other groups, considers the beginning of the year to be a nonpartying event. Indeed God's decision about who will die in the next year starts on Rosh Hashanah. If a child grows up in a Rosh Hashanah partying household what will they do in adulthood, probably join a faith that doesn't treat the beginning of the year as a very solemn occasion. Celebrating Rosh Hashanah with a party is not authentic Judaism.[10]

I had mixed emotions when I read these comments. But before I indulged them, I had to go to the dictionary and look up *syncretism*. Syncretism is the combining of, often, contradictory forms of belief or ritual practice without critical examination or logical unity. Armed with a better understanding of what I was being accused of, I let my feelings flow. I was thrilled that people were reading and debating my essay, but I was hurt and angered by the inauthentic comment. Who was this person to accuse me of not practicing authentic Judaism? Who was he to judge what was and was not an appropriate approach to religious practice? My initial instinct was to fight back with a post defending my position. I was about to do just that when, as I typed the first word of my retort, I heard a voice say, "Stop. Don't do it. Don't get in an emotional war of words with this guy." Maybe it was my inner Cameron, but the more rational side of my brain prevailed. I watched as other readers who supported my idea defended it, and I enjoyed reading the debate.

The goal of the party was not to supersede traditional observance but rather to add an informal community component. We wanted to create happy memories—not just for our family but for our friends as well. I hoped that by doing something to celebrate in a slightly different way that Sammy (and his buddies) would develop a strong connection to Judaism that would be the foundation of observance later in life. The thought was to have him associate ritual with fun and enjoyment so that as an adult he will find fulfillment and joy in continuing to practice. In addition, the lighthearted approach to the celebration was an innocuous way to extend the holiday for Cameron and our Jewish friends, who are less comfortable with ritual engagement. It seemed to work. Our friends told us how much they enjoyed the alternative practice.

"This was so much fun," said Nina. "You should make this a tradition. I mean— I'm not trying to create work for you, but it was great, and the kids had such a great time."

"It was a lot of fun," I said. "And I think we will do it again."

Now our Jewish New Year's party is an annual event, and the challenge is how to keep it fresh as our children get older. We have added a mitzvah component and ask families to bring a bag of apples that we then donate to a food pantry in order to share the sweetness of the New Year with those in need. Since Rosh Hashanah also celebrates the creation of the world, we have adopted a "Happy Birthday to the World" theme and serve cupcakes. We graduated from crafts to sports activities. This year, at Sammy's request, we will have a gaga pit. (Gaga is an Israeli variation of dodge ball that is played in an octagonal- or hexagonal-shaped pit and is popular in the United States at Jewish summer camps and day schools.) I imagine that the party will continue to evolve as our children continue to grow. That is fine. Sharing the holiday with all our friends is what makes this celebration meaningful to us.

We have seen firsthand how home and holiday rituals, communal worship, and community celebrations are an integral part of strengthening one's connection to Judaism. Without the bonds to the Jewish faith created by these things, Judaism might fade. Fishman says that the reason interaction with the varieties of Jewishness—social networks, the arts, academics, and spiritual opportunities (personal and communal)—is so critical is because in an open society, Jews need to feel that being Jewish is worthwhile. She says that contemporary Jews will only engage Jewishly "if they can truthfully answer...the...questions: 'Why be Jewish?' and 'Why does it matter if Jewish culture is transmitted to future generations?'"[11]

Intermarried couples, like other Jews today, have been asking themselves these same questions. Some Jewish partners in interfaith relationships cannot find a meaningful answer to them from Jewish institutions and agree to create a home in another faith, two faiths, or with no religion at all. Others, like us, are not only choosing Judaism but are finding compelling connections to Jewish life inside and outside of traditional Jewish establishments. Keren R. McGinity's research shows that there are more interfaith families than many want to believe who are consciously investing their time in Jewish activities in order to nurture their kids' (and their own) Jewish development. Interestingly, the Steinhardt Social Research Institute study that I cited at the beginning of the chapter says that the Jewish experiences of a Jew before marriage are a better predictor of who will live a Jewish life than the religion of a marriage partner. Exposure to home ritual, worship, Jewish social networks (community), and Jewish education is key because when "exposed to similar levels of these critical Jewish experiences as children and adolescents, adults raised in inmarried and intermarried homes look very much alike."[12]

The study shows what engaged intermarrieds already know: that it is not who stands under the chuppah but what goes on behind the mezuzah that matters. We understand the value of teaching our children the words, *Baruch atah Adonai, Eloheinu, melech haolam, asher kid'shanu b'mitzvotav v'tzivanu l'hadlik ner shel Shabbat* (Blessed are you, Adonai our God, Sovereign of the universe, who hallows us with mitzvot, commanding us to kindle the lights of Shabbat). Maybe if we allow ourselves to pay attention to these interfaith families who have found a reason to be Jewish and to transmit Jewishness to their children rather than assume that they are just an exception, we might learn about what is driving their engagement and use it to help all Jews find meaningful connections.

———•———

SEVEN

EMBRACING THE KIPPAH

I have talked about how ritual, worship, and community have supported the building of Sammy's—and our family's—Jewish identity. Education has been another pillar of our approach. We see the participation in the retelling of Judaism's stories and ceremonial practices as critical to the transmission of the faith to the next generation because it communicates our values and beliefs. To cement these learnings, it is important that they are reinforced regularly. The early rabbis understood this, and it is why we continually reread the Torah, reiterating our people's history and heritage. The hope is that the repetitiveness helps our hearts and heads absorb the lessons so that we act accordingly.

When I started this interfaith journey with Cameron, I knew that I did not have a good enough grasp on Judaism to be our child's primary Jewish educator. Cameron, while smart and a quick study, was not in a position, given his faith background, to fill in the gaps. I knew that I needed additional resources to help me in teaching Sammy about Judaism. I planned to rely on others who I felt were more religiously knowledgeable, such as my father-in-law. Even though he was not Jewish, I felt that he knew more about Judaism than I because of his time spent in theology school. As Cameron said, "When we started dating and into the early part of our marriage, if a question about Judaism came up, we called my dad. My father knew more than Jane did. It wasn't until Sammy started preschool that Jane started to build her Jewish knowledge muscle."

It is embarrassing to admit that my non-Jewish father-in-law was our go-to guy on Judaism. Not only did I not know the answers but I also was not confident that my Jewish family did either. Since I did not see anyone in my family engaged in Jewish learning beyond religious school, and we did not discuss religion, it was hard to know what they knew about Judaism. So we asked Jack. We laughed about the irony of the situation early on, but when Sammy arrived, we knew that we needed a Judaic resource to help bolster our efforts to build Jewish self-esteem. We understood that, for us, education was a key component to building a connection to our Judaism.

Dr. Leonard Saxe, Professor of Contemporary Jewish Studies and Social Policy at Brandeis University, says in "On Jewish Identity," in the Winter 2012 issue of *Contact*, that decisions Jews make regarding religion—decisions about observance, marriage, affiliation, and engagement in Jewish life—are a result of the saliency of Jewish identity. He notes that in order for Jewish identity to be important in relation to other available identities, "Jewish education" has "to be prominent and effective."[1]

We recognized the need for good Jewish instruction, but like the parents that social activist and Jewish communal leader Albert Vorspan addresses in his book, *So the Kids Are Revolting? A Game Plan for Jewish (and All Other) Parents*, we felt that the solution to our Jewish education dilemma was formal teaching handled by experienced professionals. The homeschool model of imparting Jewish religious tradition and history, as well as Hebrew, was not an option for the reason Vorspan stated in 1970 when the book was written; from a Jewish perspective, I was "a functional illiterate." But I still wanted my child to "know what it [meant] to be Jewish."[2] Since I could not tell him, I would send him to our synagogue to learn. The points Vorspan made to my parents' generation forty-three years ago were still valid.

Someone once told me that Jewish life begins at birth, not at age thirteen, and Sammy's formal Jewish education began early. When he was nine months old, we started attending a Mommy and Me class at the JCC. I cannot say that I chose the program specifically for the Judaism, which because of the kids' age was minimal, but it did reintroduce me and introduce Sammy to the Hamotzi, the blessing over bread, and blessings for other types of food, which we said at snack time. What I was mainly looking for at the time was a way to meet people after moving to Dallas. But the class did reconnect me with Jewish education, and I was able to learn about the city's Jewish preschool options from other parents that I met. We also made some great friends. A year and a half later, we were ready for the next step.

I always knew that I wanted to send Sammy to a Jewish preschool. I attended one. In fact, I have a picture in my bedroom of my mother dropping me off at B'nai Abraham preschool in Livingston, New Jersey, and I thought it would provide a positive and fun experience with Judaism before religious school. We felt this was important because, like many people, we assumed that supplementary religious education had not changed all that much from when Cameron and I went through it thirty years ago. Religious instruction and Sunday school were boring, dull obligations, where kids misbehaved and little was learned, regardless of faith. It appeared to be designed to test a child's endurance of tedium more than anything else.

At the time, there was no reason to believe that we would not subject Sammy to this same form of mild torture in order to become a bar mitzvah. We thought that it if he had a good start to Jewish learning in preschool that we would have half a chance at getting him to look forward to religious school. Upon reflection, I recognized that my other reasons for insisting on Jewish preschool had to do with a desire to inspire in Sammy a lifelong love of Judaism, to buttress his emerging Jewish identity, and to find a gateway to other facets of Jewish life for our family. We hoped that Jewish preschool would be much more than finger painting and counting. As Arthur Hertzberg stated in his March 10, 1965, address to the New York Metropolitan Region, National Jewish Welfare Board, we hoped that a Jewish early childhood education would be a place where we oriented Sammy "to a healthy acceptance" of his "Jewish identity" and "make Jewish experience crucial to" his "future outlook."[3]

Our temple has an early childhood education program that is well respected throughout Dallas. We joined our friends in enrolling Sammy in the school. It was an amazing experience for all of us. Not only did Sammy get all the usual benefits of a preschool education—exposure to important scholastic skills, such as vocabulary and the building blocks of reading and math, socialization, and group learning—but the school helped to build a connection to our synagogue and instill a love of Judaism. As we became more involved in the school's parents' association, our involvement with the larger temple organization increased. We built community.

The warmth and creativity of the preschool's programs that addressed Jewish concepts, traditions, and values made ritual observance less intimidating and encouraged us to experiment or deepen our home practice. We formed a beautiful home–school connection, with each—the formal and informal education—reinforcing the other, enabling Sammy's (and our family's) Jewish self to blossom. By prekindergarten (pre-K), Sammy was eagerly sharing his thoughts about the weekly Torah portion at school and requesting that a mezuzah be added to the entry to our house from the garage since we do not use the front door and, therefore, cannot kiss it upon arriving home. We started to say that it would not surprise us if Sammy became a rabbi. Nor would it upset us. At the same time that Judaism became more embedded in Sammy's personality, it assumed a more central place in our family life.

I was growing more comfortable in my own Jewish skin, and I was proud of the Jewish home that we were building. Still searching for approval from my mother that I was a good Jewish mom and hoping to demonstrate Sammy's connection to Judaism, I shared with her a conversation that I had with one of Sammy's teachers. "Debbie, the teacher at Sammy's school that leads the Torah unit on Fridays was saying how enthusiastic Sammy is during the discussion," I said during one of my mom's visits.

"Hmm…" she responded.

"Apparently he's quite the little scholar. I guess our conversations at our Shabbat table have resonated with him. Debbie calls him Rabbi Sammy," I continued.

147

"Oh, God, I hope he doesn't become a rabbi," my mother replied, rolling her eyes.

"Why do you say that?" I asked. "I can think of worse careers."

"He'll never make any money," she said.

"There's more to life than making money," I responded. "At least he'd do something meaningful like help people and the community."

"He'll be poor his whole life," she answered.

"It has more social value than his parents' former job, marketing high-interest credit cards to people who can't afford to pay their balance," I said. After a pause I added, "The good news is that Sammy's five, so he has plenty of time to think about what he wants to be, and I hope we're supportive of whatever path he chooses."

The conversation did not achieve much other than highlight our different worldviews. My mother has always said that I am an idealist. I am sure my comment about doing something that has value for the community did not surprise her, nor should I have expected her to have a different reaction. Yet I was hoping to get the pat on the back that, at thirty-nine, I still craved. I wanted her to say, "You are a good Jewish parent. I am so proud of you." But by engaging in verbal sparring, my message was obscured. What I wanted my mother to know was just how strongly Sammy identified with Judaism. Cameron and I were proud of this, given our interfaith status, and had put a considerable amount of effort into Jewish identity building. It was, for us, a labor of love from which we all found fulfillment. I wanted our work to be recognized, but rather than explicitly stating what I wanted her to hear, I asked my mother to try to find the correct meaning in my story. This strategy led, not to greater understanding, but to defensive responses to one another's comments.

When Sammy was four, we started talking about what his education would be post-preschool. Like many of the parents of students in Sammy's year, we felt sad that soon he would leave this wonderful, nurturing environment that had filled him with such goodness—Jewish and secular, academic and social–emotional. The school had become an extension of our family, and it was hard, but necessary, to think about the next step. We wondered how it would feel to leave our safe little Jewish cocoon. When parents started a movement to lobby the school to add a kindergarten class, delaying all of our separation for one more year, we jumped on board. We felt strongly that continuing Sammy's education in the nurturing environment he and we loved would be ideal. The fact that the curriculum would have a strong Judaic component did not faze Cameron or me because it was a place that was familiar and accepting. Given that it was a school within our own Reform congregation made us feel that Sammy would learn Jewish content from a perspective with which we were comfortable.

Hertzberg writes in "Jewish Education Must Be Religious Education" in *Being Jewish in America*, "Is there a Jewish schoolmaster anywhere who has not heard unnumbered times the parental admonition, 'Don't make my child too religious,' followed usually by, 'I don't want him to grow up to be a rabbi'?"[4] After seeing firsthand how the teaching of Jewish values, ideas, and rituals were handled during the preschool years, we were confident that the Jewish component of the curriculum would not make Sammy too religious but just right from a Reform point of view. Unfortunately, it became clear that the kindergarten option was unlikely to become a reality. Resigned to graduation, I began to research other schools in the city.

While the idea of transitioning to a new academic home was hard for Cameron and me, it was more difficult for Sammy. Each year he would grow attached to his wonderful teachers, often telling us that he would not love the next ones quite the same as his current ones, yet each fall he would quickly fall in love again. But at the end of the threes, his level of concern moved beyond being sad about leaving his teachers to verbalizing his unhappiness about leaving the temple's early childhood program. Even at age four, he recognized that he only had one year left in this comfortable environment. Shortly before the start of summer camp, his sadness came pouring out. I went upstairs to put something away and found Sammy sitting on the floor in his playroom, crying. Concerned, I asked him what was wrong.

"Bug, what's the matter? Why are you so sad?" I asked and sat down on the floor next to him. Sammy climbed into my lap, put his head on my shoulder, and started sobbing. I rubbed his back. "Can you tell Mommy what's wrong? Maybe I can help you."

Through his tears, he said, "I just finished the threes, and that means I'm leaving Ally and Elizabeth, and that I only have one year left at Temple. Then I have to go to another school."

"It's sad when we leave teachers we love, and you've been really lucky to have some pretty special ones," I said. "Remember when you told me last summer that you were never going to love anyone as much as you loved Gail?"

"Uh-huh," sobbed Sammy.

"Do you remember that after your first week of summer camp before the threes even started you already loved Ally?" I asked.

"Uh-huh," sobbed Sammy again.

"Well I bet the same thing is going to happen when you start pre-K in the fall." I said. "You're going to love your new teachers too, and it will be a great year."

"But it's going to be different," cried Sammy. "It's going to be my last year at Temple, and then I'm going to have to go to a different school, and I don't want to leave Temple. I want to stay there forever until I have to go to college, and I even wish I could go there for college. I wish it had every grade."

"I wish it had every grade too. It's a really special place. But we're going to find another school that you'll love just as much for kindergarten," I responded. "While you will need to go to a new school, we're members of Temple. I promise we can go back to your classrooms to visit whenever you want. In the meantime, I know you're going to have a great time at summer camp and a great year in pre-K."

"It's not going to be the same. I'm going to miss it so much," said Sammy.

"We all are, Bug. Good-byes are really hard."

A visit to his old teachers and classrooms on the first day of camp, coupled with a fun morning, seemed to ease his immediate sadness about leaving his former teachers and moving to pre-K, but he still shared how brokenhearted he was to be graduating throughout the next school year. The conversation drove home the importance of finding a school that was a good fit for Sammy, preferably one that was warm, nurturing, and academically engaging. We needed to make a thoughtful choice. It also highlighted for me just how attached we had all become to our synagogue's community.

Having lived in Dallas for five years at the time, we had learned about the public education system in the city and state. While there were pockets of highly regarded elementary schools, they were in neighborhoods that we could not afford. Our local school was good—but not exemplary. Even in excellent schools classes were large—twenty-two students—with legislation that enables schools to lift class-size restrictions in order to help address the district's budget crunch. We also knew that state cuts in funding for education would begin to affect schools as Sammy entered kindergarten and would continue into his early elementary years. According to the National Education Association, in the 2010–11 school year, when Sammy started, Texas ranked forty-first in per-pupil spending. In 2011–12, the state dropped to forty-fifth.[5]

In addition to budget issues, revisions to the state's social studies and history curriculums caused us concern as a family that was raising a child in a minority religion. In 2010, the Texas State Board of Education adopted changes that included diminishing the teaching of the civil rights movement and religious freedoms. These amendments resulted in the removal of Thomas Jefferson as an influential political philosopher and an increased emphasis on the Christian influences of the founding fathers.[6] These changes reflected ideas that are taught in public school Bible courses that are becoming increasingly common throughout Texas. According to the Texas Freedom Network Education Fund, which supports efforts to promote religious freedom and individual liberties, most of the "courses are taught by teachers with no academic training in biblical or theological studies."[7] Many "assume that students are Christians, and that Christian theological claims are true," and present the Jewish Bible as a deviation from the norm.[8] These things made us uncomfortable. Cameron and I are firm believers in the separation of church and state, especially in schools—the exception being in parochial schools, and even then we believe that secular academic subjects such as history and science should be devoid of any religious point of view (or at least as much as possible).

Besides economic and curriculum concerns, we took issue with the poor academic standards in the Texas public schools. The Thomas B. Fordham Institute, an education research and advocacy group, gives Texas a *C* in Math and Science and a *D* in US History standards. In its 2006 study of education reform in all states, the Institute gave Texas a *D* for student achievement, a *C-* for quality of academic standards, and a *D+* for the rigor of the state's definition of proficiency in reading and math.[9] That's not a strong case that the system is sufficiently preparing students for future success, and there is not much improvement on the horizon. A review by the Institute of the state's proposed new math standards in April 2012 found them to be only a modest improvement and still "inferior to the Common Core math standards."[10] The Common Core State Standards are an initiative to provide consistent education standards across states and are coordinated by the National Governors Association Center for Best Practices and the Council of Chief State School Officers.

Although we worried about the quality and content of the education Sammy would receive in public school and the fact that he could be the only Jew in his class in an area of the country where many people have little interaction with Jews, part of us wanted to put our ideals first and support public education. On the other hand, we were not prepared to sacrifice Sammy's learning for high-mindedness. It was a dilemma. Do we use our neighborhood elementary and try to effect change, or do we do what is best for our child? Are we part of the solution or part of the problem of families fleeing the public schools? During our discussions, I could not help but think of the famous declaration made by the great rabbi Hillel in Pirkei Avot: "If I am not for myself, who will be for me, and if I am only for myself, what am I?"[11] After weighing our concerns, we decided to send Sammy to private school, yet we continued to vote our conscience through the support of politicians and initiatives in favor of better public education.

As we started the process of creating a list of where to apply Sammy, Cameron and I agreed that I would do the preliminary visits to narrow the choices to three schools. He would visit those I suggested, and then together we would rank them. After visiting the secular schools and discussing my impressions of them with Cameron, we determined they were not a good fit for Sammy or our family. That focused our search on the city's parochial schools, which we knew had some percentage of Jewish students. These are Christian institutions, mostly with Episcopal roots or affiliations. Even though Sammy's connection to Judaism was strong, we did not consider Dallas's Jewish day schools because the perception among many area Jews is that the secular academics are not strong, due to a heavy focus on Judaic learning. The Christian schools do not suffer from the same impression, even though they also teach religion and require daily attendance at chapel.

Why do progressive Jews have an aversion to nonsupplementary Jewish education? It can be linked to Jewish history and the immigrant experience in America. After centuries of persecution, it has become ingrained in the minds of many acculturated Jews that it is safer not to display openly one's Jewishness. Having achieved assimilated status in America, some Jews are wary of doing anything that might be perceived as "too Jewy," calling attention to their otherness and threatening acceptance in the larger community. Wearing a kippah, which is required of boys attending the area's day schools, qualifies as too much. It is a public declaration of religion. Some Muslims feel similarly about wearing a hijab or headscarf.

Part of the hesitation to wear our religious identity more openly stems from what we know through our own experience and the media that America is not postreligious. Prejudice and exclusion still lurk in certain quarters, particularly in the Bible Belt. Restrictive country club policies, dance schools that "weave Christ into every aspect of class," and baseball clinics run by secular organizations that incorporate the New Testament as a way to deepen kids' knowledge of God are subtle reminders of our outsider standing—synagogue attacks and the defacement of Jewish property are obvious examples that anti-Semitism still exists. In the eyes of less religious Jews, wearing a kippah outside of a synagogue is a public announcement of their religion. In an area of the country where many people have never met a Jew and Christianity is almost a state religion, many Jews are not eager to do something to declare their otherness openly.

Another factor in the disinterest of many non-Orthodox Jews in day school is the emphasis Jews place on scholarship and academic achievement. Jews are known to be somewhat obsessive about education. A hyperachievement mindset is entrenched in us and is rooted in the history of our people. We are commanded to study in the Torah, "teach them faithfully to your children..." (Deuteronomy 6:7),[12] and we learn in order to act responsibly. "An ignoramus cannot be a righteous person," says Hillel in Pirkei Avot.[13] It is believed that Hillel is not saying that ignorant people do not want to do good but rather that they lack the knowledge to make good choices. When referring to this quote, Joseph Telushkin states in *Jewish Literacy* that people needed to be educated in order to know the right way to act.[14] He comments on how the commandment to learn impacted Jewish ideas about education as articulated in the Talmud, which forbids parents from living in a city with no schools. He says that Judaism honored study over power, and the emphasis the faith placed on education was known throughout Europe.[15] Throughout time, Jews have maintained as a core value this emphasis on education, study, and achievement and have used it to not only advance their own knowledge but as a way to improve their socioeconomic position, as was done by Jewish immigrants during the early twentieth century.

This glorification of learning appears to refute my statement that the emphasis Jews put on scholarship and achievement is a reason why they shy away from using day school. In fact, it would suggest that Jewish day schools would have the most rigorous academic standards. But today, for many less religious Jews, perception is reality. Day schools typically admit "every" Jewish student, regardless of where he or she falls on the academic spectrum. This means students who are gifted as well as remedial.

The city's secular schools, as well as some of the Christian ones, take only "qualified students" who they believe are "capable" of benefiting from the program. Many list above-average aptitude and achievement as characteristics they look for in applicants. For many non-Orthodox Jews in Dallas, the open-door admissions philosophy of the day schools is what leads them to believe that they provide only an average education. A friend has suggested that rather than using a quote from Alan Dershowitz about being able to identify day school students in his law classes to make the point that Jewish schools have rigorous academics, the schools should reject a few applicants.

The comment to which my friend refers is from Dershowitz's 1997 book *The Vanishing American Jew: In Search of Jewish Identity for the Next Century*. Dershowitz writes that his own day school education made him a better lawyer because it exposed him to two different perspectives. He also believes that immersion in the Talmud and other Jewish sources gives day school alumni a competitive advantage in college and law school. He says that they understand methods of argumentation and other thinking skills necessary for lawyers and have a substantial lead in analysis of texts due to the study of the various types of Jewish biblical interpretation.[16]

While some Dallas day schools cite these points in their admissions pitch to parents, Dershowitz, in the same book, provides ammunition to those who believe that day schools have subpar academics. He says that day schools need to upgrade their academic qualifications to attract students because academically superior schools are what Jewish parents want. He notes that the top schools have a significant number of Jewish students but are not Jewish schools.[17] For many parents, this argument confirms their opinion that day schools provide only an average education.

The last reason I see for Jewish families not using day school is what they view as the irrelevance of Judaic education. Sure, learning Hebrew and Jewish history are necessary to become a b'nei mitzvah, but parents question whether the depth to which these subjects are studied in a day school environment is needed for admittance to an American college or success in the business world. How is the study of Jewish law (Mishna and Talmud) relevant to the skills our children need to survive in the twenty-first century? Why use time teaching subjects that are not required for college admission when the time can be spent on necessary material such as reading, math, science, and social studies and enrichment in art, music, and a more useful second language, such as Spanish or Chinese? After all, many studies show that American children are far behind students from other countries in achievement in these areas. Joseph Telushkin captures this sentiment perfectly in *Jewish Literacy*, when he points out that many nonreligious Jews find the study of Talmud, the highest level of Jewish learning, irrelevant.[18] Familiarity with obscure disputes related to remote subjects hardly seems applicable to an assimilated modern life. The only Jews many of these parents know who study these texts are Orthodox, and they appear to some to cling to old, out-of-date practices.

Any Jewish education that is viewed as more intensive than congregational religious school programs touches the fear that Hertzberg articulated in 1963 and that a lot of progressive Jews still have about their child becoming too religious. As I shared through my own experience, in chapter 3, many parents are uneasy with the idea that their kid might become more observant than they are themselves. I felt the same and had similar objections to Jewish day school. That is why I did not consider looking at or suggesting a Jewish education.

I had grown up with the same preconceived notions. Therefore, I went ahead and spoke with the admissions directors of two of the Christian schools. One said that all children, including non-Christian students, were required to go to chapel and learn about Jesus and Christian teachings. I was not comfortable with that but thought that maybe I could find a way to get comfortable with it for the sake of Sammy's education. The other director was direct in her message.

"Most of our Jewish students come to us in middle and high school when they already have a Jewish identity and can better compare and contrast the religions," she said. "I think that for a young child growing up in an interfaith home but being raised Jewish, attending a Christian school will be confusing."

"Thank you," I said. "I appreciate your honesty."

After the conversation, I realized what I needed to do, but I did not want to do it. At this point in Sammy's life, it was obvious that his Jewishness was a very important part of his identity. The admissions director was right; Christian school was not a good fit for Sammy, at least in the elementary grades. I felt stuck. I had not identified one school that might be good, let alone three. I knew that I needed to expand our search to include the Conservative day school. Why was I being stubborn? Why was I acting as if I might catch an infectious disease if I even investigated it? It was not as though we were secular Jews. Even as an interfaith family, we were already fairly observant, albeit in a Reform way. I decided to talk to Cameron to get his thoughts. As a Jew, I had wrestled with this option, so I wanted Cameron's perspective. I quickly found out; he was more at ease with the idea of a day school education than I was.

"I spoke with the admissions directors today at Episcopal School South and North Episcopal," I said.

"Yeah? What did they say?" Cameron asked.

"One said that while they do have Jewish students, all students are required to learn about Jesus and other Christian teachings," I said. "The other said that she thought that sending a Jewish child from an interfaith home to a Christian school at such a young age would be confusing. She said most of the school's Jewish students were in the middle and high school and at an age when they have a stronger sense of their religious identity."

"That makes sense," Cameron said.

"I am fine with Sammy attending chapel, and I am comfortable with him learning shared Judeo-Christian values in an ecumenical way," I continued. "But I'm not comfortable with him only learning the Christian perspective since that is not his religion. As we think about sending him to a religious school, I don't see how we cannot consider sending him to one that teaches his own religion."

I was surprised by Cameron's response. "Jane, I'm fine with sending Sammy to a school that teaches the religion in which he's being raised. Look into the Jewish day school options."

My husband never stops amazing me. Even with all of our home observance and involvement in our temple, I still expect to encounter some resistance. Being married to someone who is not Jewish is not supposed to be this...easy. There are supposed to be struggles over religion in the home, observance, and engagement. After all, if you believe many in the Jewish academic and clergy establishment, families like mine are in large part responsible for the diminishing involvement in Jewish life of American Jews. While I know, because of my participation in interfaith and outreach activities, that there are many intermarried families actively engaged in Judaism, a part of me is still conditioned to believe what many in the Jewish community state: that intermarriage is a significant factor contributing to weakened Jewish identity. Yet that has not been my family's experience. I acknowledge the difficulties we have had with my family as it relates to our religious choices, and we have encountered issues about dealing with prejudice (see chapter 8), but we have not had the big, emotional battles over religion that we are led to believe make marriage between a Jew and Gentile difficult.

I know that we are lucky, and I know at moments like these how profoundly Cameron cares for Sammy and me. He has honored his commitment to ensure that Sammy knows what it means to be Jewish, and he enthusiastically participates in Jewish life. I am not sure if he understands what a gift he has given to us. Certainly, I do. As Sammy's preschool director once said, "I'm not surprised by anything Cameron does. He loves you both so much, and I know that there is absolutely nothing he will not do for Sammy." Words seem to be a terribly inadequate way to express to him my appreciation and thanks.

The following day I called the Conservative day school. When I spoke to the admissions director, I had several questions, including what percentage of the school affiliates with the Reform movement, and were interfaith families welcome. I was surprised to learn that 30 percent of the students were Reform, which was more than I expected, and that there were a number of interfaith families, especially if you expanded the definition to include those with extended families that are not Jewish. The woman I spoke with spent a significant amount of time with me, even though I gave no indication that I was even planning to visit the school. While I recognized that this was her job, her willingness to talk with me for more than thirty minutes, coupled with her seemingly honest answers about and assessment of the school, made me consider that my impression of Jewish day school might be wrong. I decided to attend an evening kindergarten open house.

Upon arrival, a middle school student (the school only goes through eighth grade) greeted me at the door and pointed out the art room and lower school library as we walked to the classroom where the meeting was being held. I appreciated the minitour, but I was disappointed that the rooms she showed me were dark. My first thought was that the visit was not off to a good start, but I also realized that my preconceived prejudice against day school might cause me to look for negatives. I told myself that I could make an appointment to visit the school during the day if necessary.

When we reached the meeting location, I immediately noticed a basket of kippot near the entrance and heard a staff member remind the men to take one if they were not wearing their own. I squirmed a little and thought that this might be too religious for me. I am ashamed to admit that my initial reaction to this display of religious identity in a safely Jewish environment was discomfort. But it was. If we had been in a synagogue, I would have felt comfortable because that is an "acceptable" place to engage in religion, but my upbringing told me that a school was an unacceptable location. It was as if the wearing of a head covering by men inside threatened my acceptance in the community outside the building.

I took a seat. After some opening remarks made by the admissions director, the two kindergarten teachers spoke. They highlighted the small class size, which at fifteen was about the same as the other private schools I had visited. Then they mentioned that there were two teachers in each classroom—a noted advantage over the other schools, which only had one. They discussed the curriculum in detail, demonstrated how language arts was taught, and emphasized that the material was customized based on each student's ability. They shared how even within the high, middle, and low learning levels that there was stratification, and the low student-to-teacher ratio enabled them to address learning differences to this degree. My discomfort was quickly turning to elation as I listened with delight. We wanted this type of learning environment for Sammy.

When the head of Jewish Studies stood to speak, I was pleasantly surprised to find that I liked what she had to say. She spoke about the school's ethical covenant and teaching of Jewish concepts. I found that I really liked the idea of the values that we were imparting at home being reinforced at school. It seemed to me that, in addition to a good secular education, Sammy would be learning to be a purposeful and responsible member of the larger world. I liked that his Jewish identity would be nurtured, and more importantly, I could picture Sammy at the school.

It appeared that I had found the perfect fit when the question-and-answer portion of the program started. The first question was from a man for whom the Judaic component of the curriculum was extremely important.

"How often do the children daven?" he asked.

Daven? Did I hear the word "daven?" The question caused the hair on my arms to go up.

Daven is a Yiddish word that means to recite prayer, and for me, it usually conjures the image of Orthodox men standing with small prayer books open in their hands, swaying and rocking while they murmur the day's liturgy in the morning, afternoon, and evening. I witnessed davening firsthand on my flights to and from Israel and during my visits to the Western Wall in Jerusalem when I was sixteen. For a Reform Jew not accustomed to this practice, it can feel foreign, remote, and like something better suited to life in a European shtetl. The words "pray" or "services" are more familiar and less intimidating.

"The children have services once a day," answered the Jewish Studies director.

The answer did not seem to satisfy the questioner, and he began a series of follow-up questions about the depth and breadth of the Judaic curriculum that were asked in an increasingly aggressive way and were sprinkled with plenty of Yiddish and Hebrew words. If the kippah-wearing made me squirm, this scared the hell out of me. I felt like the air was being sucked out of the room, and I noticed that my breathing intensified. I thought that no matter how good a fit the school initially seemed, I just could not do it. The religious aspect was too much. I was resigned to revisiting the secular schools when a current parent at the school gave a testimonial of her family's experience—her *interfaith* family's experience. She introduced herself as the Jewish half of an intermarried couple and shared her thoughts on the academics, inclusiveness of the school community, reason for returning her kids to the school after trying her neighborhood elementary, and her non-Jewish husband's comfort and involvement in her children's education. As she spoke, I let out a small sigh of relief. Maybe this could work. I took it as a sign not to give up on the school just yet.

I shared what I learned with Cameron and told him that I thought it was a good place for Sammy. I scheduled a daytime visit so that I could get a better look at the facilities and observe a kindergarten class. I liked what I saw, and the admissions director reassured me that an interfaith couple would be welcomed. Over the course of the next few weeks, she had two interfaith families call me to share their experience, including one who belonged to our synagogue. I was impressed with the outreach, and it made us feel wanted, which was a big deal for intermarrieds because so often we were made to feel like pariahs. I was certain that this was the school for Sammy and found a way to come to terms with the outward displays of Judaism. I realized that attending a school that follows the practices of a different Jewish denomination would teach Sammy respect for differences and show him the variety of perspectives within his own religion (the school is Conservative, and many of the Jewish Studies teachers are Orthodox).

I recognized how his familiarity with the Torah would benefit him in later years as he analyzed literature. This was an aspect of my own education that I felt was deficient. I always believed that I was at a disadvantage because of my religious illiteracy. I missed the biblical references in the books we read in high school English that my fellow students could identify, and I often wondered how a better understanding of the Bible might have made the stories more meaningful. I was pleasantly surprised to see the ethnic and racial diversity that existed at the school. To be sure, there were a greater variety of ethnicities than races, but both were present, and Sammy would see that Jews came in different colors and from many places. I realized that the racial and economic diversity would not be what it was in a public school, but I knew that we would be able to give Sammy more diverse experiences through extracurricular activities, camp, and volunteering.

My one remaining issue was that I needed to get over my squeamishness about Sammy wearing a kippah, but I figured that was a relatively minor detail. I asked a friend who has three children at the school, two of which were boys, if wearing the head covering at school made them want to wear it all the time. If I were honest with myself, I feared that my child might become too religious. Over coffee one morning, she said, "You know a lot of us less observant families worried about that. If you weren't raised in an environment where men covered their head all the time, it can feel uncomfortable because it just isn't familiar."

"I'm glad to hear I'm not alone on this," I said.

She smiled. "Listen, some parents tell their kids to take it off after school. But it doesn't really bother me as much as I thought. If it's still on their heads when we get home, I don't care. Frankly, I don't really notice," she said. "What I find is that more often than not the boys take it off when they get in the car because they're either hot or they just want to take it off at the end of the day. I liken it to how I felt about wearing heels with my suit when I was practicing law. I'd put them on when I got to the office, and as soon as I left, I'd put on more comfortable shoes."

Hearing these comments helped me realize that I was making a bigger deal out of this than needed. But like with many things, we tend to worry about the unfamiliar, investing time and emotional energy thinking about "what if" scenarios, only to find that our worries are unfounded. I got over my fear of the kippah and asked Cameron to visit the school. If he liked it, we would apply nowhere else. When Sammy's preschool director found out that we were looking at the school, she said, "I had no idea you were looking at day school. I can't think of a better fit for Sammy. They will challenge him, and he will love the Jewish aspect of the school. His Judaism is so important to him. I know he will thrive there."

I was anxious to hear Cameron's opinion of the school and spoke to him after his visit. "I really liked it. I think it would be a great school for Sammy," he said. "I felt very welcome. I met with the admissions director, K–8 principal, and head of school."

"Wow. I thought you were just meeting the admissions director. They seem to have rolled out the red carpet for you. How did you feel about the Jewish aspect of the school?" I asked. "It's a bonus, don't you think?"

"I think it more than a bonus," he said. "It's a really important part of the education. I think Sammy would be lucky to go to a school like this."

Tears of joy, love, and gratitude rolled down my face.

Once we made our decision, I called to tell my mom since she was interested in the progress we were making on schools for Sammy. By this point in our Jewish journey, it was easy to assume what my family's response would be to our decision to send Sammy to day school. As expected, *shocked* and *horrified* were two of the adjectives that sprang from their mouths. My mother repeatedly asked me to explain our choice, each time stating that she would like to understand how we made our decision. At the heart of the confusion over our school choice was the assumption that the state of the public school system in Texas was the same as in New Jersey, and that there were many secular private school options. I tried to educate them about the differences, often repeating the process we went through and the reasons for our selection. I could see that it was hard for my family to accept how the educational situation in Dallas was different from their own experience.

"I don't understand why you don't just move to a good school district," said one sibling.

"There have to be a number of secular choices. Why don't you just apply to those? I can think of at least five nonsectarian private schools in this area," said another family member.

Rather than continue to repeat our decision-making process, I simply listened. I realized that nothing I said would change their opinion. Over time, my mom at least seemed to accept our choice when she saw how Sammy was thriving. But once in a while, she still lets slip that she is not entirely sold on the idea that Jewish day school can provide a quality education.

"My neighbor's son just received his college acceptances. He got into Harvard, Yale, Princeton, Stanford, and the honors program at University of Texas," I said.

"That's impressive. Where does he go to school?" she asked.

"He goes to an all-boys school in Dallas. He went to public school until fourth grade and then transferred. It's one of the best schools in the area," I said.

"If it's one of the best schools in the area, then how come my grandson isn't there?" she asked curtly.

"Mom, we've been over this many times. Right now, Sammy is in the best place for him. If he is no longer challenged or we are unhappy with the education, we will move him. But there's no reason to move him from an environment in which he is thriving," I responded.

Like parents, some grandparents fear that their grandchildren will be more religious than they are themselves. In my mother's case, I think she is uncomfortable with Sammy's Jewishness because it reminds her of her very observant immigrant grandparents and their old-world lifestyle; and she shares many of the reservations about day school that I detailed earlier.

In contrast, my in-laws had no concerns about our school choice. They felt that we had done our homework and made a thoughtful decision. The Judaic aspect of the education did not seem to threaten them. They had already accepted that we would be religiously different. Their penchant for seeing the connections between Christianity and Judaism and their support of religious pluralism made the nature of Sammy's school a nonissue. In fact, they happily attended Sammy's first Grandparents' Day celebration at the school, and Pam crocheted Sammy's collection of colorful, striped kippot.

He is very proud of his handmade head coverings.

"Sammy, I just love all your colorful kippot," said the campus rabbi at carpool one morning.

"Thanks. My grandma makes them, and she's not even Jewish!" Sammy replied, smiling proudly.

"That is so cool!" the rabbi answered.

It is a little ironic that the kippah, which was the outward manifestation of my discomfort with day school and public declarations of Jewishness, is the symbol that connects my Christian in-laws to Sammy's Jewish life.

For the most part, day school has lived up to our expectations. That is not to say it has been perfect; it has not, but then no school is. Our single biggest requirement for Sammy remaining at the school has been that he is challenged and gets what he needs in the core secular academic subjects. To date we have been satisfied. We have found that there is an emphasis on learning effective oral and written communication, developing curiosity and imagination, collaborating through team assignments, utilizing critical thinking and problem solving, and analyzing information in the early elementary grades. These skills are some of the seven survival skills that Tony Wagner, codirector of the Change Leadership Group at the Harvard Graduate School of Education and author of *The Global Achievement Gap*, cites as necessary for success in the twenty-first century. He stresses the need for these competencies to be taught in high school, but we are pleased to see that these critical areas are already being nurtured.

As for the Jewish curriculum, I thought we would like it but still had the impression that some of it would feel too religious for us. But for the most part, that has not been the case. We have found that we enjoy the religious dialogue we have developed with Sammy, and we also enjoy watching the growth in his Jewish identity, knowledge, and worldview. The conversations we have based on something he learned or a question he has—Why aren't the dinosaurs in the creation story? Why don't we keep kosher? Is the Torah the word of God? to list a few—have often made us explore and examine our own beliefs and then articulate them in language understandable to a child. We watch with pride at Shabbat services as Sammy follows the prayer book and recites the Hebrew. We learn together as we read the week's Torah portion in order for Sammy to search for the answer to the school rabbi's weekly Torah trivia contest. We marvel at his deep affection toward Israel, which has already led us to discuss at a high level current events in the Jewish state. Cameron participates equally in these discussions, which are typically followed by Sammy asking the same question: "When can we go to Israel?"

As for my concerns about the school, some have been realized, and others have not. I feared that the Orthodox Jewish Studies teachers would not be welcoming to a Reform Jew. This has not been the case. The teachers seem to have embraced the students' varied practices. I received a call from his kindergarten Jewish Studies teacher, telling me how Sammy loves to talk about the things he does at his synagogue and how he asked to teach the class the melody his temple uses for Oseh Shalom, a prayer for peace.

"Shlomo (Sammy's Hebrew name) is so proud of his synagogue. He tells us all the time about the services he goes to," she said. "He asked me if he could teach the class the tune your temple uses for Oseh Shalom. I said, 'Of course! You can do it the next time you are the prayer leader.'"

We were thrilled that she was open to more than one way of doing things.

While I expected a less accepting attitude from Sammy's Orthodox instructors, I did not think that we would have any issues with the administration or students since the majority were Conservative and most had friends and family who affiliated Reform. I was surprised to find that it was from these groups that we encountered denominational and interfaith prejudice.

Between kindergarten and first grade, I cochaired for the parents' association a program that matched new families with existing ones to help ease the transition to school. As part of the matching process, we worked with the new admissions director. The woman Cameron and I worked with during Sammy's application process had left. During a meeting to go over incoming students, the conversation turned to recruitment and how to attract families that are not currently considering a day school education.

"It's a challenge getting some families to consider day school," said the director in response to one of the committee members. "We do well with families in which one or both parents went to day school. We can do a better job of making the case to pro-private-school families, but of course, the Reform don't care about Jewish education."

I was irked by the sanctimonious comment, but for the sake of a good working relationship, I did not respond. In my mind, denominational affiliation had nothing to do with how much someone cared about religious education. I know Reform families who work tirelessly to ensure that their children receive Jewish knowledge, whether it is through day school or supplementary education. I also know Conservative families who show as little interest or caring in Judaic learning as it is generally assumed that Reform Jews do. As the discussion continued, the director repeated two more times, "Reform Jews don't care about Jewish education." After the third remark, I could not hold my tongue anymore.

"I'm sorry," I said. "I'm a Reform Jew, and I'm offended by that generalization. We are not only Reform, but interfaith, and we chose this school. We have found that we are more observant than a large percentage of the families in my son's class. I don't think affiliation is a good measure. We care deeply, as do other Reform families we know, about our child's Jewish education." My cochair nodded in agreement. The admissions director gave me a look that said, "Are you finished with your outburst?" Then she proceeded to the next item on the agenda. Her lack of response annoyed me, but I was glad I spoke up. I felt that if my reaction made her choose her words more carefully in the future then it had served its purpose.

After this incident, I should have suspected that the perception that Reform Jews have a disregard for Jewish practice and education was more widespread than I thought. This stereotype was based on the practices of American Reform Jews in the nineteenth century: no head covering and little adherence to dietary and other ritual laws. But over time, the Reform movement reintroduced many of the Jewish elements that they previous rejected. I was frustrated that this woman, who previously affiliated with the Reform movement, held this opinion. I realized that I was irritated because I felt that I had let go of my misconceptions of day school and those who teach at and attend it, but that others had not rethought their perceptions of Jews like me. The remark reminded me that some still believe that Jewishness can be measured and quantified. But if the school was going to accept Reform Jews, then it needed to acknowledge and respect that "good" Jews come from all backgrounds.

Besides denominational issues, I anticipated that Sammy and our family might encounter some challenges because of our interfaith status, even though the intermarrieds I spoke with reassured us of the accepting nature of the school. Still, I believed that, at some point, it would come up, and it did. The first incident happened in kindergarten. A little girl who came over to play mentioned that Sammy was only half Jewish.

"My mom says that Sammy is only half Jewish because his dad is not Jewish," she said on the way to our house.

"No, I'm Jewish," said Sammy confidently.

"That's right. Sammy and I are both Jewish. Sammy is not half anything. His dad is not Jewish, but he and I are," I responded.

I was happy to hear Sammy's response and figured that if this was the worst thing he heard about his interfaith family then we were lucky. The issue came up again in the fall of first grade. On the way home from school, Sammy shared that his classmates said he was only half a Jew.

"I'm only half Jewish because Daddy isn't Jewish," said Sammy matter-of-factly.

"What? Who told you that?" I asked, wondering what diminished his confidence on this subject.

"Everybody," Sammy answered.

"Who's everybody—the kids, teachers?" I asked concerned.

"The kids," Sammy replied.

"What do your teachers say when they say this?" I asked, hoping that they overheard and stopped the conversation. "Do the kids say it in a mean way?"

"No, no one is mean about it. They just say because one of my parents isn't Jewish that I'm only half. My teachers don't hear it," Sammy answered.

"Sammy," I said seriously. "You are not half anything. You are as Jewish as any other kid in your school. I'm Jewish; you're Jewish. You are not less Jewish than anyone else in your class."

Concerned about how this "half-Jewish" comment might affect Sammy's Jewish identity, I resolved to discuss it at our parent-teacher conference the following week. I believed that this was not coming from Sammy's teachers, and I felt that if they knew that this was being said, they would put a stop to it. I wanted to believe that the idea that Sammy was only half Jewish was coming from the children applying their math and reasoning skills to real life or parents who mistakenly equated religion with ethnicity (a child with one Irish and one Italian parent would be one-half of each nationality). But I suspected, based on the comment made by the girl in kindergarten, the idea probably came from parents who were ignorant about interfaith families, believing the stereotypes and the negative press about intermarriage. Regardless of the source, I wanted the issue addressed.

"We haven't heard any of this," said his secular academic teachers after I shared my conversation with Sammy. "The kids are starting to talk about the winter holidays, and that's probably why it's come up. We'll listen for it and address it."

"Thank you," I said. "I don't want Sammy feeling that he is inferior or less of a Jew because Cameron is not Jewish. I want him to be confident that he is as welcome at this school—and deserves to be at this school—as much as any other child."

When I spoke with his Hebrew-Jewish Studies teacher, she made a sad face. "I didn't know; I have not heard this," she said. "I will, of course, address it. There are all kinds of Jews in this world. All are good. Variety is good. This makes me sad. I do not want him to think this." After some additional discussion, we started to leave. Before we left, she raised her hand to her chest and tapped it over her heart. She said, "My Shlomo—he is neshama."

Neither Cameron nor I knew what this meant, but we understood it to be a compliment. A little research helped us understand that *neshama* is a Hebrew term of endearment. Neshama means soul. It is the purest aspect of the soul and penetrates to the very core of our being. When used in this way, it means good Jewish soul. The meaning of the word "sham" is to give value, implying quality or worth. Knowing that she knew Sammy came from an interfaith home made her words more meaningful. I would never have guessed that we would find such warmth and receptiveness from an Orthodox Israeli. Acceptance sometimes comes from the most unlikely places.

If anyone had told me nine years ago, that Sammy would attend Jewish day school, and that Cameron would attend events such as Daven and Donuts, I would have said they were crazy. Daven and Donuts is a monthly morning service for parents and children held before the school day. Given how I feel about the word daven, I assumed that this would be too much religion for either Cameron or me, but Sammy came home and announced that he really wanted to go—with Cameron.

Cameron said, "It's a Conservative school, it can't be that over-the-top."

After the event, I asked Cameron for his impression. "What did you think of Daven and Donuts? Sammy said he had fun."

"It was good. It's really neat to watch Sammy recite all the prayers, and many of his friends were there with their dads. But there were some people who put on those straps with boxes—what do you call them?" he asked.

"Tefillin."

"Yeah, and they wore prayer shawls," he said. "It was intimidating since I'm not used to seeing it."

I assumed Cameron would not go again. But the next time the event took place he went. Afterward, he said it did not feel as foreign as it did the first time because he knew what to expect.

Daven and Donuts reminds us that the world feels less scary when we are exposed to diverse people and practices. Day school has taught Sammy, as well as us, to accept differences in religious observance. If Cameron can attend davening, then I can stop cringing every time I hear the word. This is one example of how I have become, through Sammy, more comfortable expressing my Jewishness. Our choices for Sammy's formal Jewish education have strengthened his Jewish identity and made mine more salient. In "On Jewish Identity," Saxe refers to the potential for education to do this and for it "to ignite a Jewish spark within participants' souls."[19] Learning has sparked Sammy's Jewish flame and rekindled my own. Both burn brighter because of Cameron's involvement and support.

EIGHT

A LESSON IN CONFRONTING PREJUDICE

Our day school experience has highlighted the benefit of exposing ourselves, and Sammy, to diverse experiences, even within our own faith. It has broadened our understanding of the variety of rituals, practices, and ideas that exist within Judaism and has made us more respectful and less dismissive of non-Reform traditions. In a way, it has been a minilesson on how to fight prejudice that we hope Sammy will internalize and apply more broadly when he interacts with people from various ethnic, racial, religious, and socioeconomic groups.

While we are working to ingrain in Sammy that engaging with those who are different is one of the best ways to build understanding, we recognize that diversity does not erase anger, close-mindedness, false ideas, fear, and negative opinions. The fact is that prejudice and anti-Semitism still exist. According to the Anti-Defamation League (ADL), "since World War II, public anti-Semitism has become much less frequent in the Western world" and "Jews face little physical danger," but "stereotypes about Jews remain common."[1] We are reminded that negative views of us lurk in the shadows through neighbors' remarks or colleagues' comments, even while we move with ease through our mostly assimilated daily lives. We deal with these moments in different ways: sometimes we handle them quietly, other times publicly, at times gracefully, and at other times with emotional outbursts. But regardless of how we respond to them, the memories of these encounters are etched in our minds as reminders that no matter how integrated we are into society at large, as Jews, we remain outsiders.

If our encounters with prejudice remind us of our outsider status, it is our study of our people's ancient history at an early age that begins to develop our understanding of it. As toddlers and school-age children, we learn about anti-Semitism in antiquity (BCE) through the celebration of Jewish holidays that commemorate atrocities against Jews, such as Passover (enslavement in Egypt) and Hanukkah (persecution by the Seleucid [Syrian] Empire). Purim, which celebrates the Bible story of Esther, further drives home the point that some people do not have high opinions of us. Haman, an influential advisor to the king and an ancient version of Hitler, planned to exterminate all the Jews of Shushan (the Persian city where the story took place). Esther, Queen of Shushan, learned of the plot and revealed her religious identity (which was known only to her uncle) to her husband the king, in order to save the Jewish people. The king canceled the order of execution, and Esther prevented a Holocaust-like catastrophe. The tale is marked each year with a joyous celebration that includes costumes, noise-makers, and carnivals. But while the celebration is fun, a deeper understanding of the holiday is not lost even on children. Sammy told me at age six that he "just knows" that some people do not like Jews, and they want to do bad things to us.

"How do you know that?" I asked, curious about why he felt this way since he had never experienced prejudice.

"Because of the things that have happened to the Jewish people," he said.

I assumed that he was speaking of the Holocaust, but I asked, "Do you mean the Holocaust?"

"I mean Passover and Purim. The Egyptians made us slaves, and Haman wanted to kill us."

"I wasn't thinking about those stories," I replied. As adults, we sometimes forget that long before we learn about the horrors of Hitler and concentration camps, we learn about the Jews' oppression by Pharaoh and the evil of Haman.

Not just biblical history shapes our view. As we grow and study early (Common Era) Jewish history, we become aware of other examples of religious intolerance and develop an understanding of how these events form the groundwork for later prejudice toward our people. We learn that Jews are a favorite punching bag of the Roman Empire and of Rome's crucifixion of a Jewish political rebel named Jesus. We begin to see how the story that Jesus's followers create about this event—that the Jews, not the Romans, were responsible for Jesus's death—becomes the foundation for centuries of hatred directed toward us. We connect the dots from this event to the Crusades, in which Jews suffered along with Muslims, especially in France and Germany. We recognize the link between the church's report of Jesus's death and the blood libel.

Started in twelfth-century England, the blood libel accused Jews of killing non-Jews in a religious ritual and then drinking their victims' blood. This incredulous claim persisted over time. By the fourteenth century, it had become associated with Passover with Christians claiming that Jews mixed Christian blood into matzah and wine.

We learn how the Jewish people have suffered not only because of the false claim that we killed Jesus but because we would not convert to another religion. We read about the choice given to Jews in twelfth-century Morocco and Spain—convert to Islam or die. We study the Spanish Inquisition, the period from the fifteenth to the early nineteenth century in Spain and Portugal, when Jews and other heretics were tortured in an effort to cleanse us of our impure faith. We realize how these perceptions of Jews as "Christ killers," heretics, and souls in need of saving have made it easy for governments and people throughout history to use us as scapegoats during periods of political and social upheaval, poor economic conditions, and nationalistic fervor. We understand how these concepts and events are the roots of more modern atrocities, such as the waves of pogroms (murderous attacks) against Russian Jews in the nineteenth and twentieth centuries and the Holocaust.

But our worldview is not only shaped by Jewish history highlights from abroad, it is also molded by our knowledge of the treatment of Jews (maybe our own family members) in the United States. The PBS series *The Jewish Americans* discusses anti-Semitism in this country. "Jewish Americans... flourished in America, enjoying immense freedom and opportunities...But like other minorities... have also faced prejudice, especially during periods of economic hardship or war. During World War I and the Great Depression, Jews were often targets as scapegoats.[2]

We learn about the 1915 lynching in Atlanta of prominent Jewish businessperson Leo Frank, who was falsely accused of killing a worker, and the uptick in anti-Semitic attacks that followed in the 1920s with the resurgence of the Ku Klux Klan (KKK). We read about the outspoken commentary of American industrialist Henry Ford, who used his newspaper, *The Dearborn Independent,* to blame Jews for America's problems. We develop admiration for Jewish Americans, such as Supreme Court Justice Louis D. Brandeis and baseball hall of famer Hank Greenberg, who, despite having endured bitter taunts and prejudicial treatment, achieved greatness in their respective fields.

We absorb this history into our Jewish selves, but it is our experiences, and those of our parents, that most heavily influence our perspective regarding a Jew's place in the world. In America in the years following World War II, public acts of anti-Semitism receded, and many of our families moved out of urban Jewish enclaves to the suburbs, where they lived and worked among Gentiles. But institutional prejudice was common. Our parents have memories of restricted neighborhoods; associations, businesses and social organizations that excluded Jews; limited opportunities for career advancement; and Jewish quotas at colleges, universities, and corporations. Over time, these too mostly faded away.

According to Manfred Gerstenfeld and Steven Bayme, authors of *American Jewry's Comfort Level, Present and Future,* anti-Semitism is significantly lower now than it was fifty to one hundred years ago.[3] But while anti-Semitism has become much less blatant, it has not disappeared. My generation is likely to report encountering religious slurs and stereotypes in the classroom, neighborhood, and office; lingering ideas about the role of Jews in Jesus's death; and proselytizing, as Christian groups continue to try to save our souls through conversion to the one true faith. According to the Berman Institute North American Jewish Data Bank's 2011 study on the Jewish population of the United States, bias toward Jews may have continued to decline in the past twenty years, but the American Jewish community still encounters anti-Semitism regularly.[4] The report finds that 12 percent of Jewish adults and 16 percent of Jewish households with children between the ages of six and seventeen experience prejudice in their local community annually, and it states: "It is likely that a very high percentage of American Jews experience anti-Semitism somewhere, at some time during their lives."[5] This corresponds with the findings of the 2013 Pew study of Jewish Americans, which reports that 15 percent of Jews say that they have been called offensive names or been snubbed in social settings in the past year.

My first experience with anti-Semitism took place during a seventh-grade cooking class. A girl named Lisa asked me if my mother used the blood of Christian children to make matzah. While I had no idea that she was referring to the blood libel at the time, I did not need to be a Jewish history scholar to understand the negative connotation of her question. Even at age twelve, with no prior experience with bias, I knew the sound of prejudice.

"Does your mom use Christian boys' blood when she bakes matzah for Passover?" Lisa asked.

I thought the question was absurd for two reasons: one my mother did not bake; and two, using blood in food sounded like one of the most disgusting things I had ever heard. "No, she buys the matzah at Shop Rite," I replied. "It comes in a box. Does your mom use children's blood in her cooking?"

While this was my only childhood or young adult experience with bias, I heard about others from my parents and friends. My stepfather, Joel, recounted a conversation with an acquaintance about the restrictions on membership that still exist at a country club in New Jersey.

"Jane, I got a call the other day from your friend Joe," Joel said. "He called to see if I knew someone that might sponsor him for membership at The Green Spring Club. I told him that I thought that the club was restricted, but that I would make a call to a guy I know who is a member."

"What did your friend say?" I asked.

"When I asked if the club admits Jews, he told me I was crazy; that of course Jews are admitted, but that he would ask the membership committee to confirm. He added that his daughter had just married a Jewish guy, and that if he learned that membership was restricted, he would resign. He called back ten minutes later and told me that he just resigned from the club!"

More recently, my friend Abby shared an encounter that she had during some research being done by a Dallas-area private school. She was asked to participate in a focus group consisting of parents whose children had been accepted at the school but chose to attend a different institution. Abby joined a question-and-answer session with other parents that had turned down admission.

"The researcher asked why we declined our child's admissions offer," Abby said. "A number of parents said that the school was 'too liberal.' I knew that to be code for 'too Jewish.' The researcher then asked if the number of Jewish students at the school was an issue."

"He really asked that?" I asked. Abby nodded. "How did people respond?"

"Some said yes; others said that they wanted a more 'diverse' student body. The school is known to be diverse ethnically, racially, and religiously. Jewish students account for less than one-quarter of the school's population. It appeared that greater diversity was a euphemism for too many Jews. So when it was my turn to answer, I said, 'I'm Jewish, so the number of Jewish students isn't a problem for me!'"

(It should be noted that one researcher's question and the comments of a few parents do not necessarily reflect the opinions of the school or other parents. Jewish and non-Jewish students continue to be admitted and choose to attend this institution.)

It is experiences like these, coupled with Jewish history, that frame our worldview. According to the 2000–01 National Jewish Population Survey, only I percent of American Jewish adults perceive no anti-Semitism in the United States,[6] and the Jewish Data Bank reports that "only 14 percent of respondents perceive no anti-Semitism in their local community."[7] The recent Pew study found that a substantial minority, 43 percent, feels that Jews continue to face much discrimination. It is this belief in the continued presence of bigotry that makes us alert to prejudicial innuendos and negative perceptions and sometimes causes us to respond with light-speed sensitivity to any remark or action that hints of prejudice. But even the most bias-sensitive among us is at times caught off guard when we encounter intolerance.

We continue to express disbelief when we encounter prejudice, and the events still touch a raw nerve. One reason for the surprise is that our highly assimilated lives and the infrequency of the incidents lull us into a false optimism about our level of acceptance in all segments of society. Another is that, often, stereotypical remarks come from people who appear to like us, such as a chummy coworker who lets slip that he "Jewed down" a vendor during negotiations or a close classmate who says that Jews are going to hell. These remarks are often so stunning that we are silenced.

To be honest, our experience with this type of prejudice was limited until we moved away from the New York metro area ten years ago. Having spent most of our life in the Northeast, we were accustomed to a world where prejudicial remarks were saved for private conversation. Making negative comments about minorities at work or during neighborly chatter was seriously frowned upon.

That is not to say that bias did not or does not exist in this part of the country. Joel's story about the restricted country club in New Jersey illustrates that it is present, but it is something that exists in settings that are more private. Contrast that with Abby's focus group encounter in Dallas, and it raises the question of why roll-off-the-tongue remarks about Jews are more common in some parts of the United States, while more closeted prejudice exists in other areas.

This geographical difference in the prevalence of openly prejudicial language can be explained in part by population statistics. According to the Jewish Data Bank, people who live in communities with a large number of Jews or a significant Jewish minority experience anti-Semitism less frequently. The study's authors give two possible explanations for this finding: "One...non-Jews are less likely to display anti-Semitism in an area where they know a good chance exists that someone Jewish is within earshot," and two, "more non-Jews live and work with Jews, leading to exposure and familiarity that temper anti-Semitism" in these communities.[8]

In the New York City area, we were in the company of 1.54 million Jews. (One in every six households in the five boroughs of New York, Long Island, and Westchester identifies as Jewish.[9]) In North Texas, we have fifty- to fifty-five-thousand coreligionists, or less than 1 percent of the Dallas area's population.[10] These numbers, along with the Jewish Data Bank's findings, help to explain why we never encountered an openly negative remark about Jews at work or in our neighborhood when we lived in New York and one of its suburbs, but we did in Dallas. Cameron recently confronted negative Jewish stereotypes at the office.

"Something happened at work the other day that I didn't tell you about," he said one Sunday as we drove to get Sammy at a friend's. "It was after a call with a firm whose mortgage assets we're acquiring. I was leaving the meeting with Frank, who I frequently work with, and he says, 'Those bankers on the call sounded like a bunch of Jews.'" Cameron paused and then said, "I was really angry. I didn't know what to do. I wanted to respond to him—tell him that was a negative stereotype, but I was afraid that, in my anger, I would just explode. I knew that if I did that, I wouldn't accomplish very much. He would tune out, and I wouldn't change his behavior. I want to say something, but I just don't know what."

"I think that all you need to do is let him know that your wife and son are Jewish," I said. "Down here, people don't seem to stop and consider that their comments may offend someone. They don't see their words as prejudicial. They're just verbalizing a stereotype of Jews that they assume many hold because they haven't met anyone to tell them otherwise."

A few weeks later Cameron arrived home from a meeting of an organization he is involved in, with a story about a similar incident. "I have to tell you what happened at the board meeting tonight," he said as he walked into the kitchen. "Bob Jones was giving a summary of a recent event on resume writing given by a woman whose last name sounds Jewish. He was saying how successful the event was, but that the presenter was difficult to work with. As he was sharing what made her challenging, he says, 'I don't want to use any ethnic stereotypes, but she was cheap; she shoveled extra muffins from the event into her bag, and she kept asking for more money.' I can't remember what other examples he used, but immediately my defenses went up because I know that these negative stereotypes are said about Jewish people. As he is giving his report he says again, 'I don't want to use ethnic stereotypes, but—' and this time I cut in."

I listened quietly as Cameron continued. "I said, 'I don't know what ethnic stereotype you're referring to, and I don't care, but I ask you to stop. I don't appreciate negative language being used about any group. It offends me.'"

Feeling very proud of my husband, I asked, "What happened?"

"It was quiet for a moment and then the meeting continued, but I noticed that Bob didn't speak for the remainder of the agenda, and he wouldn't look at me when I spoke, even if I were looking at him. I was nervous to speak up because I didn't want to humiliate him or make him uncomfortable. But then as he continued to speak, I realized that I didn't care if I made him uncomfortable. His language was making me uncomfortable. I wanted him to know that this kind of speech is unacceptable. Anyway, I felt really good about how I handled it, and it gave me the confidence to stand up to this stuff. After the meeting, I got a text from Bob, apologizing. I sent him this response," said Cameron, showing me his phone.

> Thanks for the note. It's incredibly uncomfortable for me to confront "innocent" ethnic stereotyping, but it is even more uncomfortable hearing because my wife and son are Jewish, which I happen to be very proud of. I don't want my son to have to endure those kinds of insults to his heritage, so I ask those I hear it from to stop...which hopefully someday it will.

Cameron smiled and added, "I feel so good about this. I think that he'll think twice before making any remark like this again. Isn't that the goal—to change behavior and make the world a better place? Bob even sent an apology to the entire executive committee. I feel really good about how this turned out."

After these incidents, I wanted to see if more than Jewish population density was causing us to encounter prejudice in Dallas. I came across an interesting finding in the Jewish Data Bank's study relating to intermarriage and encounters with anti-Semitism: "Communities with higher intermarriage rates (percentage of married couples in Jewish households who are intermarried) show higher percentages of respondents who experienced anti-Semitism."[11] I wondered why intermarriage increased experience with prejudice. I would have thought that it would have the opposite effect. The authors of the study were similarly puzzled. They stated, "This is a somewhat surprising finding as many believe that one of the reasons for the decrease in anti-Semitism...is the increase in intermarriage (which leads to an increase in the number of non-Jews with Jewish relatives)."[12]

As I considered the possible reasons why high intermarriage rates correlate with greater experience with anti-Semitism, I thought in more detail about our encounters. I speak of them using the terms "our," "we," and "us"; but really, they are Cameron's experiences that I experienced indirectly. Yet, if I were asked a question about our experience with bias, I would report on behalf of my household since everyone in the home is touched by the experience, even if Sammy or I are not party to the actual exchange. It is possible that the percent of respondents in cities with large numbers of intermarrieds that report encounters with anti-Semitism is higher because more non-Jews in Jewish homes are confronting bigotry, leading to more "Jewish" homes reporting incidences.

The Jewish partner may not have the opportunity to encounter prejudice, or his or her faith is widely known, so anti-Semitic language is not used in his or her company. But the not Jewish spouse, like Cameron, can pass in majority Christian culture. Their identity is liminal, which is an anthropological term that means "not defined, not set, in-between." Our not Jewish husbands and wives may live in a home that identifies as Jewish, and they may move in a Jewish world, but they do not publicly identify their family's religion. So, people like Cameron's coworker assume that Cameron and his family are Christian (unless Cameron has had occasion to say otherwise), and that Cameron is a "safe" person to make derogatory remarks to about Jews. Without the knowledge that Cameron has a Jewish home, there is nothing to deter his officemate from using religious slurs or negative stereotypes. The same can be true for interracial or multicultural couples.

Another reason for the high rate of experience with anti-Semitism in communities with high intermarriage rates may be that the small size of the Jewish community in some of these cities may negate any positive effect interfaith couplings have on the perception of Jews. There may not be enough intermarrieds to make a difference. Finally, as many interfaith couples know, the presence of a Jew in a not Jewish family does not eliminate ignorance. Family members "forget" that the Jew is Jewish and let a negative comment slip or share an inappropriate joke at a holiday dinner. Parents and siblings are outwardly hostile because they are upset that their kin married someone the family feels is unacceptable.

But while intermarriage will not eliminate prejudice on its own, it can play a positive role in breaking the cycle of intolerance. As more non-Jews experience anti-Semitism in a more personal way because they have a Jewish partner, child, or home, they will be faced with the decision about how to confront the offending behavior. If they learn how to address it in an assertive way, then it is likely that prejudicial comments will be rebuked more often, leading to the positive impact on the decrease in experience with anti-Semitism that the authors of the Jewish Data Bank's study assumed already existed. But in order to get to this point, we will need to educate intermarrieds about the history of religious intolerance, the forms it takes, and how to respond to it effectively.

Based on the examples of our encounters with prejudice, one might think that Cameron and I have navigated this difficult subject well. But we have struggled with anti-Semitism, specifically intolerance in the guise of proselytism. To frame our experience, it is helpful to understand the culture of where we live. Dallas is sometimes referred to as the buckle of the Bible Belt, that stronghold of evangelical Christianity that encompasses much of the Southeastern and South Central United States. It is an area where proselytizing is frequent and aggressive, and prejudicial opinions of Jews are prevalent. Religion pervades public life. Billboards advertise talent agencies for Christian performers. Missionaries from area churches ring our doorbell to share the word of God weekly. Ballet schools minister to families through Christ-centered dance. Baseball clinics teach the word of God along with batting skills. Work associates begin business discussions with conversations about Jesus. Even my jar of North Texas honey comes with a message from the Lord. A message from the proprietors says that they know that God directed my purchase. For Northeasterners unaccustomed to such public religiosity, it can sometimes feel like we live on another planet, and it has made us wonder how this part of the country became such a bastion of religion, where proselytizing is forthright, and stereotypes of non-Christians are still so widely held.

Originally, the Southeast-South Central United States was an Anglican (Episcopal) stronghold more concerned with money and commerce than with faith. It was a society in which everyone had a place. White, Christian males sat at the top of the social order, with the wealthiest holding the most power; women were submissive to men, children to their parents, and slaves to their owners. Loyalty to family and kin was prized. It was into this world that the first Baptist preachers arrived from the North in the mid-eighteenth century to spread their liberal religious views. They told slaves that they should be free and women that they deserved an equal voice in matters of religion. This message challenged the authority of the area's plantation and business owners. Rather than igniting a religious revival similar to the one taking place in the North, the ministers found little acceptance among the locals. Methodists preaching a puritanical outlook on life that shunned Southern pursuits such as cursing, dancing, drinking, dueling, gambling, hunting, and shooting followed the Baptists. They too found little support. As Christine Leigh Heyrman writes in her book *Southern Cross: The Beginning of the Bible Belt*, it took about one hundred years before evangelical Christianity "won the attention, if not the allegiance, of a majority of southern whites."[13]

Heyrman points out that evangelicalism only found success in the South after the gospel spreaders realized that to effect religious change they had to make their message palatable to the middle-aged white men who held power. They learned that to gain acceptance in Southern society, what they preached needed to mesh with the area's traditional culture. They needed to affirm the proper roles as seen by the locals, "of men and women, old and young, white and black, as well as their positions on the relationship between church and family and between Christianity and other forms of supernaturalism."[14] Women and slaves had to be marginalized, and the promises of equality and liberation made to them in the eighteenth century had to be replaced in the nineteenth century by a pledge to ensure equality and respect for all white men. Rhetoric admonishing sinful vices needed to be toned down. Guns and their related activities had to be acceptable and drinking and gambling tolerated.

These altered Baptist and Methodist teachings helped establish non-Anglican Christian denominations and became the foundation for family-values fundamentalism. Once modified to be more Southern-friendly, evangelical Christianity gained momentum during the Second Great Awakening, the period of religious revival that gripped the United States from 1790 to the 1830s. Proselytizing was central to its spread, and missionaries, preachers, and churchgoers sought to draw nonbelievers to their cause with the promise of salvation through conversion and individual piety. Jews were prime targets of this evangelical fervor, even though revivalists, like other Americans, were comfortable with Jesus being Jewish and acknowledged the contribution of "the seed of Abraham"[15] to the Christian faith. Still they were steadfast in their commitment to proclaim the gospel to the Jewish people.

Even today, many Bible Belt ministers encourage churchgoers to evangelize to Jews. In its June 1996 Resolution on Jewish Evangelism, the Southern Baptist Convention proclaimed, "that we direct our energies and resources toward the proclamation of the gospel to the Jewish people."[16] More recently, in his March 2008 column "Why Evangelize the Jews?", Stan Guthrie, an editor-at-large at *Christianity Today*, wrote that the Jews need Jesus, and Christians should renew their "commitment to...sensitively but forthrightly persuade" Jewish people "to receive the Good News."[17]

This brief history provides some context for understanding life in the Bible Belt today. It frames experiences such as one that we had several years ago. At a business dinner, Cameron was given a book about Messianic Judaism (a Christian denomination commonly associated with Jews for Jesus) written by a rabbi who converted to the faith.

I found the book on the kitchen table one morning. Cameron left it there after emptying his workbag. I picked it up and read the back cover and introduction. My blood pressure spiked, and I said angrily aloud to no one at all, "What the hell is this? Why would he ever bring something like this into the house?"

I could barely contain my feelings about the book that day and exploded on Cameron when he got home that evening. "Where did you get this book?" I demanded.

"I got it at that dinner with the management company last night," Cameron replied.

"Was this Jews for Jesus propaganda a parting gift?" I asked sarcastically.

"The CEO gave it to me. When I arrived, he came over to introduce himself. He asked immediately if I had accepted Jesus Christ as my Lord and savior."

"Didn't that bother you? This was a business function. Why the hell does it matter if you have a Lord or savior?" I responded angrily.

"I told him that I was raised Christian, but that my family is really neat because you're Jewish, and we're raising Sammy Jewish. The guy then said that even Jews can accept Jesus, and he went and got the book," Cameron said.

"Weren't you offended by this?" I asked with my voice rising. "Why didn't you tell him that you weren't interested, that you don't believe that there is only one right religion or that you have to accept Jesus to be saved?"

"Jane, I am developing a relationship with this firm. They state on their website and company materials that they are a Christian company. Working with them has the potential to turn into a lot of business. I just accepted the book. I didn't know what else to do. I didn't want to do anything to damage the chance of getting business from them," Cameron explained.

My head was now spinning and probably had Medusa-like snakes sprouting out of it. I yelled, "What else would you do to get business?" Without waiting for a response, I continued, "You need to understand that not everyone thinks our family's religious makeup is 'neat.' Not everyone is as open-minded as you and your family! We live in the Bible Belt!" I paused and then continued my verbal assault. "Your reputation should win you business, not your religion. But if you're going to share our faith, then you need to be prepared to stand up to people like this. Stand your ground and in a respectful way disagree with the idea that we all need to accept Jesus! If this person won't give you business, then screw him. This offends me!" I said, shaking the book. "I'm getting rid of it, I don't want it in this house," and I stormed off, throwing the book into the giveaway pile.

I realized that my reaction was over the top, but as anyone who has experienced intolerance in any form knows, some situations touch an emotional hot button more than others. I was hurt that Cameron would bring this book into the house, and that he was not willing to stand up to this religious bully. I knew that he did not believe that Sammy or I needed to be saved through the acceptance of Jesus, so why did he not speak up? I felt that his first loyalty should be to his wife and son, not to his business. From my perspective, he chose the dollar over defending his family. At the time, I was too angry with Cameron to consider that he might have been too shocked by the up-frontness of the proselytizing to say anything. What should have followed my outburst was a discussion of why this book and interaction caused me to react in the way I did, but it did not. We never had a constructive conversation about intolerance. I did not explain that Jews are sensitive to proselytizing because we have been targets for conversion by Christians, often by force, since the Roman Empire's acceptance of Christianity. I did not mention that I hoped—no, expected—that as someone who now participates in the Jewish faith that he would confront these situations actively. I assumed that my tone communicated all he needed to know about why a Jewish person would find a book like this offensive, so I did nothing to initiate a discussion, but neither did Cameron. We both swept the issue under the rug, which meant that the situation was destined to repeat itself—and it did. But rather than taking place in a business setting, it happened at little league baseball.

For the past few seasons, Sammy's baseball league has run a Baseball and Bibles clinic. The program is organized by Baseball and Bibles, an organization that partners with local youth leagues and churches in our area to teach children and their parents baseball fundamentals, "introduce them to [or] deepen their familiarity with the Word of God, and talk about Lessons of Life, from the perspective of baseball, and the Bible."[18] A quick glance at the organization's logo, a baseball overlaid with a gold cross, leaves no doubt that the perspective of the Bible and God's word are Christian. The league's e-mail promoting the clinic carried the innocuous subject line "Baseball Camp." It was not until the note's bottom that the actual name of this family friendly event was mentioned: Baseball and Bibles Youth Baseball Clinic. I forwarded the message to Cameron.

"Why can't it just be a baseball clinic? Why do we need to bring in the Bible?" I wrote.

Cameron responded, "I agree. That said, it's Texas, and Sammy needs to know how to navigate this challenge. I think this would be helpful stuff for Sammy, and I suspect that it's not heavy on the Bible. How about we sign him up, and I'll do it with him? I'd like to recommend it to the team as well (Cameron was the head coach). I don't think people are going to be offended. They know the drill in Texas."

I read Cameron's response with raised eyebrows. I thought, *Cameron is really missing the boat if he thinks that you develop a callus to prejudice through repeated exposure. You do not form a thick skin by purposefully putting yourself in these types of situations.* While I was agitated by Cameron's reaction, after my lunatic response to the Messianic Judaism book, I wanted to try to handle this situation in a calmer manner. Before responding, I called my friend Shari to get a second opinion about attendance at this event and my feeling that Cameron should not send this to our mostly Jewish team (twelve of our fifteen players were Jewish). She agreed that we should not feed our kids to the fire in order to toughen them up. Feeling confident that I was not overreacting, I thought about how to express why Sammy could not go and why Cameron could not recommend the clinic to the team.

While I was constructing my response, I realized that at the root of the problem was our two different worldviews: persecuted-minority-Jewish female and majority-white-Christian male. To me, this event was an example of religious intolerance. To Cameron, it was just a harmless baseball clinic run by a bunch of overzealous Bible beaters. The reason that I was surprised at his response was that I had assumed that after ten years of living a Jewish life, he had shed the privilege and perspective that comes with being part of the majority. I thought that because he lived his life as an unofficial Jew that, in a situation like this, he would think and feel like a Jew. I knew that he understood the nature of anti-Semitism when it was clothed in hate speech and negative stereotypes, so I thought that he understood that, for Jewish people, proselytizing also fell into the intolerance bucket. I wrongly assumed that he had taken this message from the Messianic Judaism incident. So, instead of explaining why proselytizing offended and angered me as much as other forms of prejudice, I focused my response on our different outlooks, even going so far as to state that his position in society prevented him from understanding the Jewish perspective.

I responded to his e-mail. "Sammy has a book club meeting. He can't go. Honey, as a white Christian male you may be turned off by this, but you don't understand. Jews in Texas may be used to this stuff, but it still is offensive, and no one on the team will appreciate you recommending that they attend. This might not be purposeful anti-Semitism, but it is pure thoughtlessness about the fact that there are non- Christians in this world and people who do not believe in their view of God (which of course is the one correct view). As Jews, we've seen this movie before. Don't be fooled—this will have a good dose of Bible. We absolutely will not put our child in this situation so it is a learning experience. He will experience plenty of prejudice in life because of his religion. There just really isn't a good way to describe this to you to help you understand. You've never been a minority. To understand the nerve things like this touch, you need to think and feel like a minority that has the scars of thousands of years of persecution burned into its DNA."

My response did not articulate why I did not want Sammy to attend or why the event could not be recommended to the team. Pointing out how Cameron's membership in the majority precluded him from comprehending how Jews view proselytizing and bias did not help to build understanding.

Cameron replied, "I guess I'm just ignorant."

I decided to talk to him when he got home from work. "Honey, you're not ignorant," I said as we were getting ready for bed. "I'm sorry that my e-mail made you feel that way. I was trying to make the point that you are thinking like a white Christian man, and that, in these situations, you need to put yourself in the shoes of—and think like—a minority. Jews have been persecuted and excluded throughout history; we carry this past with us; it makes us sensitive to this stuff."

"Bad choice of words," he replied. "You say that I live a Jewish life, that I'm so close to being Jewish. Now I can't understand. Why would you purposely make me feel like an outsider?" he asked with a look on his face that was a mix of hurt and anger.

I wanted to say, "Congratulations! You just got it. These types of things are reminders to Jews that we are outsiders. Now you know how it feels, and it isn't a pleasant feeling." But I thought that would be like adding gasoline to a fire, so instead I said, "Cameron, you do live a Jewish life, and you are Jewish in many ways."

"Apparently not," he retorted.

"Living Jewishly and understanding the sensitive nature of this issue are different things. Obviously, I am not explaining this well. Let me think about it and see if I can be more clear."

While I avoided turning into a crazy woman, I would classify this explanation of Jewish sensitivity to evangelism as a botched attempt similar to my "December

Disaster" when I blundered the communication to Sammy of Cameron's religious identity. Clearly, I needed some help developing my message. There was a big gap between my expectations of how Cameron should handle prejudice and his understanding of its many forms. But at this point, I had no idea how to bridge the divide. The following morning, I placed an SOS call to my teacher, Risa. I reached out to her because she works regularly with interfaith couples, knows Cameron, is a Jewish educator, and has lived in Dallas for over thirty years. Risa took my call, and I explained to her what happened.

"Jane, you know that your comment about Cameron not understanding because he is a white Christian male is what set him off, right?" She asked.

"Yes," I answered.

"Okay, well the first thing you need to do is apologize and reassure Cameron that he is very much a part of the Jewish community. Then you need to tell him that suggesting that the kids go to this will make the parents think that he is being insensitive and explain that these types of things remind parents, especially the ones that grew up in Texas, of times as children that they were made to feel like an outsider because they were Jewish. You're right; you cannot knowingly send your child to something like this. There is a history of religious groups and sports down here. Tell him about the Fellowship of Christian Athletes, which most of the parents on your team will know about, having grown up in Dallas. Search the Anti-Defamation League (ADL) website for information. If you can't find anything, give the local director a call and tell her you're my friend."

"Thank you. I really appreciate your help," I said.

Eager to put this behind us, I hung up and called Cameron. "I want to apologize for what I said last night and reassure you that you are very much a part of the Jewish community," I said. "I know that I did a horrible job of trying to explain why you couldn't recommend this to the team, so I called Risa for some advice this morning."

"You did?" he said.

"I did. It's important to recognize when your words are like a shovel digging a hole," I said. "Risa was better able to articulate what I wanted to say."

"I want to talk about this, but I need to go. We can talk tonight. Thanks for the call and apology."

That evening I shared what Risa had said as well as information from the ADL and the Fellowship of Christian Athletes (FCA). Founded in 1954, the FCA is the largest Christian sports organization in America and has national reach. It "focuses on serving local communities by equipping, empowering and encouraging people to make a difference for Christ."[19] It partners with area professional, college, high school, junior high school, and youth organizations, including schools—public and private, secular and parochial—to offer its programs and share its message of accepting and serving Jesus with students and coaches. I used the example of the response by the ADL to an FCA talent show in a public school, in the Phoenix area, as a way to help Cameron understand why Jewish people react the way I did to the blurring of the lines between the secular and parochial. The Jewish community's reaction to this event was chronicled in the *Jewish News of Greater Phoenix*. The piece included the response by the regional director of the ADL, Joel Breshin, to the event with professional performers "singing and preaching about Jesus." Breshin said that the "apparent breach in the wall of separation between church and state" was "a very grave matter" because it forced non-Christian children to choose between "being proselytized to by Christian missionaries or not attending a popular event."[20] In a secular environment, this type of decision should not have to be made.

We discussed that the ADL classifies proselytism as religious intolerance because of its threat to religious freedom. I shared that the idea that America needs to be "Christianized" implies that non-Christians do not belong or are not entitled to an equal place in the social order. We talked about the history of fundamentalists targeting Jews and how evangelism has the potential to fuel religious-related violence. Afterward, Cameron said, "I get it."

Like many Jews, I see proselytizing as a form of religious intolerance. But until our discussion, Cameron was less clear on where it belonged along the prejudice spectrum. Hate speech and religious slurs were easy for him to classify and confront, but evangelism seemed more like theological small-mindedness than bias.

This uncertainty about what is prejudice and how to respond to it is not unique. Many not Jewish partners in interfaith marriages are similarly tongue-tied and confused. In essays written for InterfaithFamily, Christian spouses of Jews share that, before their first encounter, they thought of anti-Semitism as a societal problem that did not affect them personally. They viewed derogatory remarks about Jews as wrong but not prejudicial. Proselytizing as prejudice was not even discussed. Like Cameron, these men and women had never been the target of intolerance and had not received any education in how to respond to it. They had to learn on the job, which can be especially difficult when there has not been a serious discussion about anti-Semitism or how to confront it as an individual or family.

As the Jewish spouse, I feel responsible for not having initiated this conversation. I know that prejudice toward me and my people is part of my heritage, and I know that my family and I will confront it somewhere, sometime.

I should have shared this, but instead I assumed that Cameron recognized anti-Semitism's existence and understood its various forms, so I never bothered to raise the issue. I thought that my religious identity implied that we would have to deal with prejudice. The events of 9/11, which happened while we were living in New York City, did not even initiate a dialogue about the subject. While we were dating, my primary focus was on how we would raise our children, and the resources we drew from to make this decision—a premarital course with clergy, books, and online material—shared our focus. They, too, concentrated their advice on subjects such as understanding different religious customs, values, and beliefs in order to make decisions about a wedding ceremony, faith of children, observance of holidays, and lifecycle events and how to deal with family pressures. Nothing encouraged me to talk to Cameron about anti-Semitism, so I should not have been surprised that Cameron was unclear about the various forms of prejudice and how to respond to them. I feel lucky that he handled his encounters as well as he did.

I wish I could say that we are unique in our avoidance of this difficult topic, but we are not. In an informal, unscientific poll of families in my interfaith network, I found that few discussed prejudice during premarital counseling with rabbis, other clergy, or counselors. If they discussed it with each other, it was in the abstract. Many stated that the not Jewish partner recognized that intolerance existed, but few saw how their pending union would make anti-Semitism personal. Only one couple discussed prejudice in any detail, and this was due to the openly anti-Semitic behavior displayed by the parents of the non-Jew toward the Jewish partner early in the relationship. Mostly the issue of prejudice arose after marriage, usually following an incident involving the couple's children. All the couples handled the situations or intolerance on their own, without professional advice, and all believe that dealing with prejudice remains an ongoing struggle for their family because it is a hard subject for people to wrap their mind around.

Part of what makes it so difficult is that there is no equivalent to anti-Semitism for Christians. Rabbi Arthur P. Nemitoff says in his June 2002 InterfaithFamily article "Anti-Semitism: Where Does It Begin...and End?" that Jews and Christians have different views of Christianity that influence what they see as anti-Semitism. "For Jews, the history of Christianity is replete with anti-Semitism, of attempts to control, convert, and exterminate Jews...For Christians, the history of Christianity is filled with noble stories" that seek to bring Jesus's message "of hope, of love, of concern for all creatures" to the world.[21] Nemitoff feels that this difference makes it challenging for not Jewish partners to understand what the Jewish partner sees as prejudicial. He notes that incidents such as synagogue bombings are easy to identify as anti-Semitic, but that comments about Jewish traits (e.g., cheapness) or body parts (e.g., big noses) and prayers at public events that invoke Jesus can be more difficult to pinpoint.

Nemitoff suggests that partners learn what upsets the other to better deal with this tricky subject. But what else can be done to assist interfaith families in building understanding so that they feel more equipped to deal with anti-Semitism? Some clergy and professionals suggest that a Jewish family member share "deep-seated fears and historical memories"[22] related to anti-Semitism. Others recommend that couples read the opening chapter of *The Intermarriage Handbook*, which talks about the persecutory history of the Jews. A social worker friend who counsels interfaith couples suggests that support groups and classes do more on the subject. She says, "The groups I've worked with touch on the topic but don't allot enough time to explore the subject in-depth, and class curriculums often encourage participants to brainstorm their own ideas about how to approach the issue but don't offer any good suggestions or references to provide further assistance."

Often it seems that intermarrieds who need guidance on this topic must find the resources, tools, and advice that they need on their own from organizations such as the ADL, Students Together Opposing Prejudice (STOP), Teachers Against Prejudice, and the Anti-Prejudice Consortium. What appears to be missing is a robust conversation about anti-Semitism, initiated by communal leaders, that helps interfaith couples move beyond the abstract to a more thoughtful dialogue about how intolerance affects (or may affect) them personally.

Is there a reason we are reluctant to speak about anti-Semitism with interfaith couples in a more meaningful way? Does exploring cultural differences and positive and negative stereotypes remind us of the controversial area of psychology called ethnotherapy, which gained national attention in the 1980s? Ethnotherapy "seeks to change negative attitudes about ethnicity and race through group interaction and self-exploration"[23] of issues such as shame, self-hatred, and assimilation. Do we fear that intermarrieds might choose a non-Jewish path as a way to escape prejudice? Do we believe that discussions about intolerance are better handled individually? Is the issue so dense that we do not feel that we can do it justice? Or have we simply prioritized other issues that we believe are of more immediate concern to an interfaith relationship?

Whatever the reason, I believe that a more proactive approach is needed. While I am not suggesting that we make dealing with anti-Semitism a central focus of our interfaith outreach, I am proposing that we engage those in interfaith relationships in a more active dialogue about all of the implications—positive and negative—of their choice of religious association. For those that choose to associate Jewishly, we need to help them find the strength and pride to re-sist prejudice. For those that choose a non-Jewish or no-religion path, we need to ensure that they understand that their choice will not inoculate them from anti-Semitism (especially for those that carry a Jewish-sounding last name or who have not chosen to convert) and help them to develop the confidence to confront bias in a positive way.

My suggestion may sound too simple. Prejudice is a complex problem with many dimensions and parallels. For example, at first glance, it might seem wise to only focus on helping the non-Jew understand anti-Semitism; but that would ignore the fact that some Jews, including those that intermarry, have prejudicial feelings toward Gentiles. A not Jewish mom I know recently shared that while she and her Jewish husband have dealt with proselytizing and other religious issues at their Jewish daughter's "Christian-leaning" public school in a positive way, her husband still denigrates non-Jews. She says, "My husband sometimes portrays Gentiles negatively as a way to strengthen our daughter's Jewish con-fidence and connection with the Jewish people. But it's hurtful to me. I know that he appreciates the enormous efforts I make to support our child's Jewish identity, and I know that the negativity stems from his great fear that our child will abandon her faith, but I suspect this will be an ongoing challenge for us."

Addressing issues and building understanding from both perspectives will only become increasingly important as the number of interfaith/interracial marriages grows. As our outreach efforts attract interfaith couples to Judaism, and as more multicultural and LGBT families become part of our faith, we will need to address prejudice in a way that takes into account different cultural histories; various understandings of religion, community, and family; and the multiple experiences with bigotry.

The discussion of prejudice needs to be a bigger part of our communal outreach to intermarrieds, from individual synagogues, clergy, and counselors to organizations that support interfaith families, such as InterfaithFamily and the Jewish Outreach Institute. To do this, we do not need to reinvent the wheel. Best practices and models are available from antibullying programs (there are plenty of parallels between the two topics) and groups such as the ADL that can be leveraged to create programs, resources, suggestions, and references to help interfaith couples deal with anti-Semitism. Intermarrieds can be empowered to deal with this issue by listening to the experiences of other interfaith couples that have dealt with it—both successfully and unsuccessfully. These stories not only let families know that they are not alone in this struggle, but they are a vehicle to share ideas and strategies for confronting the issue.

My discussion of anti-Semitism is far from comprehensive, but it was not intended to be. A full exploration of it, including parallels to other types of bias and bullying, demands more space. Instead, I chose to share my family's experience in order to draw attention to the challenge that prejudice presents to interfaith families and raise awareness that more needs to be done in this area. As we seek to engage more interfaith families in Judaism, we need to better help these families and their children deal with all of the issues they will confront along their Jewish journey. Prejudice may not seem as pressing a topic as the religious identity of a home, but anticipating the issue and talking about it early on can increase the likelihood that interfaith couples will handle future encounters in a way that facilitates closer ties to the Jewish community rather than disengagement or a distancing from Jewish life. It is time that we engage those in interfaith relationships in a serious conversation about prejudice.

NINE

A JEWISH FUTURE

Many of us can relate to the observation made in chapter 8 by the not Jewish mom about her Jewish husband's concern that his daughter might abandon her faith later in life. It is a fear that generations of parents, regardless of race, creed, or ethnicity can understand, and it raises questions such as: Will my child abandon his heritage? What will I do if she does not embrace a part of our family's identity that is important to me, and what can I do to prevent this from happening? It is why among some in the Jewish community, intermarriage is demonized, and Christmas trees are frowned upon.

As my friend alludes to, fear of abandonment of our heritage—religious, cultural, or ethnic—is often the driving force behind the things we do, both positive and negative, to strengthen a particular piece of our children's and family's identity. Our insecurity can be a good thing when it causes us to engage in education, ritual practice, and culture; it is bad when it causes us to negatively judge, preach exclusion, and perpetuate prejudice as a way to try to prevent our fears from being realized.

This past spring, at one of Sammy's baseball games, I sat in the stands, talking with two moms whose sons go to school with Sammy. During the conversation, I mentioned that I was writing about our family's experience as an interfaith family. I was surprised to learn that neither of the women knew that we were intermarried but not at all surprised that the topic of abandonment of the Jewish faith came up.

"Which one of you is not Jewish?" one asked.

"Cameron," I replied. "Obviously, we have a Jewish home, and Sammy is being raised Jewish." I thought this point was obvious since Sammy attends day school with their children, and a Jewish day school probably would not be the educational institution of choice for a family raising a child with two religions or none at all.

"But Sammy isn't really Jewish," the other said.

"Yes he is," the first one answered. "They're raising him Jewish."

"No, he isn't. He can choose which religion he is," said the second.

Hoping to settle the debate, I said, "Sammy is Jewish. We have one religion in our home."

"But he can choose what he is," the second mom answered.

"No, Cameron and I made that choice for him. Before we got married, we agreed that our children would be raised as Jews. Sammy is Jewish. He understands that Cameron is not, but that he and I are," I replied.

"Well, I guess he's Jewish since you're the Jewish one. But, what will he be when he is older? He might choose to have no religious identity or affiliate with a non-Jewish faith," she argued.

"Well, can't we all make that choice? In a way, aren't we all Jews by choice?" replied the first woman. "Everyone is free to choose another religion when they're an adult, regardless of what religion their parents practice."

"I guess," said the other mother. "But he's going to think that marrying someone who is not Jewish is—" and she stopped without completing the remark.

"Okay?" I asked.

"Yes," she answered, without looking at me.

She is right. Sammy does see that marrying a non-Jew is okay. But he also sees that intermarriage does not have to equal abandonment of one's faith. On the contrary: he lives in a home that is filled with Jewish ritual and observance, talk of spirituality, and engagement with Jewish education, community, and culture. He sees parents that nurture a strong connection to Jewish heritage, regardless of their own religion. The result of our commitment to Judaism is evident in how Sammy feels about being Jewish.

"Do you like being Jewish?" I asked one day.

"I love being Jewish! It's *awesome*," Sammy replied in a loud singsong voice.

"Why is it awesome?" I probed.

"It just is. Being Jewish is really special. Being part of the Jewish people is special," Sammy answered.

"Would you ever not want to be Jewish?" I asked.

"Mommy, are you crazy? Why would I not want to be Jewish?" Sammy asked.

"Well, maybe one day you'll marry someone who isn't Jewish and decide to be a different religion," I said.

Sammy walked over, put his hands on my shoulders, and leaned his forehead against mine. As he looked into my eyes, he said, "Mommy, I'm always going to be Jewish. You married Daddy. He isn't Jewish, and you're still Jewish, and I'm Jewish. Don't be crazy." Sammy's answer was very logical and matter-of-fact.

He thinks that conversations like these are crazy because, at this point in his life, he cannot fathom being anything other than Jewish, but I know that a time may come in his teen and young adult years when he does question his religious identity. That is why I feel it is important to start the conversation about Jewish identity and continuity early and allow it to evolve as he gets older. As I learned in an outreach program on dating, this open dialogue needs to be coupled with ritual and community engagement, both of which increase the likelihood that Sammy will make Jewish choices in the future. As is true with many things in life, actions often have more impact than words. So, it is our responsibility as parents to model the Jewish behaviors and values that we want Sammy to see as essential. I would say that the same holds true for extended family and caregivers. Sylvia Barack Fishman reinforces these points in *The Way into the Varieties of Jewishness*. Just as parents serve as important models of behavior in other areas of life, so too do they act as role models for Jewish involvement. The level of Jewish activism in a home strongly influences the type of Jewish engagement children will have as adults. Fishman says that parents have the biggest impact when they are regularly involved in and show a strong commitment to Jewish activities and regularly explain in an honest manner why they engage with Judaism.[1]

Fishman's comment highlights one of the reasons our Jewish leaders encourage us to light Shabbat candles at home and why Sammy believes that you can be both intermarried and Jewish. He does not see intermarriage and Judaism as mutually exclusive, nor does he see that only Jews can live a Jewish life and nurture Jewish heritage. This is due to Cameron's active engagement in Judaism. Sammy does not just hear about why we live Jewishly from me; he hears it from both of us. Together we articulate our hopes that he will make Jewish choices. We already discuss intermarriage openly with him and work to make Judaism a core part of his identity so that if he intermarries, he will choose to invest in a Jewish future by having a Jewish home.

Sammy shared his view of intermarriage and Jewish continuity one night during a dinner conversation about marriage, after Cameron mentioned his feelings about Sammy choosing a Jewish partner.

"I hope you'll marry someone Jewish one day," said Cameron. "I'll be disappointed if you don't."

"Why?" Sammy asked.

"Because I hope that you'll pass on Judaism to your children and help Judaism continue. I think it's easier to do that when the person you marry is Jewish too," Cameron answered.

"You're not Jewish, and you're helping me to be Jewish," said Sammy.

Sammy was right. It made me think that we needed to clarify our position. He needed to understand that just like all people are different, all marriages and intermarriages are different. We needed to make clear that our hope is that he will pass Judaism on to the next generation, not that his spouse is of Jewish lineage. Given my family's history and previous experience with choosing a spouse based on religion, not love, I could not honestly say that Jewish descent is a nonnegotiable characteristic for a future spouse, without sounding like a hypocrite. Given the fluid world we live in, that probably is not the best strategy. I do not need to look far or wide to see that inmarriage only guarantees continuity of religious DNA. It does not ensure continuity of Jewish identification or practice. If future engagement with Judaism is the goal, then it seems to me that what is important is not who Sammy marries but rather the vibrancy and saliency of his Jewish identity. I made this point.

"You're right. Daddy is helping you to be Jewish, but not everyone is like Daddy," I said. "Daddy is happy to create a Jewish home and be part of a Jewish family, as are *a lot* of not Jewish people who marry Jews. But some people aren't as comfortable with that, and that is why Daddy says it's easier if the other person is Jewish."

"Oh," Sammy replied.

"What we really want is for you to love being Jewish. We want Judaism to be so important to you that regardless of who you marry—Jew or non-Jew—that you will want to have a Jewish home and share the Jewish faith with your family," I said.

It is up to us as parents to make Judaism a core part of Sammy's identity so that transmission of the Jewish faith is a priority for him, regardless of his marriage partner. As David Epstein, an Orthodox Jew and father of five children, says to Yosef Abramowitz and Rabbi Susan Silverman in *Jewish Family & Life: Traditions, Holidays, and Values for Today's Parents and Children*, "Guaranteeing Jewish identity is the sum of everything you do when you raise your children. It's not just telling them *don't*."[2] Telling Sammy not to intermarry will not make Judaism important to him or guarantee a Jewish future. Instead, we must make being Jewish relevant to the other things that he is (male, child, athlete, volunteer, student, etc.), especially when those things are on the surface contradictory, such as interfaith and Jewish. Leonard Saxe says in his Winter 2012 *Contact* article, "On Jewish Identity," that Jewish identity will only remain relevant "if the shell that identifies individuals as Jews is filled with meaning" and helps "Jews to feel a part of something larger."[3] Fishman suggests that cultural capital—comprised of social or group activities and individual activities—is the key to Jewish identity and the transmission of Judaism to future generations.[4] Interestingly, neither says that marriage is the essential ingredient for building Jewish identity or ensuring Jewish continuity. Nor do they imply that endogamy is key. Yet, many in the Jewish community assume that a strong Jewish identity includes inmarriage and that inmarriage equals engagement.

Thinking about my own experience as a Jewish child and teenager in the context of Saxe's and Fishman's points, I see that I had few of the experiences that they suggest are critical, but the ones I did have were formative. My home did not engage regularly in ritual practice. I did not attend Jewish camp or day school. I did not have a Jewish social network. But I did have parents who were consistently involved in Jewish volunteer activities. I became a bat mitzvah. I was engaged in youth group and confirmation. I visited Israel. As the Steinhardt research that I referred to earlier in the book states, critical Jewish experiences matter. I may not have had a highly engaged Jewish life as a child, but I did have enough critical experiences to influence my choices as an adult and as an intermarried adult.

I contrast my youth engagement with my brother's. While he, too, saw parents involved at our synagogue, he did not participate in confirmation or youth group, and he did not go to Israel. This is not because he was not encouraged to do all of these things. He was. In fact, my mother strongly advocated that he go to Israel during high school and again after college. He was not interested. His Jewish involvement (outside of a major holiday observance) ended at his bar mitzvah. So, while I had a few Jewish seeds that I occasionally nurtured in college by taking classes such as Hebrew and Jewish studies, Alan had little to nourish. Now that we are both intermarried, the differences in our Jewish youth engagement are evident in the choices we have made. I have a Jewish home. Alan does not. I feel strongly about having a Jewish family; Alan does not. This brings me back to our conversation with Sammy.

If we want his Jewish identity to be important to him, if we want his Jewishness to have firm roots, and if we want him to practice Judaism, regardless of who he marries, then Cameron and I need to not only plant the seeds of Jewishness in him but also nurture them often. Saxe says, "Engagement with Jewish life is not...a straight line...enactment of Jewish identity has multiple inflection points... Contemporary Jews are not just born, they're made."[5] This idea is reflected in how we raise Sammy, but I also see it in my own Jewish journey. My Jewish seeds may not have been nourished as frequently as Sammy's, but they were there, waiting for some attention. When I got serious with Cameron, they began to get the care they needed. Falling in love with a non-Jew was the spark that reconnected me to my faith.

Instead of threatening my Jewish identity and causing me to disengage from my Jewishness, intermarriage has been an opportunity to deepen my Judaism. It has forced me to confront my own feelings and beliefs about religion, spirituality, and God and think about how they influence other aspects of my life. It has caused me to be a more mindful and deliberate Jew. As I look to be a good Jewish role model for Cameron and Sammy, I often consider when making decisions what it means to be Jewish in name *and* deed. I was not always this thoughtful. To get to this place in my religious journey, I have had to look inside myself and face my own prejudices, stereotypes, and fears as well as really think about what I believe. My story about coming to terms with Jesus, making peace with the kippah and its public declaration of Jewishness, and choosing a day school education demonstrate how I have had to move outside my comfort zone and beyond my preconceived notions of faith, Judaism, and Jewish identity in order to grow. Along the way, I have become more comfortable with my own spirituality and religious and cultural identities. I know that I would not be the involved and empowered Jew that I am today without this interfaith experience.

If I had married a Jew, I could have engaged in a similar religious exploration, but I am not sure that I would have had the same determination—the same sense of purpose—to do it. Only when I was faced with a different religious identity, or none at all, did I see just how important my Jewishness was to me. Intermarriage—and my mother-in-law, who pushed me to do so—was my catalyst to engage religiously. During one of our visits to Vermont, Pam and I were engaged in one of our discussions that meandered from family to current events to politics and religion. As our conversation turned to faith, she saw that I struggled to answer some of her questions about Judaism, and that I had many unanswered questions of my own. She said, "You know I really think you would enjoy learning about Judaism more." With her encouragement, I began to build my own religious knowledge.

I used our temple's outreach and interfaith programming to learn more about Jewish values and traditions. This led me to explore more about Judaism on my own and experiment with ritual practice in our home. I started to connect to religion in new ways. These experiences sparked an interest in adult education, and when an opportunity arose to participate in a Florence Melton Adult Mini-School Jewish education class, I took it. Two years later, I have just completed my fourth course. The classes have opened my heart and mind, have engaged me in Judaism in a way I have never been before, and have helped me to build bonds with others in the community. I am now hooked on adult Jewish learning, and I have my non-Jewish family to thank for encouraging me to engage in this way. Never in my wildest dreams did I consider that intermarriage would lead me down such an emotionally, intellectually, and spiritually stimulating path. This counterintuitive Jewish voyage has been made sweeter because I am able to share my discoveries with my family—Jewish and not Jewish, immediate and extended.

As I write this, my Melton class is on break for the summer. Without the sessions, I find that my mind is restless and misses its weekly dose of intellectual sugar. I am reading and sharing articles and discussions through my class's Facebook group, but these things do not nourish my brain in the same way as group study. But the other night, an unexpected learning opportunity presented itself. When I spoke to my mother-in-law on Mother's Day, she mentioned that she had started to read a book about the Psalms.

"I just started reading the most interesting book," Pam said. "My friend at the bookstore called to tell me that she received a two-part series on the Psalms that I might like. I had been interested in learning about them more, so I purchased the books. Anyway, I noticed that when they discussed some of the Hebrew words in the beginning of the first volume, I recognized one, *tzedakah*, from what I've learned from you and Sammy. I learned that it could be difficult to translate the exact meaning of the Hebrew because the words could have a deeper meaning or intent. Anyway, I'm just at the beginning of the book, but it seems fascinating."

"That sounds really interesting," I said. "I would love to read the books when you're done. Maybe we can even discuss them together. I think that would be fun."

"Oh, that would be fun," she replied, "but it will take me a while to get through each book. If you don't mind waiting, I'd love to share them with you."

When I hung up with Pam, I was excited to share the Psalms books with her. But as I thought more about our plan, I realized that my excitement and mental restlessness could not wait until she finished the books to start studying. I wanted to begin as soon as possible. I thought that if I were able to get a copy of the books and read them at the same time as Pam, then we could discuss them in real time, sort of like a *chevruta*. Chevruta is Hebrew for "fellowship," and it is used to describe a learning partnership in which a Jewish text is studied in pairs. The learners work together to understand the meaning of the document and how it applies to larger issues. I thought the idea of studying together might appeal to her. The next morning I sent her an e-mail.

"Pam, I'm so excited about studying the Psalms books together! We can be a chevruta, which is Hebrew for *fellowship* and is the practice of studying texts in pairs in order to understand their meaning. Can you send me the name of the books, and I will purchase? That way I can read them at the same time so that we can discuss. I can also see if our temple and Jewish Community Center libraries have any commentary that we can reference."

Pam replied: "Dear Chevruta Friend, I called the bookstore, and they said that they had ordered a second set of the books on spec because a lot of people have expressed interest in the Psalms lately. I asked them to mail them to you directly. I think this is a superb idea as it will give me more discipline than I would be apt to have! Thank you! And how nice that there is a Jewish idea of learning in pairs like this—I know of no such Christian equivalent!"

I am eagerly awaiting the arrival of the books and am excited to start this new chapter in my interfaith family's journey. I cannot help but feel lucky that, for me, intermarriage continues to open new doors to spiritual engagement and family connection. It is truly a blessing in disguise.

According to Mussar, the centuries-old Jewish practice of self-improvement, the concept of a blessing in disguise enables us to find the positive aspect in our experiences. I see the many gifts my mixed faith union has given to me, and I am deeply grateful for this twist in my Jewish journey. I have a vibrant Jewish life because of my interfaith marriage. I know many intermarrieds who feel similar and who recognize the ways in which intermarriage has reinvigorated their Jewish selves. They also approach their situations with a gracious heart and an emphasis on the positive, while acknowledging that, like all relationships, there are challenges along the way. Yet rarely do I see, outside of interfaith forums, a discussion of what opportunities interfaith relationships might present to the Jewish community. Instead, many of the Jewish leaders, as well as lay people, driving the intermarriage debate view mixed faith unions from a glass-half-empty perspective. They focus on the difficulties or hardships that intermarriage creates for couples or how it hurts the Jewish faith, even though we do not know the ultimate effect it will have on Judaism. I hope that by telling my family's story, I have provided a counter to the voices in the Jewish press and community that consistently beat the drum about the downside of interfaith relationships and those who arouse communal fears about the outcome of today's high rate of intermarriage on Judaism's survival.

The real effect of intermarriage on a Jewish future is uncertain. The intermarriage rate was similarly high in Europe before World War II. Yet it was a racist madman who almost destroyed Jewish life, not interfaith unions. As Alan Morinis, founder of the Mussar Institute and author of *Everyday Holiness*, says, in a given moment it is difficult to know what is good and what is bad, regardless of appearances.[6] Mixed marriage may seriously erode the Jewish faith and diminish the traditional congregation and denomination-centric model for Jewish involvement. It may cause Judaism to slowly bleed to death. (Although using history as a guide, I am doubtful that will be the case.) But it may also embolden our engagement and renewal efforts and buoy the emergent and non-denominational community movement. It may bolster affiliation at Jewish institutions as interfaith families seek out Jewish connection. Intermarriage may have an unseen benefit. But to find it, we will need to do as I did: we will need to confront our centuries-old fears, prejudices, and stereotypes, study our history, and wrestle with our beliefs and ideas. Only after we question and look inside ourselves both communally and individually will we be able to appreciate the blessings intermarriage has to offer and see that there are lessons to learn from those in interfaith relationships.

As I wind down my family's story, I hope that I have encouraged people to think differently about interfaith families and reframe the discussion of Jewish continuity. I want to show that the reality of the religious lives of mixed faith families is more nuanced and richly Jewish than is often portrayed through surveys, statistics, and snapshot anecdotes. I hope that I have inspired others to share their stories because our stories are what will help to move us forward. Our stories will keep us vibrant (remember that the retelling of stories is part of Jewish culture for a reason) because they touch us in ways numbers cannot. They make us see other perspectives through real people and characters with whom we identify. They teach us, inspire us, encourage us, and enlighten us. They take us outside our comfort zones and present new ideas. They help us remember, spur us to action, and ask us to consider other possibilities.

Maybe my family's story has encouraged others with mixed religious DNA in their family trees to speak up and speak out about how their family has also re-mained Jewish in the presence of intermarriage. Maybe it has inspired some to be more welcoming to interfaith couples, embrace a child's not Jewish girlfriend or boyfriend, or reach out to intermarried children and grandchildren in new ways. Maybe it has caused others to investigate ways to connect their family to Judaism, pushed them to seek out Jewish choices, or explore their own and their partner's beliefs. I hope it has done any one of these things.

While this is the conclusion of the first part of my family's Jewish journey, it is not the end. Cameron and I continue to navigate and explore individually and together our religious lives and our family's religious identity and continue to plant the seeds of Judaism in Sammy. We will not know for many years if Sammy will grow into a contemporary Jew or if he will create his own Jewish home as an adult. But rather than fear the future, we focus our energy on nour-ishing what we have planted so that we can find connection today and increase the chances that Judaism will continue to blossom through Sammy tomorrow.

EPILOGUE

With the March 2010 statement (see Preface) by the Central Conference of American Rabbis (CCAR), the Reform rabbinical organization, changing its policy toward intermarriage from prevention to engagement, there was an acknowledgment, at least by one of the progressive movements, that the Jewish community's strategy of prevention has not worked. It has not stopped intermarriage nor has it reversed the marriage trend either. The overall rate of intermarriage remains between 40 and 50 percent, and almost 60 percent of Jews who married from 2000 to 2013 chose a partner from outside the faith.

While the policy of prevention has not realized its goal of more inmarriage, it has successfully created communal hysteria, interdenominational discord, anger, scapegoats, exclusion, and fractured family relationships. Through its Task Force on the Challenges of Intermarriage, the CCAR recognized what many who participate in or work with interfaith outreach programs already know from personal experience—that it is time to change course and, at least for the Reform movement, to more fully embrace outreach. This shift reframes the intermarriage discussion in a way that allows us to focus on influencing Jewish choices before marriage and facilitating the continuation of Judaism among intermarrieds after marriage.

From my perspective, at the communal level, this repositioning emphasizes outreach and engagement and should include officiating at interfaith weddings. While officiating will not be something embraced by all clergy, it does open the door to a Jewish conversation with interfaith couples. It says, "you're welcome in our community," but more importantly, it provides the opportunity to engage mixed faith couples in Jewish life and, for clergy, to influence faith-related choices. What parameters rabbis set for officiating are for individual clergy to decide, but I think that my synagogue has a good model. The rabbis who perform interfaith marriages at my congregation do not ask the not Jewish partner to convert, but they do require that the ceremony be singularly Jewish. Couples must take our introduction to Judaism course together before their wedding. This enables the betrothed to make religious decisions collaboratively and in an informed way. It also acts as a refresher on Jewish history, traditions, and rituals for the Jewish partner, who often does not remember much from religious school, and it serves to remind him or her why it is important to have a rabbi at his or her wedding in the first place. In addition, like all endogamous couples, interfaith couples must have several premarital meetings with the rabbi. Because of this process, a significant number of non-Jewish partners go on to convert either before or after marriage. Those couples that remain interfaith develop connections to our temple, often getting involved in our young adults, social justice, outreach, and preschool communities.

As a community, we can also encourage interfaith families to embrace their Jewishness by creating safe spaces for them to explore Judaism. My congregation's Interfaith Families group is an entry point to Jewish life for many intermarrieds who are not ready to participate in general congregational programs or who have not made a decision about their family's religious identity. The group provides a way for these people to get to know a small segment of a very large congregation and build connections in an environment where the other families look like them. It also provides our synagogue the opportunity to influence religious decision making—not through pressure, but through exposure to Jewish ritual and tradition and interactions with clergy who can help these families navigate faith-related issues. We find that as intermarrieds become more comfortable with Judaism and feel more connected to our temple community, their participation in nonoutreach programming grows, especially as their children get older. "Graduates" of Interfaith Families go on to chair temple-wide holiday celebrations, lead social justice initiatives, and get involved in committee work—and not just the Jewish spouse but also the not Jewish partner.

Engaging our interfaith families does not just help them live Jewishly but also supports them in their religious journey, which we have found can lead to the later-in-life conversion of some not Jewish partners. For example, our newly installed president is a Jew by choice who lived a Jewish life with his Jewish family for twenty years before formalizing his Jewish identity. Another member, a woman active in many areas of our temple for more than twenty years, recently decided she wanted to make her Judaism official. Still another was so moved by the rabbi working with her child as he studied for his bar mitzvah that, after the child's ceremony, she began the conversion process. These are just a few snapshots of what an inclusive environment that supports a diversity of Jewish families can do. There are many more people like these men and women in our community: people who date Judaism for a long time before deciding they want to marry the faith. Of course, not every non-Jewish spouse chooses to convert, but outreach provides a gateway for these men and women to explore and connect with faith, spirituality, and Judaism in their own way and at their own pace.

At the familial level, parents, siblings, children, and grandparents need to recognize that they have the power to control their response to interfaith relationships and set the tone for them as well. Families can believe the doomsday rhetoric they hear from some pulpits and classrooms and read in the press that fans the flames of discord in the Jewish community and in homes. They can support policies of exclusion, or they can embrace the idea of engagement and work to open their Jewish tent without compromising Jewish beliefs and values. They can welcome not Jewish spouses and significant others into their homes for holidays, teach them about the rituals, and expose them to Jewish life in positive ways. They can teach a grandchild how to bake challah or make latkes or invite a daughter and her not Jewish boyfriend for Shabbat dinner or to a lecture at their synagogue. They can ask a non-Jewish daughter-in-law to go to a Jewish meditation or yoga class or attend a screening of an Israeli film, or they can facilitate the building of Jewish social networks by connecting the interfaith couple to organizations, programs, and others in the community. They can show them that there is more to being Jewish than attendance at High Holiday worship services. The fact is that there are many things families can do to engage interfaith couples and help them see the breadth of Jewish faith and culture, but the key is that they must recognize that the best way to make intermarrieds receptive to Judaism is through inviting Jewish experiences that influence, rather than pressure, the couple's religious choices.

Families and couples can also avail themselves of formal interfaith programs and support groups from organizations such as the Jewish Outreach Institute (JOI) and InterfaithFamily that communities across the country offer. The Mother's Circle, for non-Jewish moms raising Jewish children; The Grandparents Circle, for Jewish grandparents with interfaith grandchildren; How Should I Know, for Jewish men with not Jewish partners; Answering Your Jewish Children, for non-Jewish fathers raising Jewish children; and InterfaithFamily/Your Community can help immediate and extended families build bridges, connect to Judaism, and navigate interfaith family life.

I know that some Jewish leaders and academics disagree with this shift in focus. They argue that interfaith outreach is not a good use of precious resources—financial and otherwise—that my story and the anecdotal evidence from my congregation's efforts are exceptions. They cite statistics that indicate that over one-third of intermarried Jews choose to raise their children outside of Judaism, and that the creation of welcoming Jewish institutions is not a panacea.[1] But I see firsthand evidence to the contrary, and I am not alone. A 2005 study done by Combined Jewish Philanthropies (CJP) of Greater Boston found that 60 percent of intermarrieds in this area are raising their children Jewish, and that intermarrieds raising Jewish children light Shabbat candles more frequently than inmarried Reform and Conservatives families.[2] These findings are not the result of chance. They are the result of robust outreach efforts by congregations and communal organizations in the Boston area. Rather than focusing on the 30 percent of families who are not Jewishly engaged, we should be looking at those that are to understand what motivates them to make Jewish choices and leverage these lessons to reach nonpracticing and unaffiliated intermarrieds. While we are working to understand what motivates interfaith families to engage Jewishly, we may also learn, as my congregation did, something about what drives inmarried participation in Jewish life.

Several years ago, the outreach committee at my temple noticed that inmarrieds were coming to interfaith family events. It was nice to think that our outreach initiatives had broad appeal, but it made us wonder why inmarrieds wanted to participate. We identified several reasons for the crossover interest, including compelling programs, the desire for Jewish connection, and a safe environment to ask "stupid" questions. The discussions that our Interfaith Families group developed were filling the need for education on Jewish topics for *all* parents, not just interfaith ones. Programs such as "How to Talk to Your Children about God," "What is a Mitzvah," "How to Celebrate Shabbat in the Home," and "Dealing with Prejudice" were created from questions the interfaith families asked but were, in fact, of interest to *all* parents raising Jewish children. Yet outside of our outreach efforts, no one else was addressing these topics. Maybe they were not addressed because it was assumed that inmarrieds knew how to handle these issues because they were wholly Jewish, or they were not asking questions, or the calendar was just simply too full with other learning opportunities. Whatever the reason, interfaith initiatives were able to fill a need for our inmarried members too—a real bang for the outreach buck.

Interfaith programming also provided a nonthreatening learning environment for all types of Jewish families. One inmarried mom said that she felt embarrassed that she had questions about mitzvahs but felt that, in a setting where almost one-half of the participants did not know much about the concept either, it was safe to say, "I don't know." Conversely, inmarried participation helped the interfaith moms and dads feel less like outsiders because they saw that having two Jewish parents did not alleviate the challenges of raising Jewish children or creating a Jewish home. It enabled both groups to realize that they were navigating many of the same issues, and their families were more similar than different. Lastly, interfaith events offered an opportunity to connect. Interfaith Families' Hanukkah Story Time enabled intermarried and inmarried families to celebrate and connect during a very Christian-centered time of year. Similarly, inmarrieds attended Interfaith Families' Shabbat in the Park, an outdoor Shabbat experience with a song session with a leader from an area Jewish overnight camp; Interfaith Families' Tashlich in the Park, a Rosh Hashanah picnic following the congregational service; and Passover and Shabbat cooking classes with *Reform Judaism* columnist and cookbook author Tina Wasserman. After one of these events, an inmarried mom said, "I wish I could attend every Interfaith Families program. You do such cool stuff."

While it is great to be cool, these programs were designed for our interfaith families in order to help them embrace Jewish choices and feel comfortable in our temple community. We needed to be sensitive to how they felt about inmarried participation. What we found was that our intermarrieds welcomed the inmarried involvement because it made them feel welcome. Nothing seemed to say you belong like a few inmarrieds crashing an interfaith party. When one of our rabbis came with his family to the Hanukkah Story Time, not because of official clergy duty but to participate in the activity, our interfaith families thought that was "awesome." They said that inmarried participation helped them feel less like outsiders, expanded peoples' networks, and encouraged broader engagement and new friendships.

After observing the beautiful crossover, we asked if interfaith outreach were still necessary. If inmarrieds and intermarrieds wanted similar programs and enjoyed learning from each other, why continue to invest the resources? We continued our efforts because we knew that many of the interfaith families that attended our outreach groups were not ready to participate in general congregational activities. For them, joining our support group was a first step in engagement—in Jewish life—and was often made when a baby was born or a child was in preschool. Interfaith Families was a safe starting point for education and a comfortable first connection to our congregation. We did not want to lose this entryway as many of the relationships formed in this group became deep and lasting. Instead of eliminating outreach, we looked at the commingling of inmarrieds and intermarrieds as a bonus and as an opportunity to influence and educate both constituencies.

This reimagining and reframing of our relationship to intermarriage shifts our role as a community from Preventer-in-Chief to Chief Influencer and asks us to work to shape the making of Jewish choices in a more positive manner. The good news is that there are congregations, movements, and organizations that have made huge strides in the area of interfaith engagement and that are doing innovative things to bring families like mine into Judaism. But more is needed from formal organizations and individuals alike. I am hopeful that we can do it. What gives me hope is not only the interfaith families that I get to work with but also the stories and best practices that I hear from outside my Jewish bubble.

I recently attended an outreach conference in Boston where an ordained Orthodox rabbi, serving a nondenominational congregation with a large interfaith membership, talked about his solution for how to deal with patrilineal Jewish children preparing for their bar mitzvah. These children were not halakhically Jewish because their mothers were not Jews and, therefore, not technically able to participate in this important lifecycle ritual. The rabbi believed that he risked alienating these families from Judaism if he told them that their children, who they raised as Jews since birth, were not eligible to be a bar mitzvah without first undergoing formal conversion. Furthermore, he did not want to damage the Jewish identity of the kids, who only knew Judaism, by telling them that they must convert. Yet, he also did not want to compromise his beliefs. What he came up with was a way for the children to affirm their Jewishness in a way that would enable him to feel comfortable with these kids becoming a bar mitzvah.

Instead of a conversion, *all* children (matrilineal and patrilineal) participated in an affirmation of faith together before their bar mitzvahs. He took the students to Boston for a day of fun, followed by a ceremony affirming their Judaism at the Mayyim Hayyim Living Waters Community Mikveh. (A *mikveh* is a ritual bath used by Jews since ancient times. Its two most common uses are for cleansing after a menstrual period and conversion.) Each child immersed in the mikveh individually and said the ritual blessings. The reason immersion in the mikveh was significant was that it symbolized total commitment, purity, and holiness. It was also a component of all traditional conversion processes. (Interestingly, the Christian ritual of baptism was based on the mikveh.) For this rabbi, the physical act of immersion by all of his bar mitzvah students was a way for him to balance inclusivity—no child was singled out as different or not of equal Jewishness—with his own Jewish belief system. After immersion, all the children were considered Jewish under Jewish law regardless of which parent was a Jew. It also provided a memorable learning and bonding opportunity for participants (who, according to the rabbi, all spoke of the experience at their bar mitzvah ceremonies). Through this ingenious approach, he was able to get comfortable officiating at all of the children's bar mitzvahs, regardless of the gender of the Jewish parent.

It is stories and efforts like the ones I highlight that demonstrate that outreach and interfaith engagement matter. While I know that, with a little creativity, compassion, and more individual and communal effort we can create an even larger Jewishly engaged intermarried population, I do not want to give the impression that I am too Pollyannaish. Interfaith unions can challenge Judaism in many ways, and some mixed faith couples and families struggle to navigate religious issues. There is no one-size-fits-all (fill in the blank—denominational, congregational, family, clergy, or community) solution, but I see the challenges posed by intermarriage as an opportunity for innovation and connection rather than as a threat to Jewish continuity.

With the Jewish intermarriage rate nearing 60 percent for new marriages and overall religious affiliation in America on the decline, it is not in our best interest to double-down on failed policies of prevention, demonization, and exclusion. If we all really care about Jewish continuity, then it is time we viewed intermarriage through a more compassionate lens, used our protective responses to implement policies and programs that facilitate Jewish choices, and helped mitigate our fears about Judaism's survival. It is time to figure out a positive way to incorporate and engage interfaith couples and families. Because let us face it, the future of Judaism depends on it. To rephrase the Ahad Ha'am statement in chapter 6, "More than the Jewish people have kept Shabbat, Shabbat *will keep* the Jewish people." Jewish spouses will not sustain us, but Jewish engagement will.

HOW TO START
AN INTERFAITH GROUP

I meet many people who are interested in starting an interfaith families group similar to the one at my synagogue in Dallas. To get you started, I have provided you with some basic guidelines and ideas for educational, holiday, and social programs. These are suggestions based on work done by the group in which I am involved. Feel free to modify them and make them your own. Once you get started, tell me, and others, about your group at interfaithandjewish.blogspot.com/ or www.facebook.com/ interfaithandjewish. I would love to hear about your experiences.

Target Audience:
Who is your group trying to reach: couples, families, women, men, moms, dads, one-faith, dual-faith, or undecided?

The group at my congregation started as a program for moms, both Jewish and not Jewish, whose families were making Jewish choices. At the time, women, who are often responsible for religion in the home, had a greater need for connection than men. After a few years, a separate group was created for dads, based on feedback from men that they wanted a similar outlet. Over time, we combined the groups as we moved toward more family programming. Recently, we recognized that some of the young adults in our community in interfaith relationships and interfaith couples without children were also looking for connection with others in a similar relationship situation, so we added couples-only events to our calendar.

The group's evolution has been organic, changing based on the needs of the members we serve. Over the years, we have learned that our group skews toward young families (parents-to-be and preschool) and those new to our city. As these families grow with their children and begin religious school, we have found that they "graduate" to involvement in more general congregational activities.

Leadership:
The Interfaith Families group has always been led by a group of lay leaders—Jewish and not Jewish—who have a personal stake in interfaith engagement. We typically have two to four people who oversee the development and implementation of programs and events. The leadership committee changes every two to three years in order to inject fresh ideas, expand the group's reach, and get more people involved in the congregational community.

Staff and clergy support are limited to assistance with scheduling and the occasional facilitation of a program. While a staff liaison has become more involved in planning as the group has grown, the passion of our intermarried lay leaders has been the key to Interfaith Families' success.

Budget:
Interfaith engagement does not need to bust the budget. Our group started with no money. Today, it operates for less than two thousand dollars. Part of our budget is received as a grant from our congregation's sisterhood.

To keep costs low, we leverage existing communication channels, such as websites, newsletters, and e-mail databases. We use social media to promote events, including posting a group profile on Interfaithfamily.com in order to reach area families and couples outside of our temple community. But our most effective communication channel is word-of-mouth, and it is free! We encourage members to bring friends and neighbors and have added many new participants because they have heard of us through the grapevine.

Another cost-effective strategy we employ is the use of people from within our synagogue and larger Jewish community as program facilitators. We engage temple lay leaders, teachers, clergy, and members with specific professional expertise when necessary and utilize nonpulpit rabbis and Jewish camp staff who live in our city. All help at no charge or for a modest fee.

To stretch our budget even further, our programs that include a meal are typically potluck. When we do offer a catered dinner, we charge for the meal and ask participants to bring wine and dessert in order to keep the cost reasonable. This enables us to provide one free dinner event each year, our Spring Mitzvah Project and Havdalah.

<u>Programming</u>:

When Interfaith Families (Moms) started, it provided educational programs primarily, but participants asked that social events be added so that they could connect in a more casual way. Over the years we have moved between the two types of activities, sometimes leaning more heavily in one direction. Currently our calendar is focused on community building and experiential programs often tied to holidays. The key to our programming success has been to let the group's membership decide what type of experiences they want.

From a calendar perspective, there is no right amount of programs. We have met monthly, every other month, and six times per year. For our members, monthly was too much, so we now meet four to six times for group specific activities and suggest that participants get involved together in general congregational initiatives.

I have included some suggestions for educational and social programs below, but what works best is listening to your members. Design programs to meet their needs and answers their questions. Be creative and do not be afraid to experiment.

Educational Programs:
- Beyond the Mezuzah: Jewish Family, Home, and Identity (three-part series)
- Celebrating Shabbat in the Home—A How-To Workshop

- How to Be the Perfect Stranger—Lifecycle Etiquette
- How to Talk to Your Children about Death and Dying
- How to Talk to Your Children about God
- Interfaith in the Bible Belt—Dealing with Prejudice
- Jewish Cooking
- Open Forum/Hot Topics Discussion
- Preparing for the High Holidays
- Reflections and Forgiveness
- Talking to Parents and In-Laws
- What Makes a Man a Good Jewish Role Model?
- What is a Mitzvah?

Holiday Programs
- Challah Baking
- Hanukkah Sing-Along and Story Time
- Matzah Making
- Passover Cooking Class
- Shabbat Cooking Class
- Shabbat in the Park
- Spring Mitzvah Project, Havdalah, and Picnic
- Tashlich in the Park

Social Programs:
- Interfaith Couples' Dinner—Dinner at a member's home (fee for meal)
- Interfaith Dads' Night Out—Meet for drinks at a local restaurant (pay-your-own-way) or in the congregation's youth lounge (free)
- Interfaith Moms' Night Out—Casual dinner at a local restaurant (pay-your-own-way)
- Visit to the Dallas Holocaust Museum (reduced fee for admission)

Cosponsorship of General Temple Programs:
- Tot Shabbat—Interfaith Families "sponsors" Tot Shabbat one to two times per year by providing all of the baked goods for the postservice meal. Group members volunteer to bake or bring the treats.
- Congregational Sukkot Celebration—Interfaith Families lead and staff the mitzvah project for this congregational event.

Keys to Success:
- Passionate leaders
- Respect for all opinions
- Nonjudgmental environment
- Safe space to share and connect
- Time for relationship building
- Support of our synagogue and community leaders
- Ability to direct group from the bottom up

JUDEO-CHRISTIAN CARROT CAKE

(Parve without Frosting; Dairy with Frosting)

The Sisterhood of Ohavi Zedek Synagogue, Vermont's oldest and largest Jewish congregation, gave this recipe to the women of my mother-in-law's parish, St. James Episcopal Church in Essex Junction, Vermont. Courtesy of P. Larkin.

Cake Ingredients
2 cups sugar
1½ cups oil
2 teaspoons vanilla
3 cups flour, plus extra for pan
2 teaspoons baking soda
1½ teaspoons cinnamon
½ teaspoon salt
3 eggs
2 cups finely grated raw carrot
1½ cups crushed pineapple, drained, juice reserved
1½ cups chopped walnuts (optional)

Directions for Cake
1. Preheat oven to 350 degrees.
2. Grease and flour a tube pan or 9 in. x 13 in. rectangular cake pan.
3. In a large bowl, mix sugar, oil, and vanilla. Add remaining dry ingredients. Add eggs one at a time. Add carrot, pineapple, and walnuts if using. Mix until well combined. Pour batter into the prepared pan.
4. Bake for 70 minutes if using a tube pan and 55 minutes if using a cake pan. Check the center with a toothpick; it should be solid.

5. Let cake cool.
6. If frosting, prepare the recipe for Cream Cheese Frosting below while the cake cools.

Cream Cheese Frosting Ingredients

8 ounces cream cheese, softened at room temperature

1 stick butter

1 box confectioner's sugar

2 teaspoons vanilla

A splash of milk or reserved juice from crushed pineapple, if needed

Directions for Frosting

Beat all ingredients together until thick. Frost the cake when cool.

RESOURCES

A select list of useful books, media, and organizational resources for families and individuals.

Children's Activities and Books:

- Judyth Groner and Madeline Wikler, *Thank You, God: A Jewish Child's Book of Prayers* (Minneapolis, MN: KAR-BEN Publishing, 2003): A first prayer book for young children with twenty-one traditional Jewish prayers in simple Hebrew with transliteration and English translation.

- Alfred J. Kolatch, *A Child's First Book of Jewish Holidays* (Middle Village, NY: Jonathan David Publishers, Inc., 1997): An engaging introduction to the major Jewish holidays, with bright and colorful illustrations.

- Sylvia A. Rouss, *Sammy Spider* series (Minneapolis, MN: KAR-BEN Publishing): A fun way for preschool children to learn about Jewish holidays, rituals, and Israel is through the tales of Sammy Spider and his mother, who live with the Shapiros and experience Judaism through young Josh Shapiros's adventures.

- Sydney Taylor, *All-of-a-Kind Family* series (New York: Yearling, 1951–1978): A time-honored classic about an immigrant family living in New York before World War I. The books share the adventures of five mischievous sisters. The family's Jewish faith plays an important role in the story.

- *Jewish Holidays in a Box*, jewishholidaysinabox.com: Fun and interactive materials to help families celebrate the Jewish holidays. The kits give parents tools to build powerful and positive Jewish memories and show them how to be creative with their celebrations.

- *PJ Library*, www.pjlibrary.org: PJ Library is a program implemented in communities throughout North America that provides free, high-quality, Jewish children's literature and music to families with children age six months to eight years old on a monthly basis and sponsors local Jewish family programming.

Cookbooks:

- Tina Wasserman, *Entrée to Judaism: A Culinary Exploration of the Jewish Diaspora* (New York: URJ Press, 2009): A culinary adventure through the Jewish Diaspora, it is as much a history book as it is a cookbook. Wasserman explains how Jews around the world and across the ages adapted local tastes and ingredients to meet the needs of Jewish holidays and dietary laws, creating a rich and diverse menu of flavors and styles.

- Tina Wasserman, *Entrée to Judaism for Families: Jewish Cooking and Kitchen Conversations with Children* (New York: URJ Press, 2013): A follow-up to Wasserman's *Entrée to Judaism*, *Entrée to Judaism for Families* provides tools to help children learn to cook, tips for adults to make the experience fun, and recipes that tell the story of Jewish communities.

Fiction Books:

- Anita Diamant, *The Red Tent* (New York: St. Martin's Press, 1997): Diamant interweaves biblical stories with events and characters of her own creation to tell the story of Dinah, daughter of Leah and Jacob. Readers experience Dinah's life from her birth and childhood in Mesopotamia to her years in Canaan, including her initiation into the Red Tent, when she reaches puberty, and her death in Egypt.

Nonfiction Books:

- Rabbi Benjamin Blech, *The Complete Idiot's Guide to Understanding Judaism* (New York: Alpha Books, 2003): Written in a warm, conversational style, this book is a fun and easy-to-understand primer to every aspect of Judaism.

- Jon Entine, *Abraham's Children: Race, Identity, and the DNA of the Chosen People* (New York: Grand Central Publishing, 2007): Entine uses genetics to illuminate the connection between genes and individual identity, and specifically the controversial question of "Who is a Jew?"

- Sharon G. Forman, *Honest Answers to Your Child's Jewish Questions: A Rabbi's Insights* (New York: URJ Press, 2006): A helpful resource that provides successful responses to many Jewish questions children ask and summarizes Jewish thought in an easy-to-understand, readable format.

- Ranya Idliby, Suzanne Oliver, and Priscilla Warner, *The Faith Club* ((New York: Free Press, Simon & Schuster, 2006): The story of three women, their three religions, and their quest to understand one another.

- Meredith L. Jacobs, *Modern Jewish Mom's Guide to Shabbat: Connect and Celebrate—Bring Your Family Together with the Friday Night Meal* (New York: HarperCollins, 2007): An easy-to-read book that shows how the Friday night Shabbat meal can bring a family together and help them connect, even as children grow older. Includes recipes, art projects, and summaries of the weekly Torah portion with suggested discussion topics.

- James Keen, *Inside Intermarriage: A Christian Partner's Perspective on Raising a Jewish Family* (New York: URJ Press, 2006): Written by a Christian father who is helping his Jewish wife raise Jewish children. Keen provides practical advice for how to give children a clear Jewish identity while maintaining a comfort level for both parents and includes perspectives from profession-als who work with interfaith families.

- Keren R. McGinity, *Still Jewish: A History of Women and Intermarriage in America* (New York: NYU Press, 2009): An examination of intermarriage and gender across the twentieth century, based on a multigenerational study that combined in-depth personal interviews with an astute analysis of how interfaith relationships and intermarriage were portrayed in the mass media, advice manuals, and religious community-generated literature.

- Wendy Mogul, *The Blessing of a Skinned Knee: Using Jewish Teachings to Raise Self-Reliant Children* (New York: Penguin Compass, 2001): A guide for raising self-reliant children. Mogul takes stories of everyday parent-ing problems and examines them through the lens of the Torah, the Talmud, and other important Jewish teachings. She shows parents how to teach children to honor their parents and to respect others, escape the danger of overvaluing children's need for self-expression, accept that their children are both ordinary *and* unique, and treasure the power and holiness of the present.

- Alan Morinis, *Everyday Holiness: The Jewish Spiritual Path of Mussar* (Boston: Trumpeter Books: 2007): An accessible and inspiring introduction to the centuries-old Jewish spiritual tradition of Mussar, which is a set of teach-ings for cultivating personal growth.

- Judy Petsonk and Jim Remsen, *The Intermarriage Handbook* (New York: Arbor House/William Morrow, 1988): A comprehensive, practical, self-help book for interfaith couples, based on interviews of psychologists, family therapists, sociologists, religious leaders, and couples themselves.

- Milton Steinberg, *Basic Judaism* (New York: A Harvest Book, Harcourt Brace & Co., 1947): A classic work for the Jewish and the non-Jewish reader. A concise and readable introduction to the Jewish faith that makes complex theological and philosophical concepts easy to understand and contrasts various perspectives.

- Rabbi Joseph Telushkin, *Jewish Literacy: The Most Important Things to Know about the Jewish Religion, Its People, and Its History* (New York: William Morrow, HarperCollins, 2008): An indispensable reference on Jewish life, culture, tradition, and religion. It covers every essential aspect of the Jewish people and Judaism.

- Tony Wagner, *The Global Achievement Gap: Why Even our Best Schools Don't Teach the New Survival Skills Our Children Need—And What We Can Do About It* (New York: Basic Books, 2008): A thoughtful analysis of the state of public education in America and what needs to be done to transform our education system.

- David J. Wolpe, *Why Faith Matters* (New York: HarperOne, 2008): A defense of religion in America. Wolpe makes the case for faith in today's world through a discussion of the origins and nature of faith, the role of the Bible in modern life, and the compatibility of God and science.

Jewish Media:

- *CJ: Voices of Conservative/Masorti Judaism* - www.cjvoices.org: The magazine of the Conservative movement.

- *Commentary* - www.commentarymagazine.com: An opinion magazine founded by the American Jewish Committee that covers issues related to democracy; American and Western security; the future of the Jewish people, faith, and culture; and the preservation of high culture.

- *Contact* - www.steinhardtfoundation.org/publications: The quarterly journal of the Steinhardt Foundation for Jewish Life. It seeks to stimulate community-wide discussion about programs and ideas that will help to revitalize American Jewish life.

- *Heeb Magazine* - www.heebmagazine.com: A publication that covers the arts, culture, and politics for young, urban Jews.

- *Jewcy* - www.jewcy.com: A website that covers ideas that matter to young Jews, including news, arts, culture, relationships, religion and beliefs, Jewish food, social justice, and family.

- *Jewish Journal* - www.jewishjournal.com: The largest Jewish weekly in the United States outside of New York City. Contains local, national, and global news updated daily as well as blogs from noted Jewish personalities and writers.

- *Kveller: Jewish Family Life—Parenting Advice & Perspectives* - www.kveller.com: An independent and inclusive website for parents raising Jewish children.

- *Lilith* - www.lilith.org: An independent, Jewish feminist magazine that combines reporting, memoir, and original fiction and poetry to provide perspective on celebrations, rituals, and social change.

- *Reform Judaism Magazine* - www.reformjudaismmag.org: The magazine of the Reform movement.

- *The Jewish Daily Forward* - www.forward.com: Published online and as a weekly newspaper, *The Forward* is one of the oldest Jewish-American publications covering news and opinion on Jewish affairs and Jewish culture. Its column "The Seesaw," answers questions submitted by interfaith couples and families.

- *The Jewish Week* - www.thejewishweek.com: A Jewish newspaper serving the Jewish community of Greater New York with coverage of Israel, politics, culture, and Jewish life.

- *Tablet* - www.tabletmag.com: A daily online magazine covering Jewish news, politics, arts, culture, life, and religion.

Multimedia:

- *From Jesus to Christ: The First Christians* - www.pbs.org/wgbh/pages/frontline/shows/religion: A four-part historical documentary series produced by WGBH and the PBS series Frontline that tells the story of the rise of Christianity. It explores the life of Jesus, his death, and the people who created the religion we now know as Christianity.

- *The Jewish Americans* - www.pbs.org/jewishamericans: A six-hour documentary that explores 350 years of Jewish American history. It takes viewers from the first settlement in 1654 to the present and shows the tension between maintaining a Jewish identity and assimilation. Produced by JTN Productions, WETA Washington, DC, and David Grubin Productions, Inc., in association with Thirteen/WNET New York.

Adult Jewish Education:

- Florence Melton School of Adult Jewish Learning - www.meltonschool. org: The largest pluralistic adult Jewish education network in the world.

Community Mikvaot:

Community mikvaot welcome people who represent the broad spectrum of Judaism's diversity to participate in ritual immersion.

- Temple Beth El, Birmingham, AL: www.templebeth-el.net/facilities.php

- Congregation Beth Israel, Phoenix, AZ—The Stein Family Community Mikveh: www.cbiaz.org/about/about

- Rabbinical Assembly Mikveh at the American Jewish University, Los Angeles, CA: ra@ajula.edu

- Jewish Federation of Silicon Valley, Los Gatos, CA—The Gloria & Ken Levy Family Campus: Community Mikvah: mikvah@jvalley.org

- Temple Shalom Mikvah, Colorado Springs, CO: www.templeshalom. com/worship/lifecycle-traditions/mikvah.html

- Adas Israel Mikveh, Washington, DC: www.adasisrael.org/mikvah

- Congregation B'nai Torah, Atlanta, GA: www.bnaitorah.org/services-facilities/mikvah

- The Community Mikvah of the Conservative Movement, Wilmette, IL: www.juf.org/guide/detail.aspx?id=18978

- Mayyim Hayyim Living Waters Community Mikveh and Paula Brody & Family Education Center, Newton, MA: www.mayyimhayyim.org

- Beth El Congregation, Baltimore, MD: www.bethelbalto.com/mikveh

- Mikvat Shalom, Portland, ME: www.mikvatshalom.org

- Temple Israel, West Bloomfield, MI: info@temple-israel.org

- Beth Meyer Synagogue, Raleigh, NC—Libi Eir (Awakened Heart) Community Mikveh: www.bethmeyer.org/content/mikveh

- ImmerseNYC, New York, NY: www.immersenyc.org

- Temple Israel Center, White Plains, NY—Brandt Family Mikveh: www. templeisraelcenter.org/Religious_Life/Brandt_Family_Mikveh/ Brandt_Family_Mikveh

- Park Synagogue, Cleveland Heights, OH—Charlotte Goldberg Community Mikveh: www.clevelandmikvah.org

- Emanuel Synagogue, Oklahoma City, OK: www.emanuelokc.org/mikvah.htm

- Shir Ami, Newtown, PA—Goldman-Strom Mikveh: www.shiraminow.org/worship/mikveh

- Temple Beth Hillel-Beth El, Wynnewood, PA: www.tbhbe.org/religiouslife/mikveh

- Congregation Ahavath Sholom, Ft. Worth, TX: www.ahavathsholom.org/facilities/mikvah

- Temple Beth-El, Richmond, VA: www.bethelrichmond.org/temple-life/mikvah

Denominational Organizations:
- ALEPH: Alliance for Jewish Renewal - www.aleph.org: Supports the worldwide Jewish renewal movement.

- Jewish Reconstructionist Communities - www.jewishrecon.org: Supports Reconstructionist congregations and communities in North America and abroad.

- Union of Orthodox Jewish Congregations of America or Orthodox Union - www.ou.org: Supports Orthodox synagogues, youth programs, advocacy efforts, and supervision of the preparation of kosher food.

- Union for Reform Judaism - www.urj.org: Supports Reform Jewish congregations, youth programs and camps, political and legislative action, and the production of music and media.

- United Synagogue of Conservative Judaism - www.uscj.org: Supports Conservative synagogues and community organizations affiliated with the movement.

- There are many Jewish-emergent and independent minyans (groups) that are not affiliated with an established Jewish denomination. Some are lay-led or have a volunteer rabbi; others have an official rabbinic leader. Some mix egalitarian and inclusive values with learning and observance that are more traditional. Search "independent minyans" or "Jewish-emergent" on the web to locate these groups in your community.

Interfaith Organizations:
- Combine Jewish Philanthropies (CJP) Interfaith Ambassador, Greater Boston, MA - interfaith@cjp.org: Connects interfaith couples and families to programs and resources within Greater Boston. Available for private consultations.

- InterfaithFamily - www.interfaithfamily.com: An organization, and online resource and network that supports interfaith families and couples exploring Jewish life. Offers InterfaithFamily/Your Community initiatives in the Greater Boston, Chicagoland, Philadelphia, and San Francisco areas.

- Jewish Discovery Institute, Newton Centre, MA - www.jewishdiscovery-institute.org/index.aspx: A resource center for interfaith couples and others interested in exploring Conservative Judaism in the Greater Boston area. Offers programs and resources for individuals, professionals, and lay leaders.

- Jewish Outreach Institute - www.joi.org: A trans-denominational organization focused on outreach to unaffiliated Jews and intermarried families.

- Keruv - www.fjmc.org/content/keruv-understanding-intermarriage: An initiative of the Federation of Jewish Men's Clubs, Keruv provides Conservative congregations with support and programs for intermarried families.

- Reform Jewish Outreach Boston, Newton, MA - www.reformjewishout reachboston.org: Offers resources, programs and information for interfaith couples, families, and individuals exploring Judaism and the Jewish community, including educational classes, programs, and support groups.

Organizations Fighting Prejudice and Anti-Semitism:

- Anti-Defamation League - www.adl.org: The nation's premier civil rights and human relations agency. It fights anti-Semitism and all forms of bigotry, defends democratic ideals, and protects civil rights for all.

- Anti-Prejudice Consortium - www.antiprejudice.org: Provides programs that fight prejudice, increase tolerance, and promote respect among all people. Works with middle schools and communities.

- Students Together Opposing Prejudice - www.stoptheprejudice.net: A seven-week curriculum created by three faith organizations. It teaches middle school students to recognize and respond to stereotypes, prejudice, and discrimination.

- Teachers Against Prejudice - www.teachersagainstprejudice.org/index2. php: Fights prejudice, intolerance, and bigotry by helping teachers address issues of sensitivity and respect in classrooms and providing activities that teach students how to confront prejudice.

GLOSSARY

Aliyah: Going up. Refers to someone who is moving from the diaspora to Israel or is going to say the blessing over a Torah reading.

Bar/Bat Mitzvah *(plural: b'nei)*: Son (bar) or daughter (bat) of commandment. The bar or bat mitzvah ceremony is a coming of age ritual performed when a boy is thirteen and a girl is twelve. At this time, the child becomes an adult in terms of their responsibility for following Jewish law, tradition, and ethics and is allowed to participate in all areas of Jewish community life.

Book of Life: The metaphorical book in which God writes the names of the righteous. During the ten days between Rosh Hashanah and Yom Kippur God considers the good and bad things a person has done during the year and then decides, "who shall live and who shall die."

Book of Proverbs: The second book in the third section (Ketuvim or Writings) of the Jewish Bible.

Bris/Brit Milah: Covenant. Bris is the German/Eastern European pronunciation. The ritual circumcision ceremony performed eight days after the birth of a son that symbolizes the Jews' covenant with God.

Chazzan *(alternate spellings: hazzan and hazan)*: The prayer leader in a synagogue. Western Jews adopted the term "cantor" in modern times. A chazzan or cantor typically has special musical skills and training as a religious leader and educator and is an ordained clergy.

Chevruta *(alternate spelling: havruta)*: Fellowship. Describes a study partner. Jews frequently study in pairs in order to understand the meaning of a text and how to apply it to larger issues.

Chuppah *(alternate spelling: huppah)*: Covering. A wedding canopy that usually consists of a fabric top supported by four poles under which a Jewish wedding is performed. It symbolizes the married couple's new home.

Confirmation: A ceremony originated by the Reform movement and tied to the Jewish holiday of Shavuot. About age sixteen, teens affirm their commitment to the Jewish people in a group ceremony.

Daven: A Yiddish word that means pray or to recite the prayers in a Jewish liturgy.

Day of Atonement: Another name for the Jewish holiday of Yom Kippur.

Dreidel: A four-sided top spun in a game of chance during the Jewish holiday of Hanukkah. It has the Hebrew letters *nun, gimel, hay,* and *shin* or *nun, gimel, hay,* and *pei. Pei* is used in Israel, and *shin* is used elsewhere. The letters are an acronym for the saying *Nes Gadol Hayah Poh, a great miracle happened here* or *Nes Gadol Hayah Sham, a great miracle happened there.*

Etrog: A lemon-like fruit used during the Jewish harvest holiday of Sukkot. It represents the heart.

Halakha: Jewish law. Often refers to any issue related to Jewish legal matters.

Hamsa: A symbol of an eye embedded in the palm of an open hand. Its origins are mysterious, but scholars have interpreted it as a Jewish, Christian, Islamic, and pagan symbol. It has been associated with the Jewish mystical practice of Kabbalah and considered Judaic art. Also called the eye of Fatima, the hand of Fatima, and the hand of Miriam.

Hanukkah: Dedication. Known as the Festival of Lights, the happy eight-day Jewish holiday commemorates the victory of the Maccabees over the armies of the Syrian Empire in 165 BCE and the subsequent rededication of the Temple in Jerusalem.

Hashkivenu: The evening prayer usually said at bedtime. It asks God to grant a peaceful night's sleep and return one to life refreshed the following day.

HaTikvah: The Hope. It is the title of the Israeli national anthem.

Havdalah: Separation. This beautiful ritual marks the end of Shabbat and Jewish holidays, and the start of a new week. It is typically performed on Saturday night.

Goy: An often disparaging Yiddish term used to describe a non-Jewish person.

Kippah *(plural: kippot):* A small skullcap, hat, yarmulke (Yiddish), or head covering worn by men, and some non-Orthodox women, as a sign of reverence for God.

Kol Yisrael Arevim Zeh Bazeh: All of Israel is responsible for each other. The statement is the basis of the idea in Jewish law of communal responsibility—a Jew must care for the well-being of other Jews.

Lulav: A bundle of three kinds of branches—palm, myrtle, and willow—that is used during Sukkot. The palm is in the center and represents the spine (uprightness). Two willow branches that symbolize lips (saying prayer) are on the left and three myrtles that stand for the eyes (enlightenment) are on the right.

Menorah: One of the oldest Jewish symbols. There are two kinds: 1) a seven-branched candelabra used in sanctuaries to symbolize the nation of Israel and its mission to be a light or example to all others; 2) a nine-branched version used on Hanukkah to commemorate the miracle that a day's worth of oil burned for eight days. A Hanukkah menorah is often called a *hanukkiyah*.

Mensch: A Yiddish term that means a person of integrity and honor that is kind and generous of spirit.

Mezuzah: A vessel that contains a small scroll of parchment with the words of the Shema prayer handwritten on it. The prayer contains the command to set God's words on the doorpost of a house. Jews of varying observance levels hang one on their front door to identify the home as Jewish.

Mikveh *(alternate spelling: mikvah)*: A ritual bath used for immersion. It symbolizes total commitment and spiritual purity. Traditional uses include conversion, and by women before marriage and after the menstrual cycle. Today, both genders use it to mark significant events such as graduation or the end, or beginning, of a period of grieving or healing. Baptism is based on the mikveh.

Mishna: Jewish Oral Law codified about 200 CE. Laws of Jewish life are systematically presented with the majority and minority opinions of rabbinic scholars in sixty-three tractates.

Mitzvah *(plural: mitzvot)*: Commandment. Also refers to a Jewish religious obligation, good deed, or charitable act.

Mussar: A thousand-year-old Jewish practice and system for personal growth and self-improvement.

Neshama: Soul. When used as a term of endearment, it means good Jewish soul.

Oneg: Joy. An informal Jewish social gathering that follows a religious service or ceremony.

Pirkei Avot: Ethics of the Fathers. A selection of quotes from rabbinic scholars from different generations offering moral advice, instruction, and insights that is part of the Mishna. It has no laws.

Purim: The joyous holiday that celebrates Queen Esther saving the Jews from the evil plans of Haman, who schemed to kill them.

Righteous Stranger: A non-Jew who lives among Jews, adopts some or all of Judaism's beliefs and practices, but does not formally convert.

Rosh Hashanah: Head of the year. It is the Jewish New Year and anniversary of creation. It begins the ten days of repentance that ends on Yom Kippur.

Schmaltz: A Yiddish word for clarified chicken or goose fat that is used for frying or as a spread on bread in German, Eastern European, and Ashkenazi Jewish cuisine.

Seder: Order. The traditional Jewish service used on the holidays of Passover and Tu B'shvat.

Seven Circles: This Jewish wedding ritual has several meanings. Some interpretations include: The seven circuits made by the bride and her family around the groom represents a seven-fold bond, which marriage establishes between the bride, groom, and their families. They symbolize the seven times that tefillin straps are wrapped around a man's arm, demonstrating that a groom binds himself in love to his bride in the same way he does to God. They represent the seven days of creation and the seven rotations of the Earth made during that time. On the day of his wedding, the groom is compared to a king. Just as an army encircles a king, the bride encircles the groom. When she is finished, she stands to his right, because according to the Psalms, that is the side where the queen stands.

Shabbat: The seventh day of the Jewish week and the Jewish Sabbath or day of rest. The holiday central to Jewish life and the only one mentioned in the Ten Commandments: "Remember the Sabbath and keep it holy." Begins at sundown Friday and ends when three stars appear in the sky on Saturday.

Shammash: Called the helper candle, the shammash lights the other candles on a Hanukkah menorah. It is set apart from the other candles—elevated, lower, or to the side—to denote its important role.

Shavuot: Weeks. The Jewish festival marking the giving of the Torah at Mount Sinai seven weeks after Passover. It began as a harvest festival, but now focuses on Torah, education, and actively choosing to participate in Jewish life.

Shehecheyanu: A blessing of praise that thanks God for bringing us to a special moment and marks joyous occasions.

Shema: The oldest fixed daily Jewish prayer. Shema Yisrael (Hear, O Israel), Adonai Eloheinu (The Lord is our God) Adonai ehad (The Lord is one), is one of the most famous statements in Judaism.

Shiva: Seven. Also, the seven days of mourning that follow the burial of a parent, sibling, child, or spouse. It is observed in the home of the mourner or deceased. At one time, parents observed shiva if a child intermarried, signifying the child's rejection from the Jewish community.

Shomrei Adamah: Guardians of the Earth. It refers to the obligation of Jews to care for nature.

Simchat Torah: Rejoicing in the Law. It is a joyous holiday marking the end of the annual reading of the Torah. On this day, the last verses of Deuteronomy are read followed immediately by the first verses of Genesis.

Sukkah: A hut built during Sukkot to represent the ones Jews lived in when they wandered the desert.

Sukkot: The harvest holiday commemorating the forty years that the Israelites wandered in the desert.

Talmud: The book containing the discussions and commentaries on the Mishna's laws by rabbinic scholars compiled in about the fifth century CE. It follows a consistent format: a law is presented, followed by rabbinic analysis of and elaboration on the opinions found in the Mishna.

Tashlich *(alternate spelling: tashlikh)*: To throw. A Jewish practice associated with Rosh Hashanah. On the first day of the holiday, Jews go to a river to symbolically cast their sins into the water.

Tefillin: Phylacteries. Two small black boxes with black leather straps attached. Jewish men, and some non-Orthodox women, place one box on their head and wrap one around their arm during weekday morning prayers. The boxes contain a scroll with the Shema prayer.

The Exodus: The Israelites' liberation from slavery in Egypt. It is the seminal event in Jewish history. It is celebrated at the Passover seder and repeatedly referenced in Jewish liturgy.

Tikkun Olam: Repair the world. It has come to refer to the pursuit of social action and social justice.

Torah: Written Jewish law consisting of the five books of the Hebrew Bible or Five Books of Moses. It includes all the biblical laws of Judaism. Non-Jews know it as the Old Testament.

Tu B'shvat: The New Year for the Trees. It celebrates nature and is often called the Jewish Earth Day.

Tzedakah: Righteous behavior. It is often used to mean charitable contributions.

Yom Kippur: Day of Atonement. Jews fast and repent for sins committed the previous year. It is the most solemn day in Judaism and the end of the ten days of repentance.

NOTES

Preface:

1. *A Portrait of Jewish Americans: Findings from a Pew Research Center Survey of U.S. Jews*, Pew Research Center's Religion & Public Life Project (Washington: Pew Research Center, 2013) http://pewrsr.ch/16IN5U4.

2. *National Jewish Population Survey 2000-01: Strength, Challenge and Diversity in the American Jewish Population* (New York: United Jewish Communities, 2003), 16. http://www.jewishfederations.org/local_includes/downloads/4606.pdf.

3. Ibid.

4. Sue Fishkoff, "Latest salvo in intermarriage debate suggests a split in Jewish community," Jewish Telegraphic Agency (JTA), February 6, 2007, http://www.jta.org/2007/02/07/archive/latest-salvo-in-intermarriage-debate-suggests-a-split-in-jewish-community.

5. Central Conference of American Rabbis, "Reform Rabbis, Largest Group of Jewish Clergy, Address Intermarriage at 121st Convention of the CCAR" (San Francisco: Central Conference of American Rabbis (CCAR) 2010), http://www.marketwired.com/press-release/Reform-Rabbis-Largest-Group-Jewish-Clergy-Address-Intermarriage-121st-Convention-1195193.htm.

Introduction:

I. Aron Hirt-Manheimer and Joy Weinberg, "Cracking the Code," *Reform Judaism Magazine*, Spring 2008, http://reformjudaismmag.org/Articles/index.cfm?id=1321.

Chapter 1:

A portion of this chapter previously appeared on InterfaithFamily:
Jane Larkin, "Interfaith Marriage–A Blessing in Disguise," InterfaithFamily.com, May 21, 2009, http://www.interfaithfamily.com/relationships/marriage_and_relationships/Interfaith_Marriage--A_Blessing_In_Disguise.shtml.

[1] Seven Circles—The ritual of the seven circles has several meanings. 1) The seven circuits made by the bride and her family around the groom represents a seven-fold bond, which marriage establishes between the bride, groom, and their families. 2) They symbolize the seven times that *Tefillin* straps are wrapped around a man's arm, demonstrating that a groom binds himself in love to his bride in the same way he does to God. 3) They represent the seven days of creation and the seven rotations of the Earth made during that time. 4) On the day of his wedding, a groom is compared to a king. Just as an army encircles a king, the bride encircles the groom. When she is finished, she stands to his right, because according to the Psalms, that is the side where the queen stands.

Chapter 2:

A portion of this chapter previously appeared on InterfaithFamily:
Jane Larkin, "Interfaith Marriage–A Blessing in Disguise," InterfaithFamily.com, May 21, 2009, http://www.interfaithfamily.com/relationships/marriage_and_relationships/Interfaith_Marriage--A_Blessing_In_Disguise.shtml.

Jane Larkin, "Why We Chose Judaism," Parenting Blog, InterfaithFamily.com, October 11, 2013, http://www.interfaithfamily.com/blog/parenting/tag/intermarrieds.

A portion of this chapter appeared in *The Forward*:
Jane Larkin, "You Can't Be Both (Jewish and Not)," *The Forward*, November 10, 2013, http://forward.com/articles/187286/you-cant-be-both-jewish-and-not/?p=all.

1. QT-P18: Marital Status by Sex, Unmarried-Partner Households, and Grandparents as Caregivers: 2000, Census 2000 Summary File 3 (SF 3)-Sample Data, New York City, New York, United States Census Bureau, Census 2000 Summary File 3, Matrices PCT1, PCT7, and PCT8 (Washington: United States Census Bureau 2002).

2. Talmud, Shevuot 39a

Chapter 3:

A portion of this chapter previously appeared on InterfaithFamily:
Jane Larkin, "How I Became too Jewish for my Jewish Mother," InterfaithFamily.com, originally published February 2009, republished November 25, 2010, http://www.interfaithfamily.com/relationships/marriage_and_relationships/How_I_Became_Too_Jewish_For_My_Jewish_Mother.shtml.

Jane Larkin, "Our Most Favorite Day of the Week," InterfaithFamily.com, November 3, 2010, http://www.interfaithfamily.com/holidays/shabbat_and_other_holidays/Our_Most_Favorite_Day_of_the_Week.shtml.

Dohany Street Great Synagogue (Budapest, Hungary: Hidden Treasures Tours, 2006), http://www.greatsynagogue.hu/gallery_syn.html.

1. Steve Israel, "The Hungarian Jewish Community" (Jerusalem, Israel: Jewish Agency for Israel, n.d.), http://jafi.org/nr/exeres/03be0911-a79a-4f60-9e38-cb1b5d9fa4d5,frameless.htm?nrmode=published.

2. Wendy Mogel, *The Blessing of a Skinned Knee* (New York: Penguin Compass, 2001), 27.

3. Kira S. Birditt, Laura M. Miller, Karen L. Fingerman, and Eva S. Lefkowitz, "Tensions in the Parent and Adult Child Relationship: Links to Solidarity and Ambivalence," *Psychology and Aging*, Vol. 24(2), June 2009, 287–295.

4. Erich Fromm Quotes, ThinkExist.com (Fromm n.d.), http://thinkexist.com/quotation/the_mother-child_relationship_is_paradoxical_and/147603.html.

5. *Faith in Flux: Changes in Religious Affiliation in the U.S.*, Pew Research Center's Religion & Public Life Project (Washington: Pew Research Center, 2009), http://www.pewforum.org/Faith-in-Flux.aspx.

6. Deborah Dash Moore, "Assimilation in the United States: Twentieth Century," *Jewish Women: A Comprehensive Historical Encyclopedia*, March 2009 (Brookline, MA: Jewish Women's Archive 2009). http://jwa.org/encyclopedia/article/assimilation-in-united-states-twentieth-century.

7. Will Herberg, *Protestant-Catholic-Jew: An Essay in American Religious Sociology* (New York: Anchor Books, Doubleday, 1960), 27–31.

8. Ibid.

9. Fern Chertok, Benjamin Phillips, and Leonard Saxe, *It's Not Just Who Stands under the Chuppah: Intermarriage and Engagement*, Steinhardt Social Research Institute at the Maurice and Marilyn Cohen Center for Modern Jewish Studies, Brandeis

University (Waltham, MA: Steinhardt Social Research Institute, 2008), http://bir.brandeis.edu/bitstream/handle/10192/23017/Intermarriage.052908.pdf?sequence=1.

10. Marcus L. Hansen, *The Problem of the Third Generation Immigrant* (Rock Island, IL: Augustana Historical Society,1938), 9–10.

11. Will Herberg, 27–31.

12. Fern Chertok et al., http://bir.brandeis.edu/bitstream/handle/10192/23017/Intermarriage.052908.pdf?sequence=1.

13. Ibid.

14. Rabbi Joseph Telushkin, "The Ten Commandments," *Jewish Literacy: The Most Important Things to Know About the Jewish Religion, It's People, and It's History,* Revised Edition (New York: William Morrow, HarperCollins, 2008), 41.

15. Sharon G. Forman, *Honest Answers to Your Child's Jewish Questions: A Rabbi's Insights* (New York: URJ Press, 2006), 28.

16. Ibid.

17. Condoleezza Rice, Quote Details: Condoleezza Rice: Life is full of…, The Quotations Page (Rice n.d.) http://www.quotationspage.com/quote/41040.html.

Chapter 4:

A portion of this chapter previously appeared on InterfaithFamily:
Jane Larkin, "How Not to Tell Your Child Daddy Isn't Jewish," InterfaithFamily.com, January 11, 2009, http://www.interfaithfamily.com/relationships/parenting/How_Not_to_Tell_Your_Child_Daddy_Isnt_Jewish_.shtml.

1. Sharon G. Forman, *Honest Answers to Your Child's Jewish Questions: A Rabbi's Insights* (New York: URJ Press, 2006), x–xi.

2. Stephen Colbert and Jon Stewart, "Can I Interest You in Hannukah?" A Colbert Christmas (New York: The Colbert Report, 2008), http://www.colbertnation.com/the-colbert-report-videos/211033/november-23-2008/a-colbert-christmas--jon-stewart.

3. *The December Dilemma—Tips to Survive the Holiday Season*, Project Welcome (New York: Union of Reform Judaism, n.d.), 2.

4. Ranya Idliby, Suzanne Oliver, and Priscilla Warner, *The Faith Club* (New York: Free Press, Simon & Schuster, 2006), 40–53.

5. Ibid.

6. Ibid.

7. Proverbs 24:5.

8. "Beit Alpha-An Ancient Synagogue with a Splendid Mosaic Floor," Archeological Sites No. 7 (Jerusalem, Israel: Israel Ministry of Foreign Affairs, 2001), http://www.mfa.gov.il/MFA/History/Early%20History%20-%20Archaeology/Beit%20Alpha%20-%20An%20Ancient%20Synagogue%20with%20a%20Splendid.

9. Clement C. Moore, *The Night Before Christmas*, Hardcover Abridged Edition (New York: Random House, 1990), 2.

10. Rabbi Joshua E. Plaut, "Jews & Christmas: What Attitudes Toward Christmas Tell Us about Modern Jewish Identity" (New York:

My Jewish Learning, n.d.), http://www.myjewishlearning.com/holidays/About_Holidays/Non-Jewish_Holidays/Christmas/Jews_and_Christmas.shtml.

11. Rabbi Joseph Telushkin, "Theodor Herzl," *Jewish Literacy: The Most Important Things to Know About the Jewish Religion, It's People, and It's History* (New York: William Morrow, HarperCollins, 2008), 276.

12. Rabbi Joshua E. Plaut, http://www.myjewishlearning.com/holidays/About_Holidays/Non-Jewish_Holidays/Christmas/Jews_and_Christmas.shtml.

Chapter 5:

National Jewish Population Survey 2000-01: Strength, Challenge and Diversity in the American Jewish Population (New York: United Jewish Communities, 2003), http://www.jewishfederations.org/local_includes/downloads/4606.pdf.

A Portrait of Jewish Americans: Findings from a Pew Research Center Survey of U.S. Jews, Pew Research Center's Religion & Public Life Project (Washington: Pew Research Center, 2013) http://pewrsr.ch/16IN5U4.

1. Jon Entine, *Abraham's Children: Race, Identity and the DNA of the Chosen People* (New York: Grand Central Publishing, 2007), 216.

2. Ibid, 216–217.

3. Ibid, 217.

4. Ibid, 220.

5. Egon Mayer, *Love & Tradition: Marriage Between Jews & Christians* (New York: Plenum Publishing Corp., 1985), 41–42.

6. Ibid, 43.

7. Ibid.

8. Ibid.

9. Julius Draschler, *Intermarriage in New York City: A Statistical Study of the Amalgamation of European Peoples* (New York: Columbia University, 1921), 49. http://www.archive.org/stream/intermarriagein00dracgoog/intermarriagein00dracgoog_djvu.txt.

10. Ibid, 27.

11. Midrash Shir HaShirim 1:4.

12. Yehuda Bar Shalom, Address to URJ Greene Family Camp Family Retreat, March 2012.

13. Lawrence Schiffman, comments on Jewish genetic research in *Abraham's Children: Race, Identity and the DNA of the Chosen People*, by Jon Entine (New York: Grand Central Publishing, 2007), 221.

14. Keren R. McGinity, *Still Jewish: A History of Women and Intermarriage In America* (New York: NYU Press, 2009), 17–18.

15. Ibid, 6.

16. Ibid, 58.

17. Johanna Ginsburg, "Founded by Mavericks, and Still Embracing the New," *New Jersey Jewish News*, October 6, 2010. http://njjewishnews. com/article/2097/founded-by-mavericks-and-still-embracing-the-new#. T8eJIN0ZFPw.

18. Keren R. McGinity, 74.

19. Arthur Hertzberg, *Being Jewish in America: The Modern Experience* (New York: Schocken Books, 1979), xii.

20. Janet Marder, Blessing for Non-Jewish Spouses—Yom Kippur Morning. http://urj.org/cong/outreach/interfaith/honoring/?syspage=article& item_id=3707.

Chapter 6:

A portion of this chapter previously appeared on InterfaithFamily:
Jane Larkin, "Beyond the Lulav and the Etrog," InterfaithFamily.com, September 29, 2009, http://www.interfaithfamily.com/holidays/shab-bat_and_other_holidays/Beyond_the_Lulav_and_the_Etrog.shtml.

Jane Larkin, "Rosh Hashanah Party for the New Year," InterfaithFamily.com, September 11, 2009, http://www.interfaithfamily.com/holidays/rosh_ha-shanah_and_yom_kippur/Rosh_Hashanah_Party_for_the_New_Year. shtml.

1. Fern Chertok, Benjamin Phillips, and Leonard Saxe, *It's Not Just Who Stands under the Chuppah: Intermarriage and Engagement*, Steinhardt Social Research Institute at the Maurice and Marilyn Cohen Center for Modern Jewish Studies, Brandeis University (Waltham, MA: Steinhardt Social Research Institute, 2008) http:// bir.brandeis.edu/bitstream/handle/10192/23017/Intermarriage.052908. pdf?sequence=1.

2. "Campaign for Youth Engagement: Committing to the Jewish Future" (Union for Reform Judaism, 2011), http://urj.org/cye/about.

3. Sylvia Barack Fishman, *The Way into the Varieties of Jewishness*, Quality Paperback Edition (Woodstock, VT: Jewish Lights Publishing, 2009), 225.

4. Ahad Ha'am, "Shabbat v'Tziyonut (Hebrew)," 1898.

5. Milton Steinberg, *Basic Judaism*, (New York: A Harvest Book, Harcourt Brace & Co., 1947), 136–139.

6. Keren R. McGinity, "Gender Matters: Jewish Identity, Intermarriage and Parenthood," *Contact: The Journal of the Steinhardt Foundation for Jewish Life*, Winter 2012, Volume 14, no. 2, 12-13. http://www.steinhardtfoundation.org/wp-install/wp-content/uploads/2013/10/winter_2012.pdf.

7. Ibid.

8. Ibid.

9. Sylvia Barack Fishman, 226.

10. Jane Larkin, "Rosh Hashanah Party for the New Year," Reader's Comments, Interfaithfamily.com. http://www.interfaithfamily.com/smf/index.php?topic=3386.0;wap2.

11. Sylvia Barack Fishman, 226.

12. Fern Chertok et al., http://bir.brandeis.edu/bitstream/handle/10192/23017/Intermarriage.052908.pdf?sequence=1.

Chapter 7:

A portion of this chapter previously appeared on InterfaithFamily:
Jane Larkin, "Day School Education For My Interfaith Family," Interfaith
Family.com, May 15, 2011, http://www.interfaithfamily.com/relationships/
parenting/A_Day_School_Education_For_My_Interfaith_Family.shtml.

1. Leonard Saxe, "On Jewish Identity," *Contact: The Journal of the Steinhardt Foundation for Jewish Life*, Winter 2012, Volume 14, no. 2, 4. http://www.steinhardtfoundation.org/wp-install/wp-content/uploads/2013/10/winter_2012.pdf.

2. Albert Vorspan, *So the Kids are Revolting. . .? A Game Plan for Jewish (and All Other) Parents* (Garden City, NY: Doubleday and Company, 1970), 19–20.

3. Arthur Hertzberg, "Current Issues in Jewish Life in America and Their Meaning for the Jewish Community Center (address, New York Metropolitan Region, National Jewish Welfare Board, March 10, 1965), published in *Being Jewish in America: The Modern Experience* (New York: Schocken Books, 1979), 125–137.

4. Arthur Hertzberg, "Jewish Education Must Be Religious Education" (adapted from *Commentary*, vol. 15, no. 5, May 1953), published in *Being Jewish in America: The Modern Experience* (New York: Schocken Books, 1979), 86–94.

5. Terrence Stutz, "Texas Slips in Spending per Pupil," *The Dallas Morning News*, February 23, 2012.

6. James C. McKinley, Jr., "Texas Conservatives Win Curriculum Change," *New York Times*, March 12, 2010. http://www.nytimes.com/2010/03/13/education/13texas.html?_r=0.

7. Mark Chancey, *Reading, Writing & Religion II: Texas Public School Bible Courses in 2011-12* (Austin, TX: Texas Freedom Network Education Fund, 2013). http://www.tfn.org/site/DocServer/TFNEF_ReadingWritingReligionII.pdf?docID=3481.

8. Ibid.

9. Chester E. Finn, Jr., Liam Julian, and Michael J. Petrilli, *The State of State Standards 2006* (Washington: Thomas B. Fordham Institute, August 2006). http://www.edexcellence.net/sites/default/files/publication/pdfs/State of State Standards2006FINAL_9.pdf.

10. W. Stephen Wilson, *Review of Draft Texas Mathematics Standards 2012* (Washington: Thomas B. Fordham Institute, April 2012). http://www.edexcellence.net/publications/review-of-draft-texas-math-standards-2012.html

11. Pirkei Avot 1:14.

12. Deuteronomy 6:7.

13. Pirkei Avot 2:5.

14. Rabbi Joseph Telushkin, "Torah Study," *Jewish Literacy: The Most Important Things to Know About the Jewish Religion, It's People, and It's History* (New York: William Morrow, HarperCollins, 2008), 625.

15. Ibid, 625–626.

16. Alan H. Dershowitz, *The Vanishing American Jew: In Search of Jewish Identity for the Next Century* (New York: Little, Brown and Company,1997), 293–299.

17. Ibid, 332.

18. Rabbi Joseph Telushkin, 627.

19. Leonard Saxe, "On Jewish Identity," *Contact: The Journal of the Steinhardt Foundation for Jewish Life*, Winter 2012, Vol. 14, no. 2, 4. http://www.steinhardtfoundation.org/wp-install/wp-content/uploads/2013/10/winter_2012.pdf.

Chapter 8:

Marcie Cohen and Mark I. Greenberg, *Jewish Roots in Southern Soil: A New History (Brandeis Series in American Jewish History, Culture, and Life* (Hanover and London: University Press of New England, 2006).

Eli N. Evans, *The Lonely Days Were Sundays: Reflections of a Jewish Southerner* (Jackson, MS: University Press of Mississippi, 1993).

Howard M. Sachar, *A History of the Jews in America*, 2nd prt. edition (New York: Alfred A. Knopf, 1992).

Rabbi Joseph Telushkin, "Blood Libel," *Jewish Literacy: The Most Important Things to Know About the Jewish Religion, It's People, and It's History* (New York: William Morrow, HarperCollins, 2008), 518–520.

Kenneth S. Stern, *AntiSemitism Today: How It Is the Same, How It Is Different, and How to Fight It*, (New York: American Jewish Committee, 2006).

1. "Anti-Semitism," (Anti-Defamation League, 2001), http://archive.adl.org/hate-patrol/antisemitism.html.

2. "Assimilation: Anti-Semitism in America," *The Jewish Americans*, prod. and dir. David Grubin, JTN Productions, WETA Washington D.C., and David Grubin Productions, Inc., six-hour series for PBS. http://www.pbs.org/jewishamericans/jewish_life/anti-semitism.html.

3. Manfred Gerstenfeld and Steven Bayme, *American Jewry's Comfort Level, Present and Future* (Jerusalem, Israel: Jerusalem Center for Public Affairs and American Jewish Committee, 2010), 11, 15, 33–34.

4. Ira Sheskin and Arnold Dashefsky, *Jewish Population in the United States, 2011: Current Jewish Population Reports, Number 4- 2011*, (Storrs, CT: North American Jewish Data Bank, Jewish Federations of North America, and the Association for the Social Scientific Study of Jewry, University of Connecticut, 2011), http://www.jewishdatabank.org/Studies/downloadFile.cfm?FileID=2919.

5. Ibid.

6. *National Jewish Population Survey 2000-01: Strength, Challenge and Diversity in the American Jewish Population* (New York: United Jewish Communities, 2003), http://www.jewishfederations.org/local_includes/downloads/4606.pdf.

7. Ira Sheskin and Arnold Dashefsky, http://www.jewishdatabank.org/Studies/downloadFile.cfm?FileID=2919.

8. Ibid.

9. Steven M. Cohen, Jacob B. Ukeles, and Ron Miller, *Jewish Community Study of New York 2011*, (New York: UJA-Federation of New York, 2012). http://www.jewishdatabank.org/study.asp?sid=90190&tp=2.

10. Kenneth D. Roseman, "Six-Tenths of a Percent of Texas," in *Lone Stars of David: The Jews of Texas* (Hanover and London: University Press of New England, 2007), 207.

11. Ira Sheskin and Arnold Dashefsky, http://www.jewishdatabank.org/Studies/downloadFile.cfm?FileID=2919.

12. Ibid.

13. Christine Leigh Heyrman, *Southern Cross: The Beginnings of the Bible Belt*, 1st edition (New York: Alfred A. Knopf, 1997), 6.

14. Ibid, 27.

15. "Resolution on Anti-Semitism" (passed by the Southern Baptist Convention at the annual Convention meeting, May 1873), http://www.sbc.net/resolutions/resprintfriendly.asp?ID=652.

16. "Resolution on Jewish Evangelism" (passed by the Southern Baptist Convention at the annual Convention meeting, New Orleans, LA, June 11–13, 1996), http://www.sbc.net/resolutions/amResolution.asp?ID=655.

17. Stan Guthrie, "Why Evangelize the Jews? God's Chosen People Need Jesus as Much as We Do," *Christianity Today*, March 25, 2008. http://www.christianitytoday.com/ct/2008/march/31.76.html.

18. "About Baseball and Bibles," Baseball and Bibles, http://www.baseballandbibles.com/about-us.

19. "About—Mission and Vision—Sports Ministry," Fellowship of Christian Athletes, http://www.fca.org/about-fellowship-of-christian-athletes/mission-and-vision.

20. Anne Rackham and Mark Gluckman, "School Official Apologizes After Christian-Themed Talent Show Says Sponsorship Not Clear Enough," *Jewish News of Greater Phoenix*, 2007.

21. Rabbi Arthur P. Nemitoff, "Anti-Semitism: Where Does It Begin… and End?" InterfaithFamily.com, June 2002, http://www.interfaithfamily. com/news_and_opinion/synagogues_and_the_jewish_community/Anti-Semitism_Where_Does_It_Beginand_End.shtml.

22. Ibid.

23. Judith Weinstein Klein, *Jewish Identity and Self-Esteem: Healing Wounds Through Ethnotherapy*, Second Edition (New York: Institute for American Pluralism of the American Jewish Committee,1989), 9.

<u>Chapter 9</u>:

A portion of this chapter previously appeared on InterfaithFamily:
Jane Larkin, "Interfaith Marriage—A Blessing in Disguise," Interfaithfamily. com, May 21, 2009, http://www.interfaithfamily.com/relationships/mar-riage_and_relationships/Interfaith_Marriage--A_Blessing_In_Disguise. shtml.

1. Sylvia Barack Fishman, *The Way into the Varieties of Jewishness*, Quality Paperback Edition (Woodstock, VT: Jewish Lights Publishing, 2009), 220.

2. David Epstein, comments on interfaith dating and marriage in *Jewish Family & Life: Traditions, Holidays, and Values for Today's Parents and Children*, by Yosef I. Abramowitz and Rabbi Susan Silverman, (New York: Golden Books, 1997), 287.

3. Leonard Saxe, "On Jewish Identity," *Contact: The Journal of the Steinhardt Foundation for Jewish Life*, Winter 2012, Vol. 14, no. 2, 4. http://www. steinhardtfoundation.org/wp-install/wp-content/uploads/2013/10/ winter_2012.pdf.

4. Sylvia Barack Fishman, 215-216.

5. Leonard Saxe, http://www.steinhardtfoundation.org/wp-install/wp-content/uploads/2013/10/winter_2012.pdf.

6. Alan Morinis, *Everyday Holiness: The Jewish Spiritual Path of Mussar* (Boston: Trumpeter Books: 2007), 70.

Epilogue:

A portion of this chapter previously appeared on InterfaithFamily:
Jane Larkin, "Outreach Matters," InterfaithFamily.com, April 16, 2010, http://www.interfaithfamily.com/news_and_opinion/synagogues_and_the_jewish_community/Outreach_Matters_.shtml.

National Jewish Population Survey 2000-01: Strength, Challenge and Diversity in the American Jewish Population (New York: United Jewish Communities, 2003), http://www.jewishfederations.org/local_includes/downloads/4606.pdf.

A Portrait of Jewish Americans: Findings from a Pew Research Center Survey of U.S. Jews, Pew Research Center's Religion & Public Life Project (Washington: Pew Research Center, 2013) http://pewrsr.ch/16IN5U4.

1. Jack Wertheimer and Adam R. Bronfman, "Straight Talk About Assimilation: An Exchange," Opinion, *The Forward*, October 21-30, 2009, http://forward.com/articles/117307/straight-talk-about-assimilation-an-exchange.

2. Katherine N. Gan, Patty Jacobson, Gil Preuss, and Barry Shrage, *The 2005 Greater Boston Community Study, Intermarried Families and Their Children: A Report of Combined Jewish Philanthropies,"* (Boston: Combined Jewish Philanthropies, March 2008), http://www.cjp.org/local_includes/downloads/24386.pdf.

Made in the USA
Charleston, SC
13 December 2014